Redesigning Public Education

The Kentucky Experience

Also by Jack D. Foster

If I Could Make a School

Redesigning Public Education

The Kentucky Experience

Jack D. Foster

Diversified Services, Inc.
Lexington, Kentucky

Printed in the United States of America
BookMasters, Inc.

Library of Congress Catalog Card Number: 99-90867

ISBN 0-9631007-1-8

Publications Division
Diversified Services, Inc.
Lexington, Kentucky

Table of Contents

Acknowledgements

As is the case with every author, many people have contributed to this book in one way or another. In my case they are too many to mention each one of them by name. However, I want to give special recognition to the following people who took their valuable time to read and offer comments on early drafts of this book: Jane David, Charles Eison, Robert Lumbsden, Taylor Collins, Jane Lindle, Penny Sanders, Robert Sexton, Stephen Clements, Harry Owen, Thomas Boysen, Carol Stumbo, Roger Pankratz, Lois Adams-Rogers, Douglas Alexander, and Pam Coe. Some of them read only portions of the manuscript while others read most of the chapters. The book reflects many of their thoughts and criticisms for which I am greatly indebted. Obviously I bear sole responsibility for the final product.

I want to express my gratitude to Governor Wallace G. Wilkinson who appointed me as his Secretary of the Education and Humanities Cabinet in 1988. As a member of his cabinet I helped him develop and articulate his education policies. He also asked me to participate with him in the debate over the direction of school reform in Kentucky prior to the decision of the Kentucky Supreme Court to declare the public school system unconstitutional. Governor Wilkinson appointed me to the task force on education reform, which made it possible for me to actively participate in the development of this historic legislation. It also made writing this book possible.

I also want to express special appreciation to my wife Peggy for her encouragement when at times it seemed this book might never be finished. A book like this one can at times seem impossible to complete.

Finally I want to express appreciation to the many people who encouraged me to write this book. An undertaking of this kind has a duty to reflect as accurately as possible the many strands of thought that went into this massive legislation. I hope this duty has been discharged responsibly.

Introduction

On June 8, 1989, in an unprecedented judicial decision, the Kentucky Supreme Court declared the state's public school system unconstitutional. Although the lawsuit filed in 1986 by 66 mostly rural school districts sought more equitable and adequate funding for public schools, the high court went beyond these fiscal issues and found the entire system of public education deficient and unconstitutional. The Kentucky Supreme Court decision abolished every vestige of the existing system of public schools. The court ordered the Kentucky legislature to create a new system of public schools no later than April 15, 1990, the end of its next biennial session.

The task facing the Kentucky legislature involved more than making what existed better. An entire statutory code recreating a system of public schools had to be written. Throughout the 1980s many states had undertaken various reforms of public education, but none had actually recreated their institution of public education. Kentucky had a unique opportunity to "start from scratch" and build a new system based on the best wisdom and knowledge about teaching and learning.

The Kentucky General Assembly met its responsibility and enacted the most comprehensive education legislation in modern American history known as House Bill 940 or the Kentucky Education Reform Act of 1990 (hereinafter referred to as KERA). The challenge for Kentucky then became one of implementing the massive changes in how schools are to function and children are to be taught.

The purpose of this book

The Kentucky legislation drew national attention when it is was enacted. Many years after its enactment, interest in KERA remains high in Kentucky and nationally. The law and its implementation have been the subject of hundreds of speeches, articles, political debates, and research. However, as time passes, the original intent of this historic legislation can be lost. The purpose of this book is to set forth the policy assumptions underlying KERA and to understand the successes and difficulties Kentucky experienced in implementing these policies.

Special attention is given to whether a specific policy proved to be unsound or whether its implementation was flawed in some way. In some instances there are significant differences between what was intended and what actually happened. It also has become obvious that the legislation had some serious omissions that still have not been adequately addressed. Hopefully this assessment will give policy makers, educators, and the general public an authoritative understanding of what Kentucky tried to do, and thereby provide a context for interpreting what followed after KERA was enacted.

The Perspective of the Author

The analysis presented in this book is one of a "participant observer." I was Governor Wallace Wilkinson's Secretary of Education and Humanities from 1988 through 1991. In that position I provided education policy advice to him and was an advocate for the school reform initiatives he proposed. Governor Wilkinson named me as one of his six appointees to the Task Force on Education Reform created to respond to the court requirement that a new system of public education be created. In this role I participated in the development of HB 940 as a member of both the Curriculum and Finance Committees. I also was a member of the Council on School Performance Standards created by Governor Wilkinson prior to the court decision.

Following the enactment of KERA, I was appointed to the Council on Education Technology and served on the panel that reviewed the first contract to implement the Education Technology plan. I also served on the panel that selected the first Commissioner of Education and the panel that reviewed the initial contract for the design and administration of the state accountability system.

After leaving public office in 1991, I had the opportunity to work with over 50 Kentucky schools to help them understand how to implement the policies and programs of KERA. Under the sponsorship of the Kentucky Valley Education Cooperative and the Bell South Foundation, I was able to work with some of these schools for three or more years. Thus I also bring to the book my experiences of working with people at the school level as they tried to understand and implement this massive legislation. Their achievements, frustrations, and problems have given me valuable insight into just how hard it has been to make the transition. I am deeply indebted to the personnel in these schools for the understanding they have given me.

However, I bring to this endeavor more than the perspective of an insider. During the six years prior to my appointment as Wilkinson's Secretary of Education and Humanities I was involved in school reform efforts in other states. As a managing partner in State Research Associates, a national consulting firm based in Lexington, Kentucky, I participated in projects leading to major education reform legislation in Mississippi and Indiana, and was consulted by policy makers in other states on various education issues. My personal views on many of the issues addressed in KERA are set forth in *If I Could Make a School* published in 1991.[1]

This book is not a mindless defense of KERA. At some points my observations are critical of the law as originally written or the manner in which it has been implemented. However, nothing I have written should be interpreted as an attack on the thousands of people who have worked so hard to implement it. The only objective is to take a hard but constructive look at what Kentucky did in 1990 and what happened thereafter.

Many years as an educator, public policy analyst, and researcher have taught me that policies need to be continuously reevaluated in the light of experience and new research. Only time can determine the efficacy of any policy regardless of its research base at the time it was adopted. KERA was based on sound research and practice, but good policy sometimes just doesn't work the way it is intended. Obviously we are delighted when it works exactly as we wanted and with the expected result. However, a policy may turn out to be ill conceived or perhaps unworkable. Sometimes the implementation is flawed. The intent here is to examine all of these possibilities.

Although this book is published more than nine years after KERA was enacted, it is still too early to make a final judgment on many of its elements. Some aspects of the law were to be implemented over a period of up to six years and just now are reaching the point of full implementation. Therefore, the findings and observations put forth in this book should be considered interim rather than the final word. Nonetheless, many important lessons have already been learned that can be beneficial to anyone interested in knowing the impact of KERA on public schools in Kentucky. Hopefully, this book will serve this purpose.

Citations referencing the legislation are shown with the location in HB 940 and the current Kentucky Revised Statutes. The purpose of the dual references is historical. Over the years the original language has in some cases either been amended or repealed. Since the intent of the book is to reflect on the initial intent of the legislation as enacted in 1990, the language of the original bill is the most accurate reference rather than the statutory citation.

The observations and findings reported in this book are representative but not exhaustive. I wanted this book to be interesting, informative reading to a wide audience. For this reason I have not burdened it with references to everything that has been written on KERA. However, I believe the book accurately reflects the consensus of those who have studied various aspects of KERA since its enactment in 1990.

A final caveat. Attributing intent to legislation is a matter of point of view. It would be foolhardy to suggest that every legislator or even every member of the Task Force on Education Reform that shaped the legislation would share the perspectives in this book. Therefore it is incumbent on this author to alert the reader that some views I express in this book about legislative intent may be subject to other interpretations. I can only express what I believe was the consensus understanding at the time.

NOTES:

[1] Jack D. Foster, *If I Could Make a School* Lexington, KY: Diversified Services, Inc., 1991.

1. The Mandate to Change

Enactment of the Kentucky Education Reform Act of 1990 (KERA) is generally attributed to the Kentucky Supreme Court decision that abolished the public school system in 1989. Obviously, the historic action of the Supreme Court made the legislation necessary, but a court decision in itself does not assure legislation as visionary as the one the General Assembly enacted in 1990.

A major event like this one almost always is preceded by circumstances that make it possible. Therefore, the redesign of Kentucky's public school system must be understood in the context of the effort to improve education at all levels that had been going on in Kentucky for more than a decade prior to the Supreme Court decision.

The legislation that followed the Court's decision is as historic as the decision itself. It represents the most dramatic restructuring of public education in this century. However, the law was not created out of thin air. Many of the most significant elements of the legislation had roots in the public debate over school reform that preceded the decision of the high court. Thus we begin this examination of the Kentucky Education Reform Act of 1990 with a review of the events that preceded its enactment.

Beginning in the late 1970s the General Assembly embarked on a series of reforms designed to improve the existing system. Among these reforms was an effort to achieve more equitable funding for all schools. Following the lead of other southern states in the early 1980s, education rose to the top of the political agenda. Education reform was a major issue in the campaigns for Governor and Superintendent of Public Instruction in 1983. The winners of both races were former educators who offered separate agendas for change based for the most part on reforms enacted in other states. However, only modest achievements were accomplished in the 1984 legislative session largely due to budgetary constraints.

Public pressure for school reform continued after the 1984 session of the legislature yielded little results. Governor Martha Layne Collins called the legislature into special session the following year to act on an array of proposals. The prevailing view was that the current education system had identifiable weaknesses and was inadequately and inequitably funded. Programs were proposed to deal with the perceived weaknesses, and money was requested to significantly reduce the inequities between funds available for educating children in the more affluent and the poorer school districts in the state.

The legislature approved a package of programs in the 1985 session. The legislation was hailed by many as a major step in the right direction, but funding for the program initiatives in the legislation was deferred until the legislature convened in regular session in January 1986.[1] The Legislative Research Commission estimated the cost of the programs they approved to be $792 million over four years.[2] Some of this money was intended to reduce inequities in funding between the wealthier and the poorer school districts but only by a small amount. The largest single expenditure would be used to reduce class sizes in the lower grades.

The 1985 legislation was ambitious in vision, but the funding needed to underwrite it was not forthcoming in the 1986 legislative budget as expected. Instead of providing full funding, only $70 million was appropriated for this purpose by the legislature for the first of the two biennial budgets for which estimates were given. As it turned out later, the tax measures enacted fell short of their revenue projections, so even less money was available than was expected.

School Finance System Challenged in Court

The failure of the legislature to appropriate the necessary financial support for the programs it enacted in 1985 angered many educators and reform advocates. They perceived the legislature's failure to act responsibly to be a betrayal by the political leadership of the state. Subsequently, a coalition of school districts and other parties formed an advocacy organization called the Council for Better Education Inc. The Council subsequently sued the Governor, the legislature, and the Superintendent of Public Instruction, requesting the Kentucky courts to declare the school finance system unconstitutional.

The Kentucky Constitution has only a brief reference to education, which states in Section 183 that "The General Assembly shall, by appropriate legislation, provide for an efficient system of common schools throughout the state." The operative words here, of course, are "an efficient system of common schools." In ruling on the merits of the lawsuit, the court had to determine if the financial support currently provided by the legislature for public education is sufficient to satisfy this constitutional mandate.

The arguments put forth by the plaintiffs were similar to those made in other states. Gross inequities in funding along with inadequate levels of funding formed the heart of the case. Although the Kentucky Constitution does not speak directly to the method of financing a system of "common schools," other school finance cases in the United States have generally found uneven financial support to be an unconstitutional condition. It was argued that a major reason for the poor showing Kentucky students made on national tests could be attributed to the relatively low funding given to schools and to the gross inequities between funding among school districts.

The lawsuit went to trial in the spring of 1988 in the Franklin County Circuit Court, the court of original jurisdiction in such cases. Circuit Court Judge Ray Corns issued an interim opinion on the case May 31, 1988, ruling for the plaintiffs, finding the school finance system unconstitutional. On June 7, 1988 Judge Corns appointed a Select Committee of five people knowledgeable about school finance issues. He ordered the committee to examine all the relevant facts of the case, provide additional analysis, and offer for the benefit of the Court guidelines for an appropriate resolution of the plaintiffs complaint.[3]

Judge Corns received the Select Committee report September 15, 1988. The committee proposed nine principles as guidelines that the court might use to "provide the foundation for future legislative accommodation of the constitutional mandate to provide for an efficient system of common schools throughout the state."[4] These nine principles were followed with 18 more specific issues the committee members thought the court should address in its final opinion. The 42-page report also contained an historical review of education and its financial support in Kentucky, and it ended with a discussion of possible constructive and legal interpretations of the intent of the words "efficient" and "system" in the constitutional language.

A month later Judge Corns issued his "findings of fact, conclusions of law, and judgment" in which he incorporated the 9 principles offered by the Select Committee. Referencing his initial ruling, Judge Corns held that:

> *The Court has heretofore held that education is a fundamental right under Section 183 of Kentucky's Constitution; that children in the poor school districts of Kentucky are being deprived of that right; that the duty to establish an efficient system of education for the children of Kentucky rests solely on the General Assembly*

and that it has failed to establish a constitutional system of public schools.

The Court has held that the present system of financing education is unconstitutional for the reasons that insufficient funds are provided to permit the poor school districts to have an efficient system of public schools as mandated by Section 183 of the Constitution; also that the great disparity between the amount of funds available to more affluent districts and poor districts violates Sections One (1) and Three (3) of the Constitution of Kentucky.[5]

In his ruling, Judge Corns defined the meaning of an "adequate and efficient school system" as follows:

An adequate, efficient school system provides each of its students with at least the following: (I) sufficient oral and written communication skills to enable students to function in a complex and rapidly changing civilization; (ii) sufficient knowledge of economic, social, and political systems to enable the student to make informed choices; (iii) sufficient understanding of governmental processes to enable the student to understand the issues that affect his or her community, state, and nation; (iv) sufficient self-knowledge and knowledge of his or her mental and physical wellness; (v) sufficient grounding in the arts to enable each student to appreciate his or her cultural and historical heritage; (vi) sufficient training or preparation for advanced training in either academic or vocational fields so as to enable each child to choose and pursue life work intelligently; and (vii) sufficient levels of academic or vocational skills to enable public school students to compete favorably with their counterparts in surrounding states, in academics or in the job market.[6]

Moreover, an adequate system must, by definition, provide sufficient physical facilities, teachers, support personnel, and instructional materials to enhance the educational process. An adequate school system must also include careful and comprehensive supervision at both local and state levels to minimize waste and to monitor the performance of teachers, administrators, and support personnel. It is very clear from this record that the schools in Kentucky's poor districts are inadequate and inefficient when measured by these criteria[7].

Linking specific learning outcomes for students with financial support broadened the scope of the decision beyond declaring the method and level of financial support for schools to be unconstitutional. The decision held that schools also must be effective in achieving specific outcomes for students if they are to be considered an "efficient system of common schools."

Judge Corns ordered the defendants to proceed as rapidly as possible to establish an efficient statewide system of elementary and secondary schools within the guidelines laid down in his opinion. He specifically required them to appear before him on February 1, 1989, to discuss what steps they had taken to comply with this action. He said he wanted to continue jurisdiction over the case only for the purpose of enforcing his judgment. However, he urged the defendants to make an expeditious appeal of his decision so that the Kentucky Supreme Court could quickly resolve any challenges to his Judgment.

Legislative leaders promptly filed an appeal of the lower court decision with the Kentucky Supreme Court, which accepted the case directly from the Circuit Court. Governor Wilkinson and John Brock, the Superintendent of Public Instruction, were defendants in the lawsuit, but they did not join in the appeal because they accepted the judgment of the Circuit Court that the finance system was indeed unconstitutional.

The Political Environment

While this litigation was going on, a vigorous and often acrimonious debate developed between legislative leadership and then Governor Wallace Wilkinson over the best strategy to pursue to improve elementary and secondary education. The major difference between Wilkinson and the legislature centered on whether to continue with the reforms enacted in the 1985 special session or to embark on a new approach proposed by the Governor.

Wilkinson believed trying to improve the present system would not bring the improvements needed in student achievement. He argued for structural changes that involved moving primary responsibility for education reform from the statehouse to the school site, development of a method by which to hold school personnel accountable for results, and providing a significant financial reward to schools that show progress.

In his first legislative session in 1988 Wilkinson agreed to fund most of the reforms enacted in 1985, but did not provide funds to continue reducing class size in the lower grades. The Senate passed his reform Bill, but the House Education Committee refused to act on it, so it did not become law. After the 1988 legislative session ended, Wilkinson announced that he would call a special session of the General Assembly early the following year to deal with his proposal.

Anticipating a special session in 1989, the legislature moved forward to develop its own agenda and offered a set of proposals to Governor Wilkinson in February 19, 1989. The proposals they offered to the Governor essentially continued the 1985 agenda with some additions including most of Wilkinson's ideas. However, the amount of money required to finance all the proposed programs was greater than either side could support, especially with the cost of responding to the finance lawsuit that was estimated to cost at least $500 million. Furthermore, Wilkinson thought the proposals didn't go far enough to restructure the existing system, and he continued to dispute the value of reducing class size beyond what had already been done.

Consequently, the debate between the governor and legislature continued beyond the March target date Wilkinson had set for a special legislative session, with no resolution in sight. Both sides generally agreed that the issue of school finance should not be addressed until the Supreme Court ruled on the decision rendered by Judge Corns, but they agreed that other education issues should be resolved prior to the outcome of the appeal if possible.[8]

The School System is Abolished

On June 8, 1989, the Kentucky Supreme Court issued its opinion on the appeal of the decision of the Circuit Court. While upholding most elements of the lower court decision, the Supreme Court went a step further. In an unprecedented decision, the Court declared the entire system of public education unconstitutional which effectively abolished it. Chief Justice Robert Stephens who authored the opinion wrote:

> *Lest there be any doubt, the result of our decision is that Kentucky's entire system of common schools is unconstitutional. There is no allegation that only part of the common school system is invalid, and we find no such circumstance. This decision applies to the entire sweep of the system – all its parts and parcels. This decision applies to the statutes creating, implementing and financing the system and to all its regulations, etc., pertaining*

> *thereto. This decision covers the creation of local school districts, school boards, and the Kentucky Department of Education to the Minimum Foundation Program and Power Equalization Program. It covers school construction and maintenance, teacher certification – the whole gamut of the common school system in Kentucky.*[9]

The General Assembly was ordered to create a new system of "common schools" by the end of its next regular session in April 1990.

Interestingly, no particular statute in itself was declared unconstitutional. The high court, in effect, said the education system in Kentucky was in an unconstitutional condition, and that is what necessitates its abolition. The distinction is made clear in the Supreme Court's opinion as follows:

> *While individual statutes are not herein addressed specifically or considered and declared to be facially unconstitutional, the statutory system as a whole and the interrelationship of the parts therein are hereby declared to be in violation of Section 183 of the Kentucky Constitution. Just as the bricks and mortar used in the construction of a schoolhouse, while contributing to the building's façade, do not ensure the overall structural adequacy of the schoolhouse, particular statutes drafted by the legislature in crafting and designing the current school system are not unconstitutional in and of themselves. Like the crumbling school house which must be redesigned and revitalized for more effective use, with some component parts found to be adequate, some found to be less than adequate, statutes relating to education may be reenacted as components of a constitutional system if they combine with other component statutes to form an efficient and thereby constitutional system.*[10]

The position of the court is that the Constitution places "an absolute duty on the General Assembly to re-create, re-establish a new system of common schools in the Commonwealth." Furthermore, the criteria set forth in the opinion is binding on the General Assembly as it develops Kentucky's new system of common schools.[11] In this action the court left open the possibility of using existing statutes to reconstitute the public school system so long as they resulted in a condition that is constitutional, i.e. a system that is "efficient" as that term is defined in the opinion.

The justices clearly recognized the significance of this decision when they wrote the following at the end of their opinion:

> *This decision has not been reached without much thought and consideration. We do not take our responsibilities lightly, and we have decided this case based on our perception and interpretation of the Kentucky Constitution. We intend no criticism of any person, persons or institutions. We view this decision as an opportunity for the General Assembly to launch the Commonwealth into a new era of educational opportunity which will ensure a strong economic, cultural and political future.*[12]

Thus the Supreme Court set the stage for recreating a major public institution from the ground up. No vestige of the old system would remain unless the General Assembly specifically reenacted it into law. Never before in this century had a legislature faced such a daunting task or had such an opportunity for vision and greatness.

Criteria of a Constitutional System

It is necessary to know how the Kentucky Supreme Court defined "an efficient system of common schools" in order to understand the criteria the General Assembly had to meet for a new system to be considered constitutional. At the very least, these criteria would provide the parameters within which the General Assembly had to conceptualize the new system.

The court saw the need to provide such guidance to the General Assembly:

> *The impact of this decision that the system is constitutionally deficient will be to set certain standards that we believe are required by Section 183 for the establishment and maintenance of an efficient system of common schools. It will be the responsibility of the General Assembly, using its own judgment and exercising its own power and constitutional duty, to establish such a system.*[13]

The opinion found three criteria that are the foundation for such a system: (1) It is the sole obligation of the General Assembly to provide such a system; (2) It must be provided throughout the state; and (3) the system must be "efficient." It is the last element that lies at the heart of the definition of a constitutional system.

The opinion provides a lengthy review of the debates that surrounded this section of the Constitution when it was drafted. Relevant decisions in earlier Supreme Court cases also are reviewed. These decisions concluded that public schools must be "efficient, equal and substantially uniform"[14] to be considered constitutional. This court now addressed the same question. What constitutes an efficient system of schools?

An Efficient System is Defined

Citing the constitutional obligation of the General Assembly to provide for such a system, this court went on to say "the General Assembly must not only establish the system, but it must monitor it on a continuing basis so that it will always be maintained in a constitutional manner. The General Assembly must carefully supervise it, so that there is no waste, no duplication, no mismanagement, at any level."[15] In this respect, the definition of efficient means a system that is well managed. This is a somewhat common sense view of efficiency. What is interesting here is how the court appears to extend the constitutional responsibility of the General Assembly beyond just the creation and funding of the system. It must "carefully supervise it" as well. This element of the decision becomes a matter of considerable debate later on.

The second element of the court's definition of efficiency is the view that the system of common schools must be adequately funded to achieve its goals. Adequacy is not defined, but it appears that a system characterized by substantial differences in level of funding is "inadequate." Here is what the opinion says:

> *The system of common schools must be adequately funded to achieve its goals. The system of common schools must be substantially uniform throughout the state. Each child, every child, in this Commonwealth must be provided with an equal opportunity to have an adequate education. Equality is the key word here. The children of the poor and the children of the rich, the children who live in the poor districts and the children who live in the rich districts must be given the same opportunity and access to an adequate education. This obligation cannot be shifted to local counties and local school districts.*[16]

Kentucky is like most other states in that it historically has required a local tax effort to support the public schools. The Supreme Court went on to say that the statement above was not intended to forbid such a practice. It simply wanted to make clear that such efforts may not be used by the General Assembly as a substitute for providing at the state level sufficient funds to ensure an "adequate, equal and substantially uniform education system throughout the state."[17]

Expanding somewhat on earlier decisions, this court concurred with the trial court and held that an efficient system of education must have as its goal to provide each and every child with at least the seven capacities cited in Judge Corns' decision. They incorporated them verbatim in this opinion to make certain there would be no question as to goals this court thought are appropriate for an "efficient system of common schools." Thus future courts will judge the efficiency of the education system at least in part on the extent to which each and every child graduating from the system exhibits at least these seven "capacities" as the court called them.

In a footnote to this paragraph added later, the Court clarifies its position on these capacities.

> *In recreating and redesigning the Kentucky system of common schools, these seven characteristics should be considered as minimum goals in providing an adequate education. Certainly, there is no prohibition against higher goals – whether such are implemented statewide by the General Assembly or through the efforts of any local education entities that the General Assembly may establish – so long as the General Assembly meets the standards set out in this opinion.*[18]

In summary, the Supreme Court stated that:

> *The essential, and minimal, characteristics of an "efficient" system of common schools, may be summarized as follows:*
>
> 1. *The establishment, maintenance and funding of common schools in Kentucky is the sole responsibility of the General Assembly.*
> 2. *Common schools shall be free to all.*
> 3. *Common schools shall be available to all Kentucky children.*
> 4. *Common schools shall be substantially uniform throughout the state.*
> 5. *Common schools shall provide equal educational opportunities to all Kentucky children, regardless of place of residence or economic circumstances.*
> 6. *Common schools shall be monitored by the General Assembly to assure that they are operated with no waste, no duplication, no mismanagement, and with no political influence.*

7. *The premise for the existence of common schools is that all children in Kentucky have a constitutional right to an adequate education.*

8. *The General Assembly shall provide funding which is sufficient to provide each child in Kentucky an adequate education.*

9. *An adequate education is one which has as its goal the development of the seven capacities recited previously.*[19]

The General Assembly now had the task of recreating a system of public schools that would meet these criteria.

The Task Force on Education Reform

The day after the Supreme Court handed down its decision, Governor Wilkinson, Speaker of the House Don Blandford and Senate President pro tem John "Eck" Rose met to discuss how to proceed. Although the Supreme Court was clear that only the legislature had the constitutional mandate to design the new school system, both Blandford and Rose agreed that the Governor's participation was essential. Thus they agreed to create a joint executive-legislative task force to carry out the work.

The three political leaders agreed that the task was too critical to leave in the hands of the people who had previously been directly involved in the current system. The process had to be under their direct control. They further agreed to exclude the Superintendent of Public Instruction John Brock and members of the House and Senate Education Committees except for their respective chairpersons. The initial idea was to create a task force consisting of only the Governor and four other executive branch appointees and the legislative leadership of the House and Senate – a group of 15 people in all.

The exclusion of Brock was seen as necessary for several reasons. Although the constitutional office he held remained, the Supreme Court had abolished the duties of the office. It was thought improper that he should participate in the redefinition of his responsibilities. He could at any time participate in the proceedings, but not as a member of the task force.

Several times in the previous decade the legislature placed on the ballot an amendment to eliminate this constitutional office in favor of an appointed chief education officer. Although these previous attempts failed at the ballot box, it was very likely this idea would be advanced again by the legislature as part of the restructuring ordered by the Supreme Court. The presence of the holder of that office on the task force was thought to constitute a conflict of interest and could potentially be politically awkward for him and those task force members desiring to abolish his office.

The legislature's education committee membership was very large. Their inclusion would have made the size of the task force unwieldy. Furthermore, their presence on the task force would make their influence numerically dominant, something Governor Wilkinson strongly opposed. While education committee members were denied official positions on the task force when it finally was created, it was agreed later that they could participate in the discussions of the task force committees, but they would not be official members of the task force. Many education committee members did participate, but others felt offended and did not attend any of the meetings.

The original task force membership was expanded to include the chairs of the House and Senate Education Committees and Appropriation and Revenue Committees. At that point all task force members were Democrats, since they controlled both houses of the legislature. After a protest by the Republican leadership, it was agreed to add the Minority leader of both the House and Senate to the task force. The Governor then was allowed to add one more member to the task force.

After much discussion with members of his Cabinet and personal reflection, Governor Wilkinson took the extraordinary position of not appointing himself a member of the task force. The decision was intended to reduce the potential for disruptive political conflict between himself and the leadership of the legislature with whom he had serious disagreement over the direction school reform should take prior to the court decision.

Before he agreed to this action, Wilkinson secured an understanding with Blandford and Rose on several issues. Clearly the numbers were such that the legislative members would control every vote. It was agreed that all decisions would be by consensus rather than formal vote. Most important to both parties, they agreed that the final product had to be acceptable to both legislative leadership and the Governor. This agreement had the effect of giving both sides a private veto that either one could use if necessary in order to avoid a public rift over task force decisions which either side could not support.[20]

The Task Force on Education Reform, as it was later named, finally was made up of 22 people: six appointed by the Governor, and eight each from the House and Senate. Blandford and Rose appointed all the members of the House and Senate leadership, the Education and the Appropriations and Revenue Committee chairs, and the Minority leaders of the House and Senate. Governor Wilkinson appointed the Secretary of the Cabinet, the Chief of Staff, the Budget Director, the Secretary and the Deputy Secretary of the Education and Humanities Cabinet and his Cabinet Liaison as executive branch representatives on the task force.

The Task Force Structure and Process

The Task Force on Education Reform met for the first time July 12, 1989. National education experts were invited to address the task force in its early meetings to provide insight into what was happening elsewhere in school reform. A decision was then made to create three major committees to do the work, the results of which would be brought to the task force for final action. Task force members were assigned to three committees: Governance, Curriculum, and Finance. Senator Rose and Representative Blandford served as co-chairs of the task force. Each committee was co-chaired by a legislator from the House and Senate.

Initially the intent was to hire a consultant to serve as director of the task force, preferably someone from outside Kentucky. This person would develop a work plan and generally guide the work of the task force. Some members objected to not using Kentucky expertise, so the search was broadened to include applicants from Kentucky. Finally, it was decided that the work of the task force would be coordinated by Vic Hellard, Jr., director of the Legislative Research Commission, and Tom Dorman, the legislative liaison in the Governor's office. The committees then hired their own consultants. The curriculum committee employed David Hornbeck; the governance committee hired Luvern Cunningham and Lila Carol; and the finance committee selected John Augenblick.

The role the consultants played was significant, because it was their staff work that made it possible for these committees to function efficiently. They often were the source of ideas and information, but the result was in every case the decision of the committee members. The committees worked independently for the most part, but working documents were shared with all members of the task force at their regular meetings.

As the work progressed, the committees held public hearings on various ideas or proposals. Public input was invited at these hearings and many position papers were submitted to the various committees by organizations that had special interest in education. The task force also maintained a telephone "hot line" which took calls from citizens. The results of the calls were regularly compiled and were provided to committee members for their consideration.

The task force meetings for the most part were opportunities for members to discuss ideas and proposals being considered in the three committees. Also it was a time when specific individuals were invited to address the members on certain issues of common interest. Staff in the Legislative Research Commission worked on draft legislation in the background, following carefully the work of the various committees beginning in the fall of 1989.

The committees submitted their final recommendations to the task force in mid-February, 1990. On March 7, 1990 the task force approved draft legislation prepared by the Legislative Research Commission, which was then turned over to the General Assembly for action before the current session ended. The bill, known as HB 940, was massive, consisting of 945 pages of statutory language needed to recreate the public school system in Kentucky. It was necessary to repeal statutes that no longer applied as well as to enact new statutes and amend existing ones to conform to the decisions made by the task force.

The General Assembly enacted this historic legislation into law on March 27, 1990 after intense debate. Governor Wilkinson signed the legislation on April 11th and ended a long journey of education reform in Kentucky.

NOTES:

[1] Under the Kentucky Constitution, the Governor may call the legislature into session at any time to deal with a limited agenda, but the appropriation of funds can only be approved in a regular biennial session.
[2] Based on a memo from the Legislative Research Commission to the Appropriations and Revenue Interim Joint Committee dated September 25, 1985.
[3] Members of the Select Committee were Kern Alexander, Chairman and President of Western Kentucky University; John Brock, the Superintendent of Public Instruction; Larry Forgy, former state budget director and Repub-

---

lican candidate for Governor in 1987; James Melton, former finance officer in the Department of Education; and Sylvia Watson.

[4] Report of the Select Committee to The Honorable Ray Corns, Franklin Circuit Court, *Regarding Council for Better Education vs. Wilkinson, et al*, Frankfort, KY: September 15, 1988, 2-7.

[5] *The Council for Better Education vs. Wallace Wilkinson, Governor, et al*, Franklin Circuit Court, Division I, Civil Action No. 85-CI-1759, filed October 14, 1998.

[6] See item (2) under the "Findings of Fact" section of the Order. This section references two other historic school finance cases, *Robinson v. Cahill*, 355 A 2d 129, (NJ, 1976), pp. 132-133, and *Polly v. Kelly*, 255 SE 2d 859, (W. Va., 1979, p. 877) as support for this position.

[7] *Council for Better Education vs. Wallace Wilkinson, Governor, et al, Op. cit.*, 4-5.

[8] For Governor Wilkinson's view of his debate with the General Assembly over school reform, see his book *You Can't Do That, Governor!*, Lexington, KY: Walace's Publishing Company, 1995.

[9] *John A. Rose, President Pro Tempore of the Senate, et. al. V. The Council for Better Education, Inc.*, Kentucky Supreme Court , 88-SC-804-TG, 66.

[10] Ibid., 66-67.

[11] Ibid., 67.

[12] Ibid., 68.

[13] Ibid., p. 39.

[14] Ibid., p. 49.

[15] Ibid., 58, as amended by Order of September 28, 1989.

[16] Ibid., 58.

[17] Ibid., 58. Note the expanded text in the amended Order of September 28, 1989 wherein the Court reinforced the intent of the original language to mean the system is a state and not a local system.

[18] See text as modified by Order of September 28, 1989.

[19] Ibid., p. 60.

[20] See Wilkinson, *You Can't Do That Governor!*, 203-204.

2. A Statement of Principles

The Task Force on Education Reform early in the process adopted twelve principles to guide the design of the new school system.[1] The full Statement of Principles reads as follows:

I. **All students can learn and nearly all at high levels.** Our belief system must include the perspective that all or nearly all students can learn at high levels. Otherwise we are doomed to fail with many since expectations translate into self-fulfilling prophecies. If one expects a discernible portion of students to fail, one will encounter the first student with whom one has difficulty and identify that student as one of those who cannot learn when measured against rigorous criteria. That student will be literally or figuratively abandoned. Soon a second will join the initial failed child and then another and another.

II. **We know how to successfully teach all students.** This is obviously not true for every teacher in every school. This principle simply acknowledges that there are teachers and schools that are successful in serving children from every conceivable background – rich and poor, children of all and every color, the disabled and those who are not, those for whom English is not their first language and those for whom it is. What works is a matter of knowledge, not opinion. It is not a mystery. The challenge is not the challenge of discovery, it is the challenge of equipping all school staff with the knowledge to act successfully.

III. **Curriculum content must reflect high expectations and instructional strategies must be successful ones.** <u>What</u> children learn should be commonly challenging. We should provide a rigorous curriculum to all, not dumbed-down curriculum to some. <u>How</u> we teach; <u>where</u> teaching and learning occur; <u>when</u> teaching and learning take place; and <u>who</u> teaches should be different for different students, classrooms and schools. The variability should be governed by what works. When we fail

---

[1] The statement of principles was prepared by David Hornbeck for the Curriculum Committee and was adopted by the full Task Force.

with a child, a classroom or with a school, we must adopt the attitude that we do not yet have the proper mix of how, where, when, and who.

IV. **Ours must be a performance-based system.** Too often the question we ask our schools is, "Did you do what you were told?" The right question is, "Did it work?" Trying hard must no longer be sufficient. What students actually know and can do is what counts.

V. **Ours must be a system in which school performance results in appropriate consequences.** When schools succeed, rarely are their staff or the schools as institutions rewarded. When schools fail, rarely are their staff or the schools as institutions sanctioned. In measuring success, we believe the school should be the primary unit of measurement, not individual teachers. There should be a spectrum of consequences. The challenge is to have alternatives and use them in ways that are more sensitive and less blunt, making certain that all parties understand the repertoire of rewards and sanctions and the circumstances which give rise to each. The successful should be rewarded, but the unsuccessful must be more helped than punished.

VI. **School based staff should have a major role in shaping instructional strategies.** Who among us is prepared to assume accountability for our actions if we have little control over those actions? Who among us can legitimately deny our accountability if we have the authority and means to act? School accountability and school-based authority are two intertwined parts of the same proposition.

VII. **School staff must be equipped with the capacity to make good instructional decisions.** Higher expectations will not happen magically. Just as the corporate community knows that a strong outcome oriented staff development and training effort is essential to meeting its bottom line objectives, so it is with schools.

VIII. **Non-Essential regulations must be reduced significantly.** The rhetoric of school based management is empty if at the same time we bureaucratically impede or frustrate those decisions with layers of process.

IX. **Schools have responsibility for outreach to home and community.** The home has a strong school support role. Parents and guardians have the responsibility, for example, of making clear that schooling is highly valued, of assuring student attendance, of creating the expectation that children and youth will study appropriately, and helping the school with behavior issues. Some instructional strategies may require the involvement and cooperation of the community beyond the school. Some children will require health and other social service support to be successful in school. The school shall have an important role in coordinating these multiple community contacts in order to secure parental and wider community help in succeeding in the school's mission.

X. What is tested will heavily influence what is taught. This principle requires that our assessment efforts be as rich and varied and multidimensional as the high outcome expectations we have for our children.

XI. Learning begins early and does not end with high school graduation. Anyone who has watched a child from birth knows what extraordinary physical and mental leaps most children make early. We know that significant mental development has occurred by the time a child enters kindergarten or the first grade. We know that children develop at different rates which can be influenced by their environment. We also know that children today will change jobs six times and occupations three times as adults. That requires the ability to continue learning for a lifetime.

XII. There is a need to provide for a measure of independent assessment and enforcement authority. Staff at the local and state level must monitor the outcomes of school performance. They must be prepared to make adjustments to ensure successful performance. Teachers will assess and alter instructional practice as often as daily for some children. School systems must provide assistance to school based staff and even aggressive intervention in schools that are not successful. State or regional assistance from the State Department of Education, universities and, perhaps, other entities will in part result from examining school performance and being prepared to intervene. There are many forms that the independent and assessment authority can take. The point is not to suggest one or more particular instructional performance oversight vehicles at this time or to describe the breadth or character of circumstances that would lead to their use. The point is to articulate the principle that the oversight of the system should include mechanisms beyond the system itself.

3. A New Approach to Curriculum

A system of education begins with a vision of what children should learn and how they should learn it. In its written opinion the Kentucky Supreme Court set the goals for a curriculum in very broad terms when it specified seven capacities to be acquired through the system of "common schools." Obviously the Task Force on Education Reform had to conceptualize an approach to curriculum that would lead to the acquisition of these seven capacities. The challenge for the task force was to translate these seven capacities into language that others could use to create a new curriculum.

Curriculum Made a Local Decision

At the outset the curriculum committee of the task force made a major policy decision not to have a state-mandated curriculum. The task force wanted to give enough guidance in the law to ensure that a local school curriculum would at least meet the criteria set forth in the Supreme Court opinion. However, there was strong sentiment against dictating specific courses or subject matter as had been done in the past.

The guiding concept was the idea that the state should clearly define what children should know and be able to do at various points in their academic career, but leave the means to achieve these results to local education professionals. The intent was to open up the system to innovation in both curriculum and teaching strategies. The task force wanted teachers to have the ability to utilize whatever information, materials, and strategies they thought necessary and appropriate to achieve the learning outcomes set by the state.

In education terminology, the Kentucky curriculum is to be "standard based." The state establishes performance standards, which most students are expected to achieve or exceed, as opposed to defining a scope of information that students are expected to master, as was the case in the past. Decisions about the best way to help all children attain these standards are left to the faculty of each school. In other words, the content of the curriculum and the way it is taught can vary widely so long as it helps students meet the state performance standards.

Performance Goals for the New System

Section 2 of HB 940 restated the seven capacities cited by the Supreme Court justices.[1] Using these capacities as a guide, the General Assembly established six "goals" against which school performance will be measured in the future. These six goals also provide the foundation for the curriculum in the new system.

The first goal says schools should expect a high level of achievement of all students. The second goal says schools should develop their students' ability to meet six specific learning objectives that will be discussed in more detail later. The third through sixth goals require schools to increase their rate of student attendance, reduce student dropout and retention rates, reduce physical and mental barriers to learning, and improve the ability of students to make a successful transition to work, post-secondary education and the military.[2] These six goals for schools would be the foundation for the school accountability program later known as KIRIS.[3]

So there are six goals for schools and within them are six goals for student learning which schools must achieve. The six learning goals for students are based on work done by a Council on School Performance Standards created by Governor Wallace Wilkinson in February 1989 as part of his school reform agenda.[4] The six learning goals later were transformed into curriculum guidelines schools used to develop their own curriculum.

In goal 2 for schools, the task force made the six goals recommended by the council on school performance standards the six goals for student learning. These six goals are:

(b) schools shall develop their students' ability to:

(1) *use basic communication and mathematics skills for purposes and situations they will encounter throughout their lives;*

(2) *apply core concepts and principles from mathematics, the sciences, the arts, the humanities, social studies, and practical living studies to situations they will encounter throughout their lives;*

(3) *become a self-sufficient individual;*

(4) *become responsible members of a family, work group, or community including demonstrating effectiveness in community service;*

(5) *think and solve problems in school situations and in a variety of situations they will encounter in life; and*

(6) *connect and integrate experiences and new knowledge from all subject matter fields with what they have previously learned and build on past learning experiences to acquire new information through various media sources.*[5]

The first of these goals is intended to empower students with the basic learning skills: reading, writing, speaking, listening, visualizing, basic mathematics, information gathering, and how to use information technology. Obviously, communication skills are essential to success in learning. This goal previously was embodied in the "essential skills" taught in the previous Program of Studies, but it goes somewhat further in that students are expected to demonstrate these abilities in real life simulations.

The second goal is to learn the central ideas of the major spheres of human knowledge. With information (facts) growing beyond the ability of anyone to master, the school performance standards council recommended a major departure from previous curricula design by requiring students to learn how to use key intellectual concepts and processes to organize and interpret information rather than to simply memorize and recall it. The central idea is to learn the "big ideas" of the major academic disciplines rather than to master a large amount of information they have generated. The specific academic disciplines included are mathematics, the sciences, the arts and humanities, social studies, and practical living.

The third and fourth goals are to develop life skills and moral sensitivity in students. Surveys taken by the performance standards council revealed that the general public expects schools to reinforce the common value system of the community (honesty, respect for others, respect for authority, etc.) and to help students grow into responsible adults. Although some of these community values may be part of the school culture, they previously were not considered part of the curriculum. These goals presumably will require schools to formally address these values and behaviors as part of their regular curriculum.

Goals five and six focus on the so-called "higher order" thinking skills of analysis, synthesis, and evaluation of information. A lot of the emphasis in the previous curriculum was on remembering rather than using information. Students rarely were required to think about how to create new information, how to use information to evaluate the merits of an idea, or how to make decisions based on information. Surveys taken by the council indicated business and industry wanted people who could reason, solve problems, and make sound judgments based on information. This goal is intended to give students the capacity to intelligently use information, reason to conclusions, and to solve problems. Students also are expected to learn how to connect and integrate their experiences and new knowledge so they can create and invent new knowledge, works of art, technology, and so forth.

The Council on School Performance Standards

As noted above, KERA's six goals for student learning are based on the work of the Council on School Performance Standards created by Governor Wallace Wilkinson in February 1989 prior to the Supreme Court decision. Given the important role the Council on School Performance Standards played in framing the performance standards for Kentucky students and the design of the curriculum, it is important to know how it was organized and how it developed its recommendations.

Governor Wallace Wilkinson created the Council on School Performance Standards by executive order about four months before the Kentucky Supreme Court handed down its decision. The charge to the council was to advise the governor, general assembly, superintendent of public instruction and the state board for elementary and secondary education on the following matters:

1. *The extent to which the Kentucky Program of Studies will satisfy the present and future educational needs of the Commonwealth's children and youth, and what may be required to strengthen it;*
2. *Standards for student performance at various stages in a child's educational program which can provide a basis for fairly and accurately assessing the educational progress of every child in the public schools;*
3. *Appropriate methods of assessing learning, suitable for statewide use, which schools can use to document the extent to which children are acquiring all the knowledge and skills expected of them*

at specific points in their educational program, given their relative ability to do so;

4. *The extent to which the curriculum of the public schools can be appropriately adapted to the differences in learning styles of children, taking into consideration the inherent ability of children to attain the expected knowledge and skills.*

The council had to report its initial findings on or before August 1, 1989. As it turned out, this was less than two months after the Supreme Court decision was handed down.

The council membership was composed of twelve representatives of higher education, business, teachers, school administrators, state school board members, and included the superintendent of public instruction and the governor's secretary of education. J. D. Nichols, a real estate developer from Louisville who was very active in improving schools in Jefferson County chaired the council. Roger Pankratz, a professor of education at Western Kentucky University, took academic leave to direct the work of the council. The Governor appointed all council members.

The council began its work by conducting focus group interviews with business leaders, educators, students, and parents in all regions of the state. The participants were asked what they thought graduates of Kentucky public schools should know and be able to do at the end of their twelve years of formal schooling. The council then contracted with the University of Kentucky Survey Research Center to conduct a telephone survey. Using the information provided by these focus groups, the Center conducted 22-minute interviews with 838 adult Kentucky residents selected at random from several pools of respondents.[6] The Center interviewed 201 "opinion leaders" from such groups as educators, business people, and education organizations, and 637 members of the general population.

The interviewers asked the respondents, among other things, to rate the quality of education in Kentucky and to indicate the importance of such things as an ability to read, write, speak, use mathematics, solve problems, and use computers. They also were asked about the importance of teaching life skills such as those required to succeed in work, at home, and in their community.

The council analyzed the information gathered from the focus group interviews and the telephone surveys. The results were grouped into six categories that later became the six goals described in more detail below.

What is important about the process used by the council is that the goals it developed are based entirely on what Kentucky citizens said they wanted from the public schools.

The next task for the council was to translate these broad goals into more specific learning objectives. Five subcommittees were formed to facilitate the work of the council, each one chaired by a member of the council. About 75 people, mostly educators from Kentucky, were invited to work with four subcommittees of the council to develop descriptions of what children should know and be able to do at the elementary, middle, and high school levels and in vocational education to achieve the six learning goals. A fifth subcommittee worked on issues relating to the assessment of school and student performance.

As noted earlier, the council's work began about four months before the Supreme Court handed down its decision that named the seven capacities an efficient school system should provide to all children. The council immediately compared the six goals it had articulated based on the opinion surveys with these seven capacities and found they were very close in concept. After thoughtful deliberation, the council elected to keep the original six goals with some modification in language to come as close as possible to the capacities described by the Supreme Court.

The Council's Curriculum Proposals Are Adopted

The work of the Council on School Performance Standards was well advanced but not completed when the Task Force on Education Reform was created. Adoption of the work of the council by the task force would save it the long arduous task of creating something on its own. Representative Jody Richards and Senator David Karem, the co-chairs of the task force curriculum committee, saw the value of the process used by the council. Hearings on the council's report were held in late September 1989 to determine public support for it as a foundation for a new curriculum. The council's proposals received broad support in the public hearings, so the curriculum committee recommended them to the full task force which subsequently adopted them.

The task force knew that further refinement of the recommendations of the council was needed before teachers could use it to design their curricula. However, the executive order creating the council expired September 1989. The task force decided to reconvene the council in 1990, and require it to frame the six goals for schools "in measurable terms which define the outcomes expected of students." This mandate included defining and measuring both the six goals for schools and the six student learning goals. The council was required to present its final recommendations to the governor, the legislative research commission, and the board of education by December 1, 1991, after which the council would disband.

The Council Resumes its Work

The council reconvened in June 1990 to complete its work. Over the next 18 months the council conducted its work with 11 task forces chaired by educators from Kentucky who were recognized as leaders in their fields and were highly respected by their peers. The council extended a statewide invitation to Kentucky teachers and administrators to serve on these task forces.

Over 450 educators volunteered to participate. From this number, 125 people were selected by the council's executive director to serve as task force members or committee chairs. The result was involvement of a cross-section of Kentucky educators by type of school (elementary, middle, etc.), academic discipline, ethnicity, and region of the state. More than 200 of those who were not selected to be task force members served on various task forces in an advisory capacity. The challenge given to these participants was to identify the most important ideas and skills associated with their respective fields as they relate to the six learning goals of KERA. Experts were hired to help with this work. The on-going work of national panels that were designing model curricula at that time was reviewed.

Drafts of ideas under consideration by the council were circulated to every Kentucky school district for review and comment. Focus groups were again used to get in-depth reaction to the council's work. Public hearings were held throughout the state to increase awareness of what was under consideration.

In November 1991 the council presented a summary report to the state board of education. The board of education was required by law to adopt the product of the council without modification.[7] The rationale for this action was to ensure the integrity of the product by keeping all elements intact. The board of education could return the document to the council with a request for specific changes they felt strongly about. However, the board accepted the product of the council as presented to it in December 1991. The council report subsequently became the conceptual basis for the Kentucky school curriculum and a system of accountability for schools.

The Conceptual Design of the New Curriculum

The six learning goals were global in nature. It was necessary to provide educators and others something more specific about what children should known and be able to do in order to meet each of the six goals. In keeping with the philosophy stated above, the council created 76 "valued outcomes" for the six goals.[8] An *outcome* is something you expect as a consequence of learning. These 76 outcomes define in broad terms what students are expected to do with the knowledge and skills they acquire during their 12 years in public education. The outcomes are stated in performance terms. Mastery of these 76 outcomes constitutes successful attainment of all six learning goals.

The 76 outcomes were still very broad, so the council subsequently identified 373 specific *concepts and processes* associated with the 76 *outcomes*. The assumption the council made was that mastery of these 376 *concepts and processes* over the course of 12 years of schooling would constitute achievement of all 76 *outcomes*. Students are expected to demonstrate that they both understand and can use these 376 concepts and processes in "real world" situations. As a link to the former program of studies in Kentucky, the council grouped the outcomes and their related concepts and processes under traditional academic headings like reading, writing, mathematics, and science.

Few people in Kentucky or elsewhere have seen the final product of the council that became the foundation on which Kentucky schools were expected to create the new performance-based curriculum. Therefore, it is important to take some space here to examine some of the technical aspects of the council's work in order to understand the nature of the information initially made available to educators to guide their curriculum development in the early years of KERA implementation.

The conceptual design for the new curriculum is found in a 249-page technical report released by the council in 1991.[9] The technical report provided a chart for each of the 76 outcomes. Each chart is designed to communicate the essential elements of each outcome. Each chart has four elements that are described and illustrated here.

First there is a general statement that describes what the student is learning to do. This is the *outcome* statement. Next is a list of specific academic *concepts and processes* to be learned under each outcome. Examples of assessment tasks are given to illustrate how students can document their understanding of and ability to use one or more of these concepts or processes at grade levels 4, 8, and 12. Finally criteria are suggested for grading the assessment tasks.

Here is an example of each of the elements of a typical chart. This example is based on an *outcome* called "visualizing" that deals with *concepts and processes* associated with geometry in a traditional curriculum. First you have a definition of the *outcome* followed by the specific *processes and concepts* associated with the outcome called "visualizing":

> **BASIC MATHEMATICS**
>
> **Visualizing**
>
> **Valued Outcome:** Students organize information and communicate ideas by visualizing space configurations and movements.
>
> **Related Processes/Concepts:** Recognizing, naming, and drawing geometric shapes (e.g., circles, squares, triangles, rectangles) and solids (e.g., cubes, cones, cylinders, pyramids, spheres) and their attributes; demonstrating congruency, similarity, and symmetry; using angles; construction, comparing, and generating irregular figures; describing position and movement in multiple dimensions; constructing scale drawings.

As can be seen in this example, students mastering the outcome called "visualizing" must be able to use a large number of *concepts and processes* by the time they complete their 12 years of schooling. Initially, the council expected that students will achieve the *valued outcome* by learning the related *concepts and processes* such as being able to recognize, name, and draw various geometric shapes and solids. As they progress they will learn how to compare and contrast these shapes and solids. Finally, they will learn to use them to describe, understand and explain the physical world.

Learning Must be Demonstrated

A unique characteristic of this approach to curriculum design is the expectation that students be able to demonstrate their ability to use what they learn in real life situations. As noted earlier, the curriculum design is "performance-based" meaning students are expected to document their understanding of an academic concept or process by successfully performing one or more tasks requiring them to use the concept or process. The performance task is expected to simulate what students might find in the world outside the school. Here is how the council proposed that student mastery of a concept or process could be determined at each of three grade levels:

Sample Assessment Tasks

Grade 4

Event Task. Students arrange sets of counters to determine how many different rectangular arrays can be made with each set.

Portfolio Task. Students use a geoboard to reproduce closed shapes and transfer shapes to dot paper. Students create 5 other shapes on the dot paper and transfer representations to geoboards.

Event Task. Students arrange tangram pieces to match an image of a boat, cat, etc.

Grade 8

Event Task. Given cubes, grid paper, and four views of a structure, students construct a model of a building.

Portfolio Task. Given regular polygon stencils, paper, and pencil, students explain why some regular polygons tessellate and others do not. Investigate and describe where these patterns occur in our world.

Event Test. Students give a set of directions so a friend could reproduce drawn figures identical to the ones they have.

Grade 12

Event Task. Given appropriate information about the size and speed of a Ferris wheel, students develop a mathematical model that describes the relationship between the position of a rider and time.

Event Task. Students determine a relationship, which shows how the length of rope between the tie ring and a boat determines how far the boat is from the dock.

Event Task. Students produce drawings or physical models to represent configurations, based on given information.

Once an assessment task is performed, the teacher will evaluate it. In the past this usually meant determining if the result was correct. However, a quality performance has other elements than just getting the right answer. One often can get a correct answer by pure chance without ever understanding why it is correct, especially if the only thing required is to select the correct answer from a list of possible correct answers. The council members envisioned a richer evaluation of performance. Here is an example of the criteria the council suggested teachers might use to evaluate any of the performances described above:

General Performance Criteria

The extent to which students:

- Select and apply appropriate strategies
- Use appropriate mathematical notation and terminology
- Use reasonable deductions and arguments
- Provide quality explanations for the solution given
- Present a variety of appropriate solutions
- Prove an accurate solution

The information in these charts does not constitute a curriculum, but rather defines the expected results of the educational process. This means among other things that Kentucky defines what students must demonstrate, most at a high level, if a school is to be considered successful. It is the responsibility of each school to develop a curriculum, teaching strategies, and classroom instructional practices that enable its students to achieve the defined outcomes.

The curriculum committee of the task force recognized the need to provide assistance to schools to help them focus their curricula on the 76 learning outcomes and their related concepts and processes. The task of transforming the council's curriculum design into a model curriculum framework was assigned to the department of education. The primary objective of the curriculum framework was to give local districts and schools a methodology for the development of their own curriculum based on the conceptual design developed by the council on school performance standards.

As spelled out in KERA, the department of education was asked to identify appropriate teaching and assessment strategies, useful instructional resources, ideas on how to incorporate the resources of the community, provide a directory of model teaching sites, and suggest alternative ways of using school time.[10] The curriculum framework was to be completed by July 1, 1993, which gave the department of education 18 months to prepare and disseminate the framework to schools for their use.

The Role of Subject Content

When the department of education finally released the curriculum framework,[11] the issue of the relationship between the concepts and processes identified in the outcomes and subject "content" was raised. Facts appeared in examples in the curriculum framework, but teachers were not told what "facts" now were important and which ones were not. Therefore, teachers continued to struggle to find a balance between teaching what they formerly taught and teaching what they considered new — concepts, processes, and outcomes.

The absence of any discussion in the council's report about the role of specific information in the new curriculum probably was a major contributor to the belief by some that learning specific information was no longer important. Many sources of information could be used to illustrate a concept or process, and the council assumed teachers would understand that. Furthermore, the council assumed the department of education would make the connection between a concept and facts that illustrate it when the curriculum framework was developed.

The importance of the "content" issue was underscored when teachers complained that the new state accountability test seemed to presume that students had been exposed to certain information, which was not part of the curriculum, as they understood it. They presumed the focus of the state would be on a student's ability to use the concepts and processes identified in the 76 outcomes rather than on remembering information about them. When some items in the new accountability test presumed the student had a working knowledge of certain information, many teachers were upset because they had not been told that such information would be required for the test.

The working assumption of teachers was that any information needed to prepare a response to a test item would be provided as part of the test since the objective now was to determine what students could do with information they were given or able to discover. Subsequently, teachers demanded that the state clarify the information domain on which the state test items would be based so they could properly prepare their students in the future. This was a legitimate concern on their part. Furthermore, this situation sent an inconsistent message from the state over the role of specific information in the new curriculum, and how information should relate to the 373 concepts and processes students were expected to learn and use.

Shortly after release of the curriculum framework the department of education developed what it called "content guidelines." The goal of this effort was to provide guidance as to what information students should be expected to know in addition to the concepts and processes identified in the council report. The intent was to identify a domain of knowledge all students should be familiar with in each of the subject areas addressed in the council's technical report. The first of a series of "content" documents was distributed in September 1994, about a year after release of the curriculum framework. The department prepared additional documents as it continued its effort to provide the curriculum guidance teachers requested.

Although the content guidelines clarified somewhat the relationship between specific information and the outcomes in the curriculum design, teachers still are expected to select the sources of this information and to determine how it is to be presented to students.

Objections to the Term "Outcomes"

A problem arose when several conservative groups alleged that the outcomes were a liberal attack on education and neglected the basics in favor of teaching values they contended should be left to families and religion. The conservative Eagle Forum in Louisville and the Family Foundation in Lexington launched a campaign to have the new curriculum design dismantled or significantly modified. In a series of letters to editors of the state's major newspapers and in appearances at state board of education meetings, representatives of this viewpoint contended the new curriculum neglected what they called the "basics" and focused too much on "fuzzy, feel-good" ideas about human relationships.

The challenge was directed primarily at the concepts included in student learning goals three and four that deal with helping students become self-sufficient individuals and responsible members of a family, work group, or community. The contention essentially was that these are "social values" and not academics and therefore not appropriate for a school curriculum. There was a belief that focusing on these behavioral matters took valuable class time away from the study of the traditional academic disciplines. Furthermore, they took the position that socialization was not an appropriate role for public education.

In a personal effort to quiet the critics, Education Commissioner Thomas Boysen initiated a review of the language used in the original 76 outcomes to see if there might be a better way to communicate what the new curriculum approach was designed to accomplish. Representatives of the groups most vocal in their criticism participated in the review process. At the conclusion of its work, the department of education released a new list of 57 "academic expectations" which replaced both the form and terminology of the original 76 "valued outcomes."

The new "academic expectations" were essentially the original outcomes except that some of them were combined and the behavioral ones were modified to eliminate the term "values" in the language. There also was some editing of the original language for purposes of clarification. Commissioner Boysen made a pledge to the conservative critics that the state would not include items from goals three and four in the state accountability test. As noted above, these are the two goals that address citizenship and social behavior.

Notwithstanding this effort by Commissioner Boysen to satisfy their concerns, opponents of the new curriculum design sought support for their position from members of the General Assembly. However, after considerable public debate over the perceived virtues and vices of the new curriculum in its 1994 session, the General Assembly left things as they were. The debate was resumed again in the 1996 session, but this time the legislature and governor agreed to create a task force patterned after the original one to review all aspects of KERA including the curriculum. Criticism of the new curriculum was again debated by the new task force, but by this time the primary concern had shifted away from the curriculum design to the problems with the testing system. In the end, the essential nature of the curriculum design remained intact.

As I examine the arguments these opponents put forth alleging that KERA did not support teaching the basics, I have come to believe this view can be traced at least in part to confusion about what is supposed to be taught through the new curriculum approach. The very first student learning goal in KERA is focused explicitly on acquiring competent skills in communications and mathematics. There is no factual basis to argue that KERA or the academic expectations (valued outcomes) on which the curriculum is to be focused somehow neglect the "basics" of reading, writing, and mathematics. Examination of the academic expectations and the related concepts and processes required by the state should confirm that students cannot be successful in achieving them unless they have a reasonable mastery of all the basic learning skills.

The Role of Textbooks in the New Curriculum

In most American schools the education process historically consisted primarily of covering material in a textbook, usually one selected by a state textbook commission. This was true of Kentucky as well. Among the benefits of textbooks are uniformity in the information studied by children, high quality scholarship, and ease of use. As a child moves from one school to another the textbooks used are likely to be the same. All teachers work within the same subject framework. Little more is required of teaching than to find interesting ways to motivate students to learn what is in the textbook.

The use of textbooks as a primary source of information has been criticized for many years, primarily because the information in many subject areas is not challenging enough and often is outdated. Critics allege that many textbooks are "dumbed down" so they will not be too difficult for the average child. Others maintain that rapid changes in fields like science and social studies cause many textbooks to be outdated by the time they are published. It is difficult for textbook publishers to keep up with the rapid growth in knowledge in these fields. Thus students often are looking at maps, charts, and graphs that do not reflect recent historical data, events, or discoveries. Either the teacher has to supplement the textbook or students are left to struggle with old information.

Because textbooks are costly, they usually are replaced only about every six years. Prior to KERA, the textbook commission annually reviewed the current offerings from textbook publishers to find new textbooks for the ones that were scheduled for replacement that year. Given the time lag created by the selection process, a textbook that took three years to prepare and publish would be as much as eight years out-of-date before it would be replaced in the classroom. If the textbook was published several years before the commission adopted it, the textbook could be as much as ten years out-of-date before it is replaced.

Most textbooks are written to the curriculum of a few large purchasing states like California, New York, Texas, and Florida. States like Kentucky always had to adopt a textbook published with another state's curriculum in mind and then adapt it to its own curriculum. The unavailability of textbooks written from the perspective of the new approach to curriculum envisioned in KERA would pose a serious problem.

While innovative teachers always supplemented textbooks with other materials, the essence of what is taught in most classrooms is what the textbook covers. The issue the task force had to resolve was whether the benefits outweighed the negatives of a heavy reliance on textbooks as the primary source for what Kentucky children should learn in the new system.

These concerns notwithstanding, the task force recreated the state textbook commission. However, in keeping with a policy to delegate instructional decisions to local school personnel, KERA authorizes the Kentucky Board of Education to grant local school districts permission to use textbooks not on the approved list. The alternative must meet the selection criteria used by the textbook commission, a policy that was in place prior to KERA. Local school districts are reimbursed the cost of the alternative textbooks, which later was expanded to include other instructional materials such as computer software.[12] The result has been that many schools have opted to use instructional materials not on the approved list, and a growing number are replacing textbooks with performance-based learning materials.

NOTES:

[1] See HB 940 Section 2. [KRS 158.645]

[2] See HB 940 Section 3. [KRS 158.6451

[3] The acronym KIRIS stands for Kentucky Instructional Results Informa-

tion System. KIRIS is discussed in detail in the chapters on accountability later in this book.

[4] Wilkinson, Governor Wallace, Executive Order 89-151, February 1989.

[5] See HB 940 Section 3 (1) [KRS 158.6451 (1)]

[6] For specific details regarding the sampling design and research procedures described here, see Council on School Performance Standards, *Preparing Kentucky's Youth for the Next Century: What Students Should Know and Be Able to Do and How Learning Should be Assessed.* Frankfort, KY: Kentucky Department of Education, 1989.

[7] See HB 940 Section 3 (1) through (3)

[8] The council called them "valued outcomes" because both students and adults consider them very important. See Council on School Performance Standards, *Op. cit.*, p. v.

[9] Council on School Performance Standards, *Kentucky's Learning Goals and Valued Outcomes: Technical Report.* Frankfort, KY: Kentucky Department of Education, November, 1991.

[10] See HB 940 Section 3 (3). [KRS 158.6451 (2)]

[11] Kentucky Department of Education, *Transformations: Kentucky's Curriculum Framework.* Frankfort, KY, 1993. A second edition has been developed and was released in September 1995.

[12] See HB 940 Section 32. [KRS 156.345 and KRS 156.433] This provision was modified in 1992 to allow schools to use textbook money to purchase of instructional materials such as computer programs.

4. The Curriculum in the Classroom

The central idea underlying the new approach to curriculum is that the state defines a set of things students should be able to demonstrate after 12 years of schooling, and educators at the school level create a curriculum that will produce these results. The only requirement the state imposes on the local school is that the curriculum it creates be designed to achieve these specific results rather than just cover certain subject matter.

Curriculum is now a local creation that can be easily adapted to a local community environment and culture. The curriculum can vary from school to school as long as the intended result is the same. The *specifics* of what is taught are not to be standardized in Kentucky, but the *objectives* of the curriculum are to be essentially the same throughout all schools. The state-mandated outcomes are the only required common element in all curricula across the state. Everything else can vary. The policy intent of this local flexibility is to enable each school to create a curriculum that reflects its own social and cultural environment. This approach to curriculum seems simple in concept but it proved to be very complex in execution.

The Implementation Timetable in KERA

The only timetable in KERA for implementation of the new curriculum applied to the council on school performance standards and the release of a curriculum framework. Implementation of the new curriculum began with the council on school performance standards, which was given 18 months from the time KERA was enacted to prepare its report to the state board of education. The department of education was given an additional 18 months to develop and disseminate a curriculum framework based on the council's work.

Presumably teachers would need at least two more years to align their curriculum with the new standards. Based on this sequence of events, it would be at least five years after KERA became law before teachers could be expected to have a new curriculum in a condition to use. Then it would be at least several more years before students could be held accountable for learning it.

According to this timetable, full implementation of the new curriculum could not be expected until at least the 1995-96 school year, and its full effect on student learning could not be expected until at least the 1997-98 school year. Given the timeframe for implementation of the curriculum, it is unreasonable to conclude that perceived changes in student performance during the first eight years after passage of the law can be attributed solely to implementation of the new curriculum.

Three serious problems were encountered during the implementation phase. One problem was the absence of a clear plan for the implementation of curriculum changes at the school level. My personal observations indicate that most teachers seemed to believe these changes were expected immediately after KERA was enacted. As noted above, this clearly was not the intention. A second problem was a gross overestimation of the ability of teachers to create a new curriculum at the school level. However, the most serious problem was the accelerated timeline for implementation of the accountability system that presumably was to be based on the new curriculum. The timeline for these two major elements of the reform was not properly coordinated.

Unstructured Implementation at the School Level

There is no mention in KERA about when the task force expected local schools to make changes in their curricula. Furthermore, there was no plan in the law or in the working papers of the task force for an orderly transition from the current curriculum to one based on the work of the council on school performance standards. Absent any explicit guidance in the law, many teachers proceeded immediately with curriculum changes without the benefit of all the information they needed for this task.

Keep in mind that nothing was available to teachers for the first three years after KERA was enacted except the technical report prepared by the council on school performance standards. Each school district central office received a copy of the council's technical report shortly after the board of education accepted it in December 1991. However, most teachers never saw the document. Broader dissemination of the technical report might have helped teachers make sense of the list of outcomes, but the cost of reproducing the 249 page report apparently was a deterrent to local districts making it more widely available to their teachers.

It appears that many teachers were making curriculum changes long before they should have been expected to do so. They did their best to transform into a teachable curriculum the briefly stated outcomes that were widely distributed based on the initial work of the council on school performance standards. In spite of all this confusion and lack of helpful information and guidance, many schools did a very credible job of analyzing their curriculum and making adjustment in these early years, notwithstanding the limited information and resources available to them.

The pressing demand by teachers for curriculum information resulted in people not directly involved in the development of the curriculum design offering opinions about it before the official framework was made available by the department of education. Some things teachers were told about the new curriculum were not accurate. Anecdotes provided by teachers to the author illustrate the nature of some of the misinformation they received.[1]

For example, some teachers were told KERA required them to throw out their old textbooks, which of course was neither in the law nor in the council's technical document. Others were told that the "big ideas" were all that was important. Teaching facts was passé, they said, which also was not the case. Certain teaching approaches like "whole language" were said to be part of the new curriculum even though the council never addressed teaching strategies. Nonetheless, these opinions were taken as fact and resulted in curriculum changes at the school level that were not necessarily what was intended or desired.

The process of curriculum redesign at the school level became more systematic once the curriculum framework was released. In 1994 the department of education required all schools to engage in a process called "curriculum alignment," which consisted mainly of making sure all the items in the framework were being properly addressed in the classroom. Some schools had already done this, but others found the task still very difficult because the teachers didn't fully grasp yet the difference between teaching to a standard instead of covering subject matter.

The development of a totally new curriculum takes enormous effort and time. On the fastest track possible, it still took Kentucky more than three years just to conceptualize the design and promulgate the guidelines for a new curriculum. Then teachers were expected to take this information and create a curriculum dramatically different from anything they had ever known, and do it within a very short period of time. This was a challenge few educators were prepared to face.

The primary responsibility for this confusion belongs to the task force, which failed to provide for an orderly transition from the old curriculum to a new one. Specific dates for implementation at the school level could have avoided at least some of the confusion and frustration teachers faced during the initial period of change. Also, much more guidance was needed to help teachers create for the first time a curriculum that is school-based.

Inadequate Curriculum Development Skills

Even with the curriculum framework in hand, many teachers had difficulty figuring out what they were expected to teach.[2] The task of creating a school-based curriculum turned out to be far more difficult than anticipated by any of us. Many teachers told me they never were professionally prepared to actually develop a curriculum. Clearly a program of professional development should have been created to give teachers the intellectual and technical skills they would need to productively engage in curriculum creation and revision. Obviously just giving them a conceptual framework was not sufficient in itself.

The department of education responded to these problems in a variety of ways such as the release of content guidelines. The department also prepared high school course outlines in 15 subjects, which was distributed to all public high schools. It also prepared two documents titled *Unit of Study Development Criteria* and *Unit of Study Reviewing Guide* to help teachers create new teaching units aligned with the academic expectations. State education leaders believed that some of the complaints would begin to subside once teachers took advantage of these materials. However, all of this assumes teachers have the proper understanding and skills to create and update their curricula on an ongoing basis—something that now seems to be a questionable assumption.

I also observed in those early years a perception among teachers that everything now had to change. Nothing they had taught in the past had any value in the new system. In reality, the change has more to do with the focus of teaching than its content. Much of what was taught before could continue to be taught, but with the objective of using this information to help students to demonstrate their ability to use what they learned as prescribed in the outcome statements.

In retrospect, the task force probably should have required the state education agency to help schools make this transition by building a "bridge" between the old and the new, to help dispel the notion that the new is to replace the old *in toto*. This was in fact what started to occur after release of the curriculum framework when schools were required to engage in curriculum alignment. We also should have provided the training needed to help teachers make the transition from teaching to memory to teaching to a performance standard. This should have been done before teachers were asked to create a standard-based curriculum such as was envisioned in KERA.

The Impact of the Accountability Program

The state accountability program, initially known as the Kentucky Instructional Results Information System (KIRIS) and renamed the Commonwealth Accountability and Testing System (CATS) in 1998, was expected to impact what is taught because it would determine the percentage of students who could demonstrate all the learning outcomes required by KERA.[3] This statistic would be used in part to determine the effectiveness of the school and the consequences it would receive under the accountability program. Not only was it expected to influence teaching, the accountability test was expected to help communicate by example how to assess a performance.

It is important to understand that the task force members clearly recognized that the state accountability test would have a direct and powerful impact on what teachers would teach in the classroom. Prior experience with the earlier Kentucky Essential Skills Test (KEST), and experience generally with "high stakes" testing programs, clearly shows that teachers will teach what they expect these tests will cover. Given the consequences of the accountability program, we knew the accountability test would provide a very strong incentive to change what is taught and how it is taught.

On the other hand, we also wanted to avoid having the accountability test dictate the curriculum. We wanted the curriculum to address all the academic expectations whether or not they are covered in the state accountability test. Otherwise, the curriculum in the classroom will likely be little more than a reflection of what the state chooses to include in the annual accountability test. Obviously, how to ensure that teachers address all areas of the curriculum and not just what they anticipate will be on the state test is problematic from both a policy and implementation standpoint. We presumed the assessment consultants employed to design the specifications for the assessment system would appropriately address these concerns.

The curriculum and the assessment system are intended to mutually reinforce each other. Therefore, the design of the accountability test should have occurred after the design of the curriculum framework to ensure there would be agreement between what is taught and what is tested. However, this did not happen. Ironically, it was this lack of planning on the part of the task force that turned this objective on its head.

The accountability program got out of step with the design and implementation of the new curriculum right from the beginning. The timelines we established for implementing the accountability system made coordination with development of curriculum at the school level impossible. In the grand scheme of things, schools were not expected to make curriculum changes until the curriculum framework was completed in 1993. However, the accountability test was introduced in 1993 before many schools had even begun to modify their curricula.

Students were tested that first year with items based on a curriculum that had not yet been developed at the school level. Furthermore, the initial accountability test instruments were developed by the assessment contractor with little more to go on than the technical report of the council on school performance standards and the preliminary working documents of the group preparing the curriculum framework.

The discontinuity between what was on the accountability test and what students were actually being taught was a major problem for everyone. Even though the results of the initial KIRIS test were only to be used to create a baseline, being confronted with a new test without appropriate time to prepare students was unfortunate. It produced unnecessary anxiety in teachers who felt their careers and professional pride could be jeopardized by the test results.

Clearly it is highly desirable when drafting such comprehensive legislation to map out the time when each element is supposed to happen so that each element is properly integrated with all the others. This is especially critical when the elements involved are as synergistic as the curriculum and the state accountability test. In this case, we failed to do this. This failure had nearly catastrophic consequences for both the curriculum and accountability programs that are so central to the reform.

The timing problems associated with the accountability test can be attributed to the conditions under which the task force was working when the legislation was drafted. There was strong sentiment among members of the task force that the public would quickly demand data on how much schools were improving as a result of the reforms that were being enacted. The large increase in tax support for schools would have to be justified at some future date. Furthermore, there had been no testing program since KEST was abolished two years earlier. Thus the timing for implementation of the new accountability system was pushed up to the earliest feasible date. In retrospect, more patience at that point would have been more helpful politically as well as pragmatically.

Not all influences of the accountability test were negative, however. For example, the accountability test requires students to prepare writing and mathematics portfolios containing examples of their work. Although there have been complaints by both students and teachers about the time such activities require, early studies of curriculum changes indicate that schools are in fact giving much more attention to writing than was previously observed.[4] The math portfolios are much newer and the requirements are still undergoing change, but one would expect a similar change in the teaching of mathematics.* Clearly this is an example of teachers doing what is necessary if they know the results will be evaluated. In this instance they are doing what we hoped they would do.

Some Final Thoughts

It is not clear yet that a new curriculum is in place in all schools in Kentucky. Comprehensive data on what is actually being taught in Kentucky schools is not available. What is known is based on direct observations, anecdotal information, and a few studies of classroom behavior in a small number of schools. Furthermore, most of these studies were conducted shortly after the curriculum framework was released, so their observations and conclusions reflect for the most part what occurred during the initial years after KERA, well ahead of the time when the impact of the new curriculum could be expected. The full effect of the new approach to curriculum is still not known.

Neither the task force nor the department of education adequately understood what skills and knowledge teachers would have to acquire in order to create their own curricula using only the outcomes as their guide. This error in judgment proved to be a nearly fatal flaw in our effort to make the transition to a standards-based approach to curriculum, while at the same time requiring each school to create its own curriculum. It now seems that we were very naïve to think teachers could make this transition on their

---

* In 1998 the General Assembly made significant modifications to these assessment practices. These changes are discussed elsewhere in this book.

own with the help of a well-designed "framework" within which the content of teaching could be added by individual teachers.

It is easy to confuse what is taught with how it is taught. When the policy decision was made to move instructional decisions to the school site, a diversity of teaching practices was to be expected and encouraged. We wanted educators to discover and use the best instructional practices available to help all students master the new curriculum without interference from the state.

We understood that the new approach to curriculum would require significant changes in teaching techniques and strategies. However, we took the position that pedagogy is the domain of educators and not policy makers. Consistent with this policy, the task force did not address the how of teaching—only the end result of teaching. Therefore, there are no references in the law to such things as phonics, mathematical tables, whole language instruction, or any other teaching methodology.

NOTES:

[1] For results of teacher interviews on this situation see Corcoran, T. "Changes in classroom practices under KERA: A preliminary report on a five-year study of ten schools." Presented at the Annual Meeting of the American Educational Research Association. San Francisco, CA., 1995. Also see Appalachian Educational Laboratory, *The Needs of Kentucky Teachers for Designing Curricula Based on Academic Expectations.* Frankfort, KY: The Kentucky Institute for Education Reform, 1995.
[2] See the results of opinion surveys appearing in Wilkerson, T. & Associates. *The 1995 Statewide Education Surveys.* Frankfort, KY: The Kentucky Institute for Education Research, September, 1995.
[3] KERA requires an accountability test be given annually to students in three grades (originally 4th, 8th, and 12th) to determine how much progress the school has made in increasing the proficiency of its students in understanding and using the concepts and processes identified in the curriculum design. Schools receive cash rewards or face possible state intervention based on measured improvement in student scores on the KIRIS test among other things.
[4] See Corcoran, T. "Changes in classroom practices under KERA: A preliminary report on a five-year study of ten schools." Presented at the An-

nual Meeting of the American Educational Research Association. San Francisco, CA., 1995; and Appalachian Educational Laboratory, *The Needs of Kentucky Teachers for Designing Curricula Based on Academic Expectations.* Frankfort, KY: The Kentucky Institute for Education Reform, 1995.

5. Academic Performance Standards

It is not sufficient to simply define what students should know and be able to do. One must also define what constitutes evidence that students know it and can do it. Identification of the 373 concepts and processes was only one of several steps required to develop this new approach to curriculum. Also required are standards by which to measure competence in the performance of tasks designed to demonstrate an understanding of and ability to use each of these concepts and processes in situations similar to what students will encounter as adults.

Standards are essential from two perspectives. First, standards guide instruction. They focus teaching on what students must be able to know and do in a specific context. The curriculum must embody the standards. Second, standards provide the basis for assessing learning. They constitute the criteria against which a student's performance is to be judged.

What are Performance Standards?

Standards are the criteria that define a performance. For example the performance might be to jump over a hurdle. Standards for the hurdle jump establish the characteristics of the jump such as the hurdle's height, width, and placement, and the length of the runway before and after it. A successful performance of a "hurdle jump" is defined as the ability to jump over a hurdle that meets the "standard" without disturbing it. In reality, performance standards usually are much more complex than this, but this illustrates the idea.

In a performance-based curriculum, students are expected to demonstrate their understanding of and ability to use specific concepts and processes by performing a specific activity or task, often called a "performance event." A performance event usually consists of requiring students to do something that involves using one or more of the concepts or processes to be demonstrated. In order to successfully complete all elements of the activity, the student must have a sound understanding of the concepts or processes on which the activity is based. Successful performance of the activity documents the student's understanding and use of these specific concepts or processes.

Standards usually vary based on a student's stage of instruction, and his or her level of intellectual and physical development. For example, the standards for a "hurdle jump" will be lower for 4th year students than 8th year students. Standards become more rigorous with each increment in instruction, and in physical and intellectual development. The educational goal is to prepare a student over 12 years to meet or exceed the standards set for 12th year students. Ideally, teachers always should be aware of the ultimate standards even though their students may not be expected to meet them at this time. Standards represent the performance goals against which student progress is to be measured over time.

The concept of continuous progress in this type of system means that students are expected to show steady improvement in their ability to meet the standards applicable to their educational status. Students who make steady progress toward the applicable standards, although less than proficient, are considered to be on track to meet the standards within the expected time. Students who are not steadily improving will most likely have difficulty meeting the appropriate standards in a reasonable time. Such students will require special instruction.

Students who consistently and predictably perform at or above the standards for their educational status are considered to have met the current instructional objectives. Students who can perform at or above the next incremental standard is considered advanced. Instruction of such students should be adapted to their advanced ability and understanding to assure their continued progress even if this means placement with other more advanced students in certain curriculum areas.

Standards for an academic performance usually involve multiple criteria such as accuracy, a coherent explanation and proper documentation of the methods used to produce the result, and an explanation or interpretation of the result. Total mastery of a specific concept or process means the student's performance must satisfy all the standards and criteria applicable to that concept or process. Likewise, attainment of a specific academic expectation requires meeting the standards for all the concepts and processes associated with that academic expectation (outcome).

Progress toward mastery of a concept or process usually is uneven. Certain standards might be mastered earlier than others. Thus the instruction of students needs to concentrate on those elements of the performance that are not yet up to standard. Mastery of a concept or process means all of its elements are performed at or above the applicable standard. In writing for example, a student may meet the standards for grammar, but not punctuation, spelling, and organization. A written piece is not considered "up to standard" until all of the elements of the written product meet the relevant writing standards.

The Standard Setting Process

The task of setting standards for the 373 concepts and processes the council on school performance standards identified was enormous. The process took several different paths at various points, which I will attempt to briefly describe here.

The task force on education reform delegated the initial work of defining standards to the council on school performance standards and then to assessment consultants to be hired by the Kentucky board of education. The board of education also was charged with responsibility to approve new graduation requirements prior to the 1994-95 school year.

There were some precedents for academic performance standards. National organizations were working on standards for mathematics and writing. Standards for other disciplines were expected in future years. However, the KERA mandate for early implementation of a performance-based curriculum and assessment system in Kentucky did not permit the luxury of waiting for these efforts to bear fruit. Thus the challenge faced by the department of education was to proceed using the best standards available at the time. If standards did not exist, they had to be created. If national standards are developed at some later date, the Kentucky standards could be modified at that time.

As noted earlier, the council on school performance standards took the first step in the development of performance standards. The council's technical report contained general performance criteria for each of the 76 outcomes. These criteria were applicable to all the tasks related to the specific outcome. In the view of the council, a student performance should be assessed in terms of the extent to which it exhibits <u>all</u> the characteristics described in the criteria. However the council's report did not provide a method by which to determine the extent to which a performance is satisfactory in a holistic sense if all the criteria are not met. Must the student satisfy all criteria to be considered "successful"? This task was left to the assessment experts that would be employed later by the board of education.

The department of education was expected to expand on the work of the council in the curriculum framework it was required to issue. The department of education in 1993 released the two-volume curriculum framework.[1] It offers examples of "demonstrators" for each concept or process that are suitable for elementary, middle, and high school students. These demonstrators are in most cases a rephrasing of the tasks described in the council's report. The framework document also suggested teaching and assessment strategies that are essentially one or two word examples of something students might do to use the concept or process in the classroom. However, nothing was presented in these documents that represented a clear set of standards of performance.

As things evolved, the major effort at standards development was shaped and driven almost exclusively by the state accountability test. The department of education and the assessment contractor enlisted the help of several hundred Kentucky teachers and curriculum specialists, who worked in committees for many months to develop the standards that shaped the state accountability test items. It should be emphasized that Kentucky educators and curriculum experts created the performance standards, not the testing company. But these were not curriculum standards for general use by classroom teachers.

The primary task of these committees was to develop standards to be used in evaluating student performance on the state test. While the intention was that eventually these standards would reach the classroom teacher, this would only occur after they were used in the state test. Because of time and fiscal constraints, training in the use of these standards was limited to those teachers recruited to help with grading student performances on the state test. Presumably, other teachers would eventually learn how to use the standards from these test proctors and assessment specialists. However, there was no plan for systematically training all teachers in the use of standards to assess student performance in the classroom.

The Evolution of Performance Standards

Standards took two distinctly different forms and semantics. The initial assessment standards were called "scoring rubrics." Rubrics are the observable elements of a performance that are to be evaluated. Each element is compared with examples that represent different levels of accomplishment. These examples are called "exemplars." A score is given for each element based on the exemplar to which it is most comparable. The entire performance is given a "holistic" score, which is the sum of the scores for each element.

Students are asked to demonstrate their understanding and use of a concept or process in any of three ways: events, portfolios, and open-ended questions.[2] The assessment contractor prepared scoring guides for each type of demonstration, which initially were used only by people hired to score the accountability test. These guides along with sample test items later were released to teachers to help them understand the state assessment process and thereby better prepare their students for the state accountability tests.

In an effort to make a rather complex assessment system more intelligible to students, parents, and the public, the department of education defined four generic types of performance, which they named novice, apprentice, proficient, and distinguished. A specific performance falls into one of these categories based on the holistic score it receives. Novice, apprentice, proficient, and distinguished are categories, not standards. They are terms that show where a student's performance falls on a continuum from the lowest to the highest, and was intended to replace the familiar "A, B, C, etc." grading scale.

As can be seen from this description, the development of standards was less than systematic after the initial work done on them by the council on school performance standards. The most intensive work has been done in conjunction with development of the state testing system, but classroom teachers were expected to incorporate these standards into the curriculum. They could not do this under the circumstances. Consequently, teaching and assessment became disparate rather than integrated activities at the school level.

Still absent are standards for all concepts and processes that teachers can use as a guide to classroom instruction. I believe it is unfortunate that we did not require this as part of the contract for the state assessment system. Standards are an essential part of the design for the new curriculum. Until standards are created for all outcomes it is unrealistic to expect students to demonstrate them in the classroom or on the state assessment tests. This means at the very least that many of the learning objectives that are at the heart of KERA will not be met. It also is highly likely that at some future point the lack of standards will be used by opponents of KERA to discredit this approach to curriculum.

Problems with Standards

Standards-based education is emerging nationally, and Kentucky has been a leader in this regard. However, every effort to set standards for academic performance of which I am aware has run into similar problems. The most obvious is to get agreement on what constitutes a "standard" and what the standards should be in various academic fields.

National groups had just begun to work on standards when Kentucky launched its own effort. To the extent it was practical, Kentucky adopted national standards in fields such as writing and mathematics. In other subjects Kentucky teachers and national experts in the respective fields developed the standards. The most progress in developing a consensus on standards has occurred in the fields of writing and mathematics. Teachers in Kentucky have participated in many workshops and training sessions based on the national writing and mathematics standards. In fact Kentucky educators have been called upon to share their experiences with others at the national level.

It appears that Kentucky has both benefited from and contributed to the national effort to create standards that can be integrated into the school curriculum. However, various studies indicate that the understanding and use of standards among Kentucky teachers is uneven. Teachers who focused on recognition and recall of specific information as their primary approach to assessment in the past found teaching to standards a difficult transition. They point to a lack of prior experience with standards and the absence of good training and materials to guide them as a serious problem.

The department of education felt tremendous pressure to launch the performance-based elements of the accountability testing program. The integration of curriculum with performance standards was an underlying assumption of KERA, but the shifting of effort to develop standards for the curriculum to standards for the state assessment system resulted in a disassociation of the curriculum from the performance standards at both the state and classroom level.

For the most part, curriculum alignment occurred without school-level standards for measuring whether students are learning what the curriculum now requires. Teachers essentially had only the previous experience with state accountability tests and released test items as guides to the performance standards they should use in their classroom instruction.

I believe those of us who conceptualized the accountability program for KERA expected the council on school performance standards and the assessment contractor to collaborate to develop standards for each academic expectation (valued outcome). These standards would form the basis for both instruction and assessment. Whether the standard was called "proficient" or any other term was relatively unimportant. What was important was that teachers, students, and parents all know and clearly understand what is expected in a performance in qualitative (i.e., observable) or quantitative terms.

The collaboration did not occur. Instead the assessment contractor and department of education relied on groups of Kentucky teachers and experts to establish criteria for each performance level at each accountability grade. While the final product might not be significantly different from what would have been produced if the collaboration had occurred, the task might have been easier and continuity would have been assured if the experience of the council members had been utilized in this process.

High School Graduation Requirements

Recognizing the need to define graduation requirements in terms of mastery of the elements of the new curriculum, the task force required the state board of education to review graduation requirements prior to the beginning of the 1994-95 school year.[3] Deferral of this review until four years after KERA became law was intended to provide ample time for local curricula to be fully developed and put in place before changes were made in graduation requirements. KERA left the time when such changes would become effective to the discretion of the board of education.

There was broad recognition among observers of Kentucky schools that the greatest change was occurring at the primary level and the least change was at the high school level. Commissioner Boysen thought that development of new graduation requirements should be concurrent with structural changes in high schools. At his request the Kentucky Board of Education authorized creation of a High School Restructuring Task Force in July 1992. The commission was asked to make recommendations about the structure of high schools as well as graduation requirements. As it would turn out later, this would be the first of two groups that would be commissioned to recommend graduation requirements to the board of education.

The 51-member high school restructuring task force was composed of citizens and stakeholders. One year later the task force presented its report.[4] A key recommendation was to create "developmental sites" funded by mini-grants to promote experimentation with alternative ways to structure secondary schools. These developmental sites would function for two years after which the state board of education would determine the most appropriate course of action to take. This recommendation was later implemented and almost one-third of Kentucky's high schools participated in the demonstration projects in some form.

The restructuring task force recommended that local schools have the option to develop their own graduation requirements. The state should provide criteria that local graduation requirements must satisfy, but the requirements (standards) could be exceeded if a local school or school district desired this. Furthermore, the group offered some innovative proposals about what might be done to make the requirements something more than naming courses to be taken. For example, they suggested requiring students to develop an integrated academic portfolio or to develop and complete a "culminating project" designed by the student. A culminating project would be a major undertaking in the senior year through which the student would demonstrate an ability to integrate information from many academic disciplines.[5]

Although KERA gave no specific direction to the board of education as to what the graduation requirements should be, it was expected that they would be framed in "light of the expected outcomes for students and schools set forth in Section 3 of this Act."[6] Obviously, the new curriculum would have to be cross-linked somehow to the Carnegie unit[7] concept to enable schools to communicate to post secondary institutions what Kentucky students had studied that is equivalent to the traditional courses on which the Carnegie system is based.

The board of education missed the statutory mandate that graduation requirements be established by the beginning of the 1994-95 school year. In part this was due to a desire to await the results of the restructuring task force report. It also was a recognition that the curriculum framework had just been issued. Only now were high schools actively engaged in curriculum alignment. In the meanwhile, Commissioner Boysen resigned and the new commissioner Wilmer "Bill" Cody inherited the task of creating graduation requirements.

In 1996 Commissioner Cody created a Commission on High School Graduation Requirements to specifically examine the extent to which current high school requirements addressed the six learning goals and 57 academic expectations and to propose ways to hold districts and schools accountable for student achievement. The commission examined national standards and reviewed comments from 41 focus groups and eight regional forums.

The commission concluded that:

> *First and foremost, ... Kentucky's existing graduation requirements, as embodied in the Program of Studies for high school students, are profoundly out of sync with the state's Learning Goals and Academic Expectations. Although these goals and expectations have been in place for several years, no aspect of the current assessment and accountability structure provides a reliable measure of whether high school graduates are meeting them. For parents, post-secondary institutions, prospective employers and the public, there is little certainty about what skills and knowledge the current high school diploma guarantees a student possesses.*[8]

The commission recommended a three-strand strategy aimed at bringing graduation requirements into line with the state's goals and academic expectations:

1. Each local board of education working with the state's minimum requirements will create a new program of studies that will promote the achievement of the state's learning goals and academic expectations by all Kentucky high school students.
2. An expansion of the state's assessment and accountability system focused on providing reliable individual student results at two levels — mastery of the state's Goal 1 skills in communications and mathematics, and mastery of the remaining learning goals and academic expectations.
3. Redesign and expansion of the high school transcript in order to provide a more useful, comprehensive picture — for parents, employers, post-secondary institutions and other key publics — of the full range of knowledge, skills and abilities with which a student leaves high school.

The commission proposed that these recommendations be implemented on a timetable that would apply them to the graduating class of the year 2002.

Implementation of the second recommendation was complicated by public controversy over the validity of the accountability test, so the recommendation applicable to assessment of student proficiency had to await resolution of broader technical and policy issues addressed in legislation enacted in 1998. It is assumed that this recommendation will be addressed again as the replacement of KIRIS occurs.[9]

Obviously the state board of education had to promulgate graduation requirements before these assessment issues would be resolved. After reviewing his commission's report, Education Commissioner Wilmer Cody recommended to the Kentucky Board of Education in January 1997 that new requirements be approved effective for the graduating class of 2002. The proposal continues the use of the Carnegie unit and traditional course names.

The new requirements strengthened minimum course requirements, particularly in language arts and mathematics. Each student must complete an individual graduation plan (IGP) which incorporates emphasis on vocational studies and consists of at least 22 credits for graduation. There also is some flexibility given in terms of substitution of more rigorous courses for those with traditional names.

Local boards of education must prepare a local policy on high school graduation requirements that describes among other things how it addresses career development and the 57 academic expectations. A letter of assurance of compliance and a copy of the local policy must be submitted to the department of education. The local board also must establish a policy which requires that high school transcripts include at least the following: (1) courses completed and grades; (2) attendance records; (3) achievement test results; (4) vocational aptitude assessment if available; and (5) employability skills information if available.

Presumably the main argument for continuing to use the Carnegie unit system for graduation requirements is to avoid making Kentucky an academic "island" in the higher education world. Since the outside world has not changed after KERA, it is argued that Kentucky must continue to use the rules which higher education dictates. This no doubt is a prudent course to take from a practical standpoint, but it also means that high school faculties must be diligent about the task of curriculum alignment. The state board of education has left this task to the local school district, but the department of education has acknowledged local districts will need technical assistance to align traditional course work and titles with the 57 learner outcomes.

Perhaps adoption of the new graduation requirements will give an impetus to the curriculum alignment process in the high schools, which seems to be lagging behind the lower grades. If an alignment is not made soon, the complaint of the secondary school teachers will be that the lower grades have not properly prepared students for high school. The new curriculum as taught in the lower grades then will be declared a "failure" from their perspective.

Obviously this is a self-fulfilling prophecy. If the high school curriculum is not aligned with the curriculum being taught at the lower grades, a "train wreck" will inevitably occur when these students enter high school and are faced with traditional courses, textbooks, and content expectations. In fact, this already is beginning to occur. This could in turn create a situation in which parents of "college bound" students demand that middle grade schools return to a more traditional curriculum and the whole curriculum reform effort will unravel.

Likewise, the higher education institutions in Kentucky have been slow to accommodate to the changes in the school curriculum. They continue to require transcripts to report student grades according to traditional academic disciplines and in some cases disregard other intellectual products such as portfolios and performances. High schools are caught between what they are expected to do to meet the requirements of KERA on the one hand, and still provide information to colleges and universities that is based on a traditional curriculum no longer expected of Kentucky students. This issue presents a dilemma for the high schools that they have no power to resolve.

NOTES:

[1] *Transformations: Kentucky's Curriculum Framework*, Frankfort, KY: Kentucky Department of Education, 1993. A second edition was released in 1995.

[2] The KIRIS test did contain some multiple-choice items, but the focus here is only on the development and use of performance-based standards by classroom teachers.

[3] See HB 940 Section 31 (1c) [KRS 156.160 (c)]

[4] Task Force on High School Restructuring, *Task Force on School Restructuring Final Report*. Frankfort, KY: Kentucky Department of Education, 1993.

[5] See the Task Force's final report at pages 22-24 for more details.

---

[6] HB 940 Section 31 (1c). [KRS 156.160 (c)]

[7] The Carnegie unit was developed early in this century to standardize high school transcripts. Most colleges and universities use the Carnegie unit to define their entrance requirements.

[8] Commission on High School Graduation Requirements, *Clear Connections and Shared Responsibility: A New Approach to High School Graduation Requirements*, July 24, 1996, 1.

[9] The legislature abolished the KIRIS system in 1998. It is currently being redesigned to overcome many of the problems described elsewhere in this book.

6. Monitoring Student Progress

"Continuous assessment" is the term used in KERA to refer to the ongoing assessments teachers make of student progress using tests that they devise for this purpose. It is essential that teachers use assessments based on the performance standards set for each of the concepts and processes on which the curriculum is based. Such assessments also should be similar to those used in the state accountability tests to measure the progress of their students. Otherwise there is little likelihood that these students will perform well when it comes time for them to take the state tests. More importantly, assessment of learning against common standards on a continuing basis is at the core of the desired approach to teaching under KERA.

The task force considered continuous assessment of students to be an essential part of the overall teaching and learning system. Teachers are expected to regularly document that their students are making steady, continuous progress toward mastery of the learning expectations as required by the state. The task force addressed this issue by giving the state board of education the responsibility to help local school districts and schools develop and use whatever continuous assessment strategies are needed to assure student progress.[1] Unless each school is able to monitor the progress of its students toward each of the academic expectations, it will be very unlikely the school can continue to improve its success rate each year. The task force considered continuous assessment to be a critical element of the reform.

It was the hope of the task force that giving school districts the responsibility to develop their own assessment programs with state assistance would result in local commitment to a process of continuous assessment that would be fully integrated with the local curriculum. Hopefully this approach would result in more support among teachers and parents. Likewise, the task force believed there had to be a clear distinction between the state accountability assessment program and the school-based assessments designed to evaluate individual student progress at all grade levels on a regular basis. If the state developed the continuous assessment program, it would inevitably be considered part of the accountability assessment rather than as a tool of instruction and evaluation.

The state assessment program was intended to measure school success and was to be done only once a year at three grade levels. A district-based assessment program is intended to measure student progress at frequent points in the year and at all grade levels. The district continuous assessment program should give teachers in every school a way to measure the progress of each student as he or she moves toward the grade of accountability. However, we wanted the information produced by the district assessment program to be used primarily to refine and improve the instructional process, not just to prepare students for the state accountability tests.

In addition to developing a continuous assessment program, KERA also requires local school boards to publish an annual performance report in the newspaper with the largest circulation in the county by October 1 of each year. At a minimum, we expected them to report district accomplishments and activities pertaining to performance goals, including but not limited to retention rates and student performance, and to publish the district's performance goals for the succeeding year.[2]

We assumed that the student performance data in the annual report would be based on the results of the continuous assessment program required by KERA. We expected that school districts would report the data in a manner similar to the state accountability program report, i.e. as a proportion of students who demonstrated various levels of proficiency on all the academic expectations (or valued outcomes) taught in the district and measured by the district continuous assessment program.

Problems with Classroom Assessments

Performance standards serve two equally important purposes. On the one hand, they are presumed to be the objective of instruction. That is to say, instruction should be focused on helping students learn how to use the various concepts and processes associated with the 76 academic expectations that are the heart of the curriculum. On the other hand, the standards are also the measure of learning that has occurred. Standards are the measure teachers should use to determine if their students can demonstrate the ability to understand and use these concepts and processes under "real world" conditions.

Not only did teachers struggle to develop and teach a performance-based curriculum, they also had to acquire new assessment skills. It no longer was a matter of students getting the correct answer. They also had to be able to explain the process they used to get the right answer. The old "true or false" or multiple choice testing methods could not be used to evaluate most performances. Furthermore, the use of terms like novice and apprentice by the state, rather than the traditional "A, B, C, etc." letter grades, required teachers to use new ways to communicate levels of student achievement.

Teachers in Kentucky had very little professional training in assessment prior to KERA. The only assessment models available were the tests they experienced in their own education, most of which were so-called "objective" or standardized tests. Many of the tests teachers used prior to KERA were commercially produced by test or textbook publishers. Teachers who created their own tests often modeled them after tests they found in textbooks or in commercial tests. Only a few teachers had exposure to standards-based assessment, mostly teachers in the performing and creative arts, special education, and technical education.

The vision of a performance-based continuous assessment system at the classroom level was simply that—a vision. The transition from a traditional form of assessment to performance assessment as a regular practice in the classroom required an enormous amount of retraining for nearly all teachers. In spite of the great importance of performance assessment, KERA made no provision for preparing teachers to do performance assessments in the classroom. All of the state's assessment resources went into development and implementation of the state assessment system, leaving teachers to struggle with this new assessment approach with almost no preparation.

Implementation of Continuous Assessment

The department of education essentially took the position that it didn't have either the mandate under KERA nor the financial resources to provide direct training to all teachers in the field of performance assessment. A "trickle down" theory prevailed that basically assumed that over time all teachers eventually would come to understand performance assessment through the state accountability program. As the state test was developed, teachers would be exposed to various methods of performance assessment and standards of performance.

Undoubtedly, using the state testing system as a model had an important influence on local school assessment practices. In the absence of any other means of learning about this approach to assessing what students know and can do, teachers demanded that the state release to them test items that would not appear in future tests. At the very least these items would serve as examples of the various forms this type of assessment can take.

After the initial testing period, the department of education did release some test items to school districts. Also the testing contractor sold to school districts "continuous assessment" tests that resembled the state test. However, the content of these tests did not change over the first three years which led to complaints from the purchasers. In 1995 the state assessment contractor, with approval of the department of education, subcontracted this work to Data Recognition Corporation which took over the sale and scoring of these tests. The assessment contractor did agree to create updated tests over the next year.

Anecdotal reports and my personal observations indicate that many teachers quickly adapted these items to classroom use, particularly teachers in the accountability grades. As time passed, more teachers were given training as assessors in the state testing program. This training gradually was shared with other teachers across the state. In this sense, the trickle down theory was at work as predicted. However, this was not a completely satisfactory or an efficient way to achieve the end of preparing all teachers to do performance assessments in their classrooms.

For one thing, in the absence of any formal training in performance assessment, classroom assessment practices were slow to change in the initial years of KERA. Furthermore students were being tested by the state in ways unfamiliar to both students and their teachers. Teachers found themselves trying to figure out the new testing approach on their own while their professional standing was at risk. Teachers responded with anger and frustration. Even when teachers in the accountability grades quickly adjusted to the new approach, their students often had not been previously exposed to the new assessments because teachers in the other grades had not yet made the transition. This further aggravated an already difficult situation.

The absence of standards and examples of assessments for all academic areas in the state accountability test also posed a serious problem. The state could not test every concept or process every year. Therefore, teachers were only exposed to the performance standards for those concepts and processes the state chose to include in the state test. Some subject areas were not included in the test until four or six years after the state testing program was launched. Thus teachers in fields not yet included in the state test were left to find examples of performance assessment by other means, or else defer the transition until the state began to include them in the state test. Clearly, this was not what the creators of KERA wanted to see happen.

The state assessment system has been extensively researched and critiqued. There are technical flaws in some of the early elements of the state test. These problems caused considerable concern among teachers who had tried to emulate them. Over time these problems at the state level had a negative effective on the movement to performance assessments at the classroom level. It may be some time yet before we fully understand just how serious this problem might be.

The Impact of Continuous Assessment

Unlike the state assessment program, continuous assessment at the school level has not been carefully studied. Perhaps the most informative study of classroom assessment practices in Kentucky was conducted by the University of Louisville in 1995. This study focused on performance assessment at the school level.[3] The findings of this study are based on a limited number of schools and classrooms, but they probably represent the best information yet available regarding implementation of continuous assessment in Kentucky schools.

The university study found great variation in the use of performance assessment among and within schools. At least 70 percent of the teachers they interviewed indicated they had used to varying degrees documents prepared by the department and the state test items to help them with performance assessment. However, the observers found a range of differences in the level of understanding teachers have of what is required of a particular type of assessment and how it should be implemented.

This study found that nearly all teachers in the schools they visited used oral and written open-ended questions on a regular basis, and eight of ten teachers reported using portfolio tasks within units of instruction. However, they also found that the use of performance assessment for many teachers is primarily in preparation for the state accountability test rather than as an integral part of their daily instruction. Use of performance assessment also varied by length of tenure as a teacher, with nearly all newer teachers using it compared to 50 percent for teachers with more than 10 years experience.

The researchers found that high implementers of performance assessment were much more likely to: (1) use assessment to drive instruction; (2) use technology and hands-on test activities more frequently; (3) provide challenging and engaging assessments; and (4) provide content that covers multiple academic expectations. These teachers appear to have more closely linked instruction and assessment than teachers who primarily use more traditional forms of assessment.

Problems with Continuous Assessment

Assessment is just as important as instruction because it indicates the success of the instruction. It is the measure of learning. Assessment results should trigger intervention when learning does not occur. It also should indicate to a teacher when a particular instructional approach is not working with certain students. Corrective action should be taken based on the data provided by the assessment.

A common complaint I heard about using performance assessment is the time it requires. Previous testing methods were efficient in that they only required checking for correct answers in most cases. Answer templates often could be used to overlay a test so that the teacher didn't even have to read the question in order to grade the answer. Performance assessments require extensive time to conceptualize, prepare, execute, and evaluate. When teachers believe they do not have enough time to cover their instructional material as it is, they are loath to decrease it by devoting more classroom time to assessments like the ones envisioned in KERA.

It is my observation that assessment generally has low value for many teachers regardless of the method used. Assessments, or "giving out grades" as many teachers refer to it, is done primarily for the benefit of students and parents. Unfortunately all too many teachers do not value assessment as a clinical tool for evaluating their own effectiveness or that of the instructional practices they employ. The cause of a failure to learn is generally attributed to the student rather than the instruction.

The defense given for this belief seems to be that some students were able to learn, so the method must be effective. Many teachers contend that some students simply do not choose to learn or, more seriously, cannot learn what is being taught. Although this might be true in some cases, this is not a satisfactory rationale for not using assessment as a tool for improving the effectiveness of instruction even with students who appear to be learning.

These observations indicate that implementation of a policy of continuous assessment using performance-based tests requires more than training. It requires changes in school culture and professional values. Such a change can begin with schools of education, but it also must occur at every school. States that are trying to move in the direction of performance assessment must take these issues into account.

NOTES:

[1] See HB 940 Section 4 (3) [KRS 158.6543 (3)]
[2] See HB 940 Section 4 (4) [KRS 158.6543 (4)]
[3] University of Louisville School of Education, *The Implementation of Performance Assessment in Kentucky Classrooms.* Frankfort, KY: Kentucky Institute for Education Research, 1995.

7. A Fair Start for Every Child

The first goal in KERA says schools are to expect a high level of achievement for all students.[1] This goal reflects what the Kentucky Supreme Court said in its opinion:

> *Each child, every child, in this commonwealth must be provided with an equal opportunity to have an adequate education. Equality is the key word here. The children of the poor and the children of the rich, the children who live in the poor districts and the children who live in the rich districts must be given the same opportunity and access to an adequate education.*[2]

Although this particular passage probably was meant to apply to funding inequities, it also applies to the quality of the instruction children receive because the court also determined that an efficient system of common schools must provide all children with the seven capacities cited in its opinion. Not only should there be equality in opportunity and access, there also should be equality in expectations.

Over the years policy makers heard educators attribute the poor performance of some students to various factors ranging from low motivation to race or family socioeconomic background. In practice this translated into lowered expectations for certain children based on their personal or social characteristics rather than innate ability. One could argue that if little is expected of someone then not much will be attempted by that person.

It was the opinion of many members of the Task Force on Education Reform that too often standards are lowered rather than expectations raised. We wanted educators to understand that the education policy of Kentucky is to set high standards for all children and then find creative ways to help them meet these high standards regardless of their social, economic, ethnic, or racial background. Academic expectations of children based on anything other than innate ability are no longer acceptable. Probably this aspect of KERA speaks as much to school culture as instructional practice, but it is an important social as well as educational public policy.

Failure of Students and Dropouts

Many task force members saw retention in grade as evidence of a pattern of academic failure that developed for many Kentucky children as early as Kindergarten. Some of us believed that certain students were literally forced out of the system either because teachers didn't want to teach them or they were problems to the school. We also believed that these "dropouts" all too often end up in prison or on the welfare rolls because they are unqualified for most jobs. In our view, schools in the new system had to work harder to keep students in the system and to find effective ways to help them learn.

If grade-level retention were to be significantly reduced, changes would have to occur in the way teachers handle children who do not learn in the traditional manner or exhibit behaviors that interfere with learning. Including these items in the accountability system is intended to ensure that teachers and others in the school give appropriate attention to these children. It no longer will be acceptable to just make them go away.

However, more needed to be done than to simply hold schools accountable for dropouts and grade retention. A whole new approach to teaching and learning had to emerge that would ensure every child a fair opportunity to learn. Given that children begin school with obvious differences in preparation, intervention had to begin in the early grades. It was on this premise that the Primary School Program was created.

The Primary School Program

The primary school program is defined in KERA as "that part of the elementary school program in which children are enrolled from the time they begin school until they are ready to enter fourth grade."[3] With these few words, the first four years of school experience for Kentucky children was significantly altered. Without doubt the Primary School Program had an immediate impact on teaching and learning.

The philosophy of the non-graded primary program goes back many years in the history of American education, but it gained renewed attention in 1988. The National Association for the Education of Young Children published a position statement regarding developmentally appropriate practices for children of ages 5-8 based on "the most current knowledge of teaching and learning as derived from theory, research, and practice."[4] The Association specifically urged teachers to recognize the rapid but uneven intellectual, physical, social, and psychological development of children during this period in their life. The Association statement stressed the importance of giving children instructional experiences appropriate to their level of development rather than their chronological age.

Although not specifically proposing creation of a primary program, Governor Wilkinson contended in his reform proposal prior to the Supreme Court decision that it was time to alter the structure of the school to enable teachers to work more effectively with children who have different learning styles, aptitudes, or interests. Wilkinson contended that the traditional school leaves the educational needs of many children unmet because it is not flexible enough to meet their different learning needs. He observed that children learn in different ways, express themselves in different ways, and are motivated in different ways. A classroom in which everyone is studying the same thing at the same time is not one that can easily adapt to individual differences in either learning style or ability.[5]

With this as the background, David Hornbeck, consultant to the curriculum committee of the Task Force on Education Reform, made the following recommendation to the committee:

> *I recommend that we abolish grade differentials up until entry into the 4th grade. That will eliminate the possibility of "failing" kindergarten or the first grade. The basic school will, thus, extend from age 4 through roughly age 9, with the objective being to have all youngsters ready to enter the 4th grade by age 8 - 10.*[6]

The curriculum committee accepted the recommendation with no discussion at the time. The language remained unchanged in subsequent drafts of Hornbeck's recommendations to the task force until they were incorporated into HB 940.

I believe the reason this proposal was not debated by the task force was because most members believed it was unreasonable to "flunk" children at such an early point in their schooling. These members thought a major reason for such a poor showing so early in the school experience of these children lies primarily in the fact they didn't have the preschool experiences enjoyed by some of their peers. In reality it was an equity issue. All children do not begin their schooling experience on the same level. Some will know their numbers and alphabet or even be able to write their names when they first enter school. Other children may not be able to do any of these things. The members believed that the non-graded primary program would provide a reasonable amount of time for schools to equalize the learning of these children.

The Primary Program is Conceptualized

KERA gave little guidance regarding the form the primary program should take. Therefore, the program as it evolved reflects more the vision of the people in the state education agency who developed the regulations and guidelines for the program than the vision of the task force or the legislature. Here is a review of how the program developed and its essential characteristics.

Clearly, there was one central idea on which the primary program was to be based—continuous educational progress without regard to chronological age or number of years in school. Continual progress means, at the very least, educators are expected to monitor the learning progress of every child and create learning experiences appropriate to each child's demonstrated ability and mastery of the ideas and procedures being taught. No child should have to wait for other children to "catch up" before moving forward. Likewise, children should not be "held back" because they do not keep pace with other children their age in certain areas. How this is to be done was left to the education profession.

The department of education began work on the program as soon as KERA was passed by the General Assembly and signed by the Governor. Many issues had to be quickly resolved as various interpretations of "non-graded" began to surface. The language of the statute was vague and there was no significant discussion of the concept by the task force or in its working documents. The immediate task for the department was to "put meat on the bones" and give elementary school administrators, teachers, and parents a clear picture of what a non-graded school setting should look like.

The concept of a non-graded primary school program had been around for decades, but there were few examples of it in Kentucky. A team of professionals in the education department was assembled to work on the project. Among other things they reviewed the existing literature on primary programs and conferred with people who had experience with them elsewhere. A group of practicing teachers also was assembled to participate in the initial design of the program.

The primary program evolved over the next eighteen months. The department of education compiled resource materials on primary schooling and non-graded education. Staff also conferred with principals from non-graded elementary schools in Kentucky. Several groups of Kentucky educators were assembled to help create a set of "principles" and "best practices" that could provide the basis for program training materials, guidelines and regulations.

The first product of this effort was a document called *The Wonder Years*, published by the department of education in 1991. In this document is a position statement which describes the department's vision of what a non-graded classroom experience might be like.

> *An appropriate primary program for all children recognizes that children grow and develop as a "whole," not one dimension at a time or at the same rate in each dimension. Thus, instructional practices should address social, emotional, physical, aesthetic, as well as cognitive needs. The primary program flows naturally from preschool programs and exhibits developmentally appropriate educational practices. These practices allow children to experience success while progressing according to unique learning needs and also enables them to move toward attainment of the educational goals and capacities of the Kentucky Education Reform Act in an environment which fosters a love of learning.*[7]

The Wonder Years identified seven "critical attributes" of a primary program that eventually were incorporated in department regulations governing the primary program. The seven attributes of a primary program are important because they represent the official definition of what constitutes a primary program in Kentucky. The words in quotes are the attributes followed by their official definition.

(1) *"Developmentally appropriate practices" means instructional practices that address the physical, aesthetic, cognitive, emotional and social domains of children and that permit them to progress through an integrated curriculum according to their unique learning needs.*

(2) *"Multiage and multi-ability classrooms" means flexible grouping and regrouping of children of different age, sex and ability who may be assigned to the same teacher(s) for more than one (1) year.*

(3) *"Continuous progress" means a student's unique progression through the primary school program at his own rate without com-*

parison to the rate of others or consideration of the number of years in school. Retention and promotion within the primary program are not compatible with continuous progress.

(4) *"Authentic assessment" means assessment that occurs continually in the context of the learning environment and reflects actual learning experiences that can be documented through observation, anecdotal records, journals, logs, actual work samples, conferences and other methods.*

(5) *"Qualitative reporting methods" means progress is communicated through a variety of home-school communiqués, which address the growth and development of the whole child as he progresses through the primary school program.*

(6) *"Professional teamwork" means all professional staff in the primary school program communicate and plan on a regular basis and use a variety of instructional delivery systems such as team teaching and collaborative teaching.*

(7) *"Positive parent involvement" means the establishment of productive relationships between the school and the home, individuals, or groups that enhance communication, promote understanding and increase opportunities for children to experience success in the primary school program.*[8]

The Kentucky Board of Education later adopted regulations that further clarified certain aspects of the primary program and gave more substance to the seven attributes initially identified. The relevant section of the regulation is reproduced here to illustrate the official context within which educators at the school level were to frame their primary school program:

Section 3. Students in the Primary School Program.

(1) *Children who attend the primary school program shall not be described as enrolled in a specific grade level. Students who transfer from a school system that uses grade levels of kindergarten through third grade shall be enrolled in the primary school program and placed according to their developmental needs.*

(2) *Each elementary school shall design the primary school program to address the learning needs of all children who meet the entry age for the primary school program and who are*

not ready to enter the fourth grade. Individual placement decisions for children who are eligible for special education and related services shall be determined by the appropriate admissions and release committee, pursuant to 707 KAR 1:051.

Section 4. Curriculum

(1) *The curriculum of the primary school program shall address the goals of education and the model curriculum framework set forth in KRS 158.6451.*

(2) *Instructional practices in the primary school program shall motivate and nurture children in diverse cultures; shall address the social, emotional, physical, aesthetic and cognitive needs of children; and shall be based upon the following principles of how young children learn:*

(a) *Young children learn at different rates through different styles.*

(b) *Young children learn as they develop a sense of self-confidence in a positive learning environment.*

(c) *Young children learn best with "hands on" experiences where they are encouraged to question, explore and discover.*

(d) *Young children learn best through an integrated curriculum by engaging in real-life activities and learning centers.*

(e) *Young children learn best in a social environment where they can converse with others to expand their language and their thinking.*

(3) *Students enrolled in the primary school program shall progress through the curriculum at their individual learning rates.*

(4) *Parents and legal guardians of children enrolled in the primary school program shall receive regular reports at a minimum of four (4) times per year regarding their children's individual progress in meeting the goals of education set forth in KRS 158.6451(1) and successful completion of the primary school program.*[9]

With the attributes of a primary program now defined and other issues clarified, the task facing the department of education, school districts, and local schools was to figure out how to turn these ideas into reality in Kentucky classrooms.

Implementation of the Primary School Program

KERA required all elementary schools to implement the primary program by the beginning of the 1992-93 school year.[10] The program is open to any child who is five years of age on or before October 1 of the school year, so Kindergarten is part of the primary program.[11] The department of education had roughly two years after passage of KERA to develop the regulations required to implement the program and to provide professional development and guidance to the elementary school teachers and administrators who had to implement it.

The department of education initially proposed a three-step plan for implementing the primary program. According to Betty Steffy who was Deputy Superintendent of Instruction at the department at the time, the first stage immediately followed passage of KERA and was called Exploration. Steffy described this as "a time for districts to implement awareness activities that would enable faculty to gain an understanding of the changes necessary to move from the traditional elementary concept of schooling to the 'success oriented' Primary program."[12]

The second phase occurred during the second school year (1991-92) after passage of KERA and dealt with preparation for change. School districts were required to develop an action plan for each school describing how the district intended to achieve full implementation of the primary school program by the beginning of the 1995-96 school year. The intention was to give districts and schools up to three years to fully implement their plan. The third and final stage was to be actual implementation of all elements of the district plan.

During the 1992 session of the General Assembly, this three step plan for phasing in the primary program was challenged by key legislators who believed the intent of the law in 1990 was for all elementary schools to "fully implement" the primary program in the 1992-93 school year. Legislators were concerned that the three-year delay might encourage some schools to put off making any progress until the last minute. Subsequently, KERA was amended in the 1992 legislative session to add language that said "the program, in its entirety, shall be fully implemented for all students who have not entered the fourth grade in every elementary school in the district by the beginning of the 1993-1994 school year."[13] The practical effect of this change was to delay the full implementation date by one year.

The department of education accepted the new deadline and the Kentucky Board of Education adopted the necessary regulations shortly after the close of the 1992 legislative session. Each school was required to submit an action plan to the department of education by June 15, 1992, describing the steps to be taken to begin implementation of a primary program in the 1992-93 school year and fully implement it by the following school year.

Support for Implementation of the Primary Program

Obviously, the most difficult challenge was to prepare the nearly 6,000 elementary school teachers for the transition that had to occur within a period of two school years. The department used every avenue available to it to disseminate information about timelines and procedures and to answer questions. The Kentucky Educational Television network was used to inform large numbers of teachers about various aspects of the program. Staff members of the department gave talks or briefings at almost every organizational meeting of professional educators, citizens, and parents during the first 12 months following passage of KERA. The newly created state Regional Service Centers all had people trained to help school personnel implement the program.

A Primary School Institute was convened in October 1991 in Louisville, the first of two major training programs sponsored by the department of education for all interested educators in the state. A second Institute was held in the spring of 1992 where more informational materials were distributed to educators and others. The Institute also provided opportunities for educators to share their experiences and knowledge.

As mentioned earlier, all elementary schools had to submit an implementation plan to the department of education. These plans were reviewed and approved during the 1992-93 school year for full implementation the following school year (1993-94). Department guidelines for preparation of the plan were specifically designed to help local school administrators and teachers think through how they would create a school environment that had the seven attributes of a primary program.

Levels of Implementation

Except for the state accountability system, no other element of KERA probably has had a greater impact on teaching and learning than the primary program. The changes were to be almost immediate and complete —probably an unreasonable expectation on the part of the policy makers. Implementation of the primary program has received considerable attention from researchers as evidenced by over 30 studies of it reported as completed or in progress in 1996.[14] These studies range from broad surveys to in-depth examination of a small number of elementary schools that have tried to implement the primary program. All of these studies provide useful information even if they do not represent a full picture of what has happened in every school in Kentucky. Based on my personal observations in the field and the results of these formal studies, certain conclusions can be drawn about the probable impact this program has had on teaching and learning up to the present time.

All of these studies consistently indicate there is wide variation from teacher to teacher and school to school in the manner and degree to which the components of the primary program are being implemented. The percentage of teachers or schools that have adopted various elements of the program vary over time and from one study to another, but the evidence reported by these researchers and my personal observations clearly confirm that much has occurred that is positive. However, Kentucky still has a long way to go before it can declare that the primary program is "fully implemented" in all its elementary schools.

Some change has occurred in almost every elementary school in the state. However, in as many as two-thirds of Kentucky schools, some teachers are still using very traditional methods of instruction even after adopting some of the physical attributes of the primary program such as the use of learning centers and flexible grouping of children. Teachers appear to be selectively implementing various elements of the program, probably based on what they feel most comfortable with. The result is a hodgepodge of the old and the new throughout the state whereas the task force envisioned a holistic transition from one form to another.

Although this might appear to be a pessimistic assessment of this element of the reform, there are examples of schools that have fully implemented primary programs and significant changes have occurred even in schools that still have not implemented every element of the program. The point is that fully implemented primary programs still are not the norm in Kentucky, notwithstanding that the statutory deadline for full implementation was passed five years prior to this evaluation.

The Kentucky Institute for Education Research has conducted annual progress reports on the implementation of the primary program since 1993. The 1995 progress report indicates that the following practices were in use to a significant degree by at least two-thirds of the teachers or school sites studied:

- flexible use of space;
- student use of non-textbook printed materials;
- student initiated communication with other students;
- two-way student and teacher interaction;
- positive discipline;
- qualitative evaluation of student performance over a broad range of subjects;
- regularly scheduled parent/teacher conferences and frequent communication between teacher and parents;
- children remaining with the same teacher for two or more years;
- qualitative progress reports to parents; and
- instructional planning with their colleagues.[15]

These practices are encouraged by the state and appear to be in wide use in Kentucky primary schools.

Other studies indicate that in many elementary school classrooms, researchers observed children engaged in hands-on activities, reading literature, writing compositions, and involved in conceptually based mathematics activities, all of which are good indicators of instructional practices consistent with the seven attributes of the primary program.[16] Of course it is not known how many of these practices existed in these schools prior to the primary program, but it is reasonable to assume that some of them could have been found in some schools prior to KERA. In any event, it appears that most elementary schools exhibit many of the instructional practices desired in the primary school program.

On the other hand, appearances can sometimes be deceiving, as several in-depth studies have shown. In some cases teachers adopt the form without the substance of an element of the primary program. For example, teachers create learning centers where children can work together in small groups, an innovation that has been encouraged by the state. The purpose of a learning center is to give students an opportunity to have hands-on experience with something being taught. However, the activities in some learning centers are not directly related to instruction. Some are only taking the place of "seat work" which previously was assigned to keep students busy while the teacher does other things such as grade papers. Thus it might appear that the teacher is implementing a learning center approach but actually is only substituting one form of "busy work" for another.

The elements of the primary program that have been most difficult for teachers to implement deal with multiage and ability grouping, focusing instruction on the state learning expectations, and making continuous and qualitative assessments of learning.[17] Even though these concepts are at the heart of the intent of the primary program, they are the elements that appear to have the weakest implementation. It seems that it is very difficult for teachers to put into practice the concept that children ought to be allowed to learn at the fastest rate they can.

The department of education defined "continuous progress" as a student's unique progression through the primary school program without comparison to the rate of others or consideration of the number of years in school. By extension, this implies flexible grouping and regrouping of children of different age, sex and ability known as "multi-age and multi-ability classrooms."

Here is a classic case of form not following function. In some schools mixing students of different ages and ability levels was an end in itself rather than a tool to be used judiciously to group and regroup children throughout the day and week in ways that would further their continuous progress. I personally observed the mindless grouping of children from 5 to 8 years of age without regard to their learning needs or abilities. These teachers thought KERA mandated that they group children of all ages at all times regardless of the pedagogic problems such groupings might create.

Actually, KERA makes no such requirement. The policy intent of the primary program clearly is for teachers to disregard age or years in school as the primary basis for organizing students for instructional purposes. The abolition of "grade levels" is to provide a legal basis for continuous progress, but it also is intended to remove the one structural element of the school that most symbolizes movement of students as a group rather than on the basis of their individual progress. Retention and promotion within the primary program is incompatible with the concept of continuous progress. It was the hope of the framers of KERA that this approach would benefit the best as well as the poorest students by allowing both to advance in their learning at the fastest pace of which they are capable during their most formative years.

Failure of so many teachers to understand the basic intent of the primary program has resulted in some unintended consequences for teachers, students, and parents. Many schools have essentially recreated a "grade level" structure by dividing the primary program students into two age groups typically referred to as P1 and P2. They have simply replaced one form of age grading with another, clearly not what was originally intended. In other schools there are times when students are placed in multi-age groupings, but often it appears that the purpose is not related in any way to instruction or student learning needs. Rather, the purpose is to "comply with KERA."

Probably the most controversial aspect of multiage grouping is the inclusion of kindergarten children in these groupings. The law is clear that kindergarten is considered part of the primary program. The main reason for the inclusion of kindergarten was to prevent "failing" of children after their first year in school. The kindergarten is still supposed to be what it always has been—an orientation to the school experience. However, in the spirit of continuous progress, there should be a seamless transition from kindergarten into the non-graded primary school classroom. A kindergarten child who is well advanced in certain skills like reading or writing could benefit from being with older children with similar skills, but a compulsory mixing of kindergarten children with 8 year old children was never the intent of KERA.

Mixing children of different abilities was in part intended to mainstream children with disabilities as required by federal law, but it also was considered to be a potentially good experience for certain students who need the challenge provided by better performing students. The merits of mixing ability levels will always depend on the range of ability that must be bridged in a single classroom and also whether the experience will leave a student feeling even more inadequate if placed in direct competition with more able students.

It was expected that teachers would make appropriate judgments about the benefits and downsides of placing students in multi-ability classrooms. Unfortunately, students sometimes appear to be placed in a classroom based on age to meet the need to create a multi-age classroom and end up in a multi-ability situation that is developmentally inappropriate. This is an excellent example of meeting a "requirement" instead of doing what is professionally appropriate.

In response to persistent complaints from teachers and parents about multi-age and multi-ability grouping, the General Assembly in 1994 amended KERA as follows:

> *A school council established pursuant to KRS 160.345 or if none exists, a school may determine, based on individual student needs, that implementing multi-age and multi-ability classrooms need not apply for every grouping of students for every activity throughout the entire day. The school council or school shall revise the action plan to reflect any changes in the primary program's design.*[18]

The General Assembly in the same legislation also addressed the issue of kindergarten children being included by amending the statute to "allow for grouping of students attending their first year in school when determined to be developmentally appropriate."

After passage of this legislation, the Kentucky Board of Education issued a position statement on multi-age and multi-ability grouping in the primary program which said:

> *The focus on developmentally appropriate practices and individual student needs in making grouping decisions will most often result in multi-age and multi-ability classrooms.*
>
> *For instructional purposes, there may be time during the day or week when students are in single age groupings based upon developmentally appropriate practices meeting individual student needs. The school council, or the school in the buildings without a council, may decide how to appropriately use the flexibility permitted in grouping students. It is unlikely that this type of grouping would result in any one student remaining with the same group of students for an extended period of time.*
>
> *House Bill 187 does not permit councils or schools to decide not to implement an appropriate primary program, which continues to include multi-age and multi-ability grouping.*[19]

Perhaps this special legislation might not have been needed had the focus in the initial implementation of the primary program been more on the "why" rather than the "how" of multiage and multi-ability grouping. The intent of KERA to have students make continuous progress through the primary program was not communicated well.

Assessment of Continuous Progress

The concept of continuous progress relies on a teacher's ability to appropriately assess each student's learning progress in order to properly place that student in the most appropriate group. This is another area where teachers seem to have great difficulty. The career-long practice of teaching to a class instead of to individual students leaves teachers with habits of mind that are difficult to change. Even where teachers are using developmentally appropriate instructional practices, there sometimes is little indication that they are attending to the individual development of the children in their classes.[20]

It is important to note here that the department of education has done more to help primary teachers with continuous assessment of students than for any other group of teachers by developing the Kentucky Early Learning Profile (KELP) for their suggested use. Assuming that teachers are creating authentic assessment activities for their students, teachers can use the KELP to measure student progress. However any authentic assessment methodology is acceptable.

Among other things, KELP requires teachers to keep "anecdotal records" which represent ongoing classroom observations of the progress of individual students. The idea behind the anecdotal records is to give teachers information they need to improve instruction and to alter their approach to children who are having difficulty with certain concepts or processes. However, researchers have reported that this is difficult even for teachers who believe this is an important aspect of their professional practice.[21] The common complaint is the amount of time it takes to just keep the records leaves little time to evaluate what they mean. Thus KELP in many schools is a time consuming record keeping system which teachers methodically maintain but is disconnected from their instructional decisions.

While time is clearly a valid issue, in many situations it masks the more fundamental issue of the seeming failure of teachers to see the importance of individualizing instruction based on clinical data they collect on student performance. The mode of operation still is to continue teaching to the class rather than the individual student even when appropriate assessments are being made on which to base individualized instruction.

Overall, Kentucky teachers and administrators deserve much credit for responding with dedication and persistence to perhaps the most demanding element of KERA even in the face of unreasonable deadlines. The fact that there are still gaps in implementation of the primary program should not lead one to conclude that it cannot succeed or that it has not had a positive impact on both teachers and students. Recent surveys indicate that many teachers now report they would not return to some of the old methods of teaching even if the primary program were suspended because they see many benefits from it for their students.[22]

Exit from the Primary Program

The only aspect of the primary school program to receive any significant discussion by the Task Force on Education Reform was the issue of ensuring readiness to move out of the program into the fourth grade. What concerned the curriculum committee was how to ensure that students in the primary program attain at least the minimum competencies necessary to continue their learning before moving on. At the last moment, the following language was added to HB 940 in an attempt to ensure that children would not be allowed to progress beyond the primary program unless and until they had acquired at least the basic skills necessary to successful learning:

> *Notwithstanding any statute to the contrary, successful completion of the primary school program shall be a prerequisite for a child's entrance into fourth grade. The State Board of Elementary and Secondary Education shall establish, by regulation, methods of verifying successful completion of the primary school program pursuant to the goals of education as described in KRS 185.6451.*[23]

Obviously, "successful completion" has to be defined before it can be verified. This provision requires the state board of education to make that standard clear and enforceable.

When thinking in terms of continuous progress, the performance goal is presumed to be the highest level of performance one could reasonably expect from a child after four years of formal schooling (kindergarten through the traditional third grade). When a standard is meant to be a "gatekeeper" rather than a goal, it represents the minimum that one will accept rather than the highest performance that one wants a student to strive to attain.

In a sense this exit requirement is a contradiction in policy. It appears that the legislation has asked the Board to send two signals. On the one hand, all students should be encouraged to do the best they are capable of doing, but on the other hand we will accept something less and call it "success." The Kentucky Board of Education had to handle this mandate with great skill. Setting a threshold at less than the highest performance desired has in the past always led to mediocrity, with far too many students continuing to move through the system with very marginal skills. Nonetheless, a regulation had to be prepared that would be responsive to this mandate but avoid the pitfall of setting standards of performance for all students that are less than challenging.

The regulation the Board adopted says that a determination of successful completion of the primary program is to be made on an individual student basis. Evidence to support the determination should include teacher observations and anecdotal records, student products or performances, and evidence of student self-reflection or assessment. The regulation then itemizes 18 specific items that must be addressed in making the determination.[24] The regulation leaves to individual schools or their districts the determination of was constitutes a "successful" performance on each of the18 items that must be addressed.

The 18 items listed in the regulation are descriptive rather than quantitative in nature. It is like saying that students should be able to jump high without defining how high is "high." The state has yet to define what constitutes a desired level of performance on each of these 18 items before a child can be declared to have successfully completed the primary program. The Board regulation only requires that local standards "be consistent with performance expectations which would support student success in the fourth grade."[25]

It appears that specific minimum levels of performance for exiting the primary school will not be forthcoming from the state any time soon. Exit decisions will continue for some time to be based solely on local judgments by teachers about what level of performance constitutes "success."

In one sense, the situation now is no different than it was before KERA and creation of the primary school program. Teachers have for decades measured the performance of students against their own standard of success and then issued a letter grade based on this standard. Students were either promoted or retained based on local definitions of what a letter grade of "A" or "F" represented.

At some future time, Kentucky's educational leadership must address the issue of performance standards for at least the fourth, eighth and twelfth grades if for no other reason than to provide an objective foundation for the state accountability tests. In any case, objective performance standards for primary school students can only be prepared after standards for the fourth grade are established. How else can primary school teachers determine that their exit criteria would support student success in the fourth grade as is now required of them?

Obstacles Encountered in Implementation

Although the primary program was seemingly non-controversial when KERA was enacted, some aspects of its implementation have been problematic or quite controversial. Among the more important obstacles were the timetable, insufficient meeting and planning time, training which often was not focused on the most immediate needs of teachers, lack of parent support for the non-graded classroom, and the practical problems creating and managing multi-age groups.

It is obvious in retrospect that administrators and teachers needed more than a year or two to rethink their profession and adopt very different methods of work. Some of the changes inherent in the primary school program necessitate retraining and acquiring new knowledge. Unfortunately, KERA did not include a special program to specifically prepare existing teachers and administrators to implement the concepts on which the primary school is based. Furthermore, the official school calendar did not make enough days available for primary school teachers to participate in all the training opportunities that were available.

Notwithstanding the intensive efforts of the department of education to prepare school personnel for the transition, most primary school teachers still felt unprepared to make the changes required of them by the deadline set in the legislation. In 1992 the General Assembly increased the number of days in the school year available to all teachers and administrators for professional development to help ease the problem of time to acquire new skills and knowledge. Still there was no systematic retraining program put in place for primary school teachers, so the additional days were not necessarily used in a manner best suited to help schools make the transition.

Time for retraining obviously was an important issue with teachers in the early years of the program, but I also found what they wanted most was the opportunity to visit and observe a primary program in operation. I was repeatedly asked, "where can I see in practice what you are talking about." The idea of establishing pilot sites throughout the state was discussed at the department of education at one point during the planning for implementation, but the deadline for "full implementation" did not allow enough time to create such sites. Certainly they could have been helpful and they might have led to a more timely and consistent implementation of the program.

While increasing the number of days for professional development was important, it did not provide the time teachers need for activities other than "professional development." Primary school teachers are expected to do joint planning, develop instructional practices that are developmentally appropriate, organize their classrooms to accommodate children of different ages and abilities, perform qualitative assessments, confer with parents about the progress of their children, and keep detailed records on every child. All of these activities are complex and time consuming, and they require quality time during the school day on a regular basis *after the primary program has been implemented.*

The typical school day prior to KERA was organized to maximize the amount of time teachers spend with students. Little time was left during the day for anything other than instruction of children. The need for time for non-instructional professional activities during regular school hours has now been addressed by most elementary schools, usually by altering class schedules to make planning or meeting time available during the day. Still many primary school teachers continue to meet in work sessions in the late afternoon or during brief (usually 30 minute) periods while students are in special classes such as music, art, or physical education.

While teachers appreciate any non-instructional time, my personal observation of how this time is used has convinced me that it generally does not provide the quality time teachers need to do the business at hand. I believe time for non-instructional activities remains a serious problem for all teachers, but especially for the primary school teachers. A 30 minute "planning break" during the day surely will not be sufficient over the long haul. Clearly more thought has to be put into how to structure a school day so that teachers can engage in the many professional activities required of them during the course of the workday rather than always at its end. More will be said about this later on when the general work environment for teachers is discussed.

The time demand on primary program teachers during the first several years became a serious morale problem in schools where teachers in all grades were not engaged in "after-school" planning or other professional activities. Most of the primary school teachers I worked with were excited about the promise of the program in the beginning and seemed willing to devote whatever time was needed to be successful. However, after the first year or so I started to hear some of them complain about their colleagues who did not teach in the primary program leaving the building after the children were dismissed while the primary school teachers were expected to stay, often for several hours, to meet or work on various elements of the primary program. Obviously these teachers thought this was grossly unfair and blamed KERA for the "added burden."

Another obstacle facing the primary school program was the weak support for it among parents in the early years. After KERA was passed and parents of elementary school children became more aware of the abolition of the first three traditional grades, teachers and administrators were deluged with questions about how this aspect of KERA would affect their children. Since the details of the program had not yet been worked out, there was little information that teachers and administrators could provide in answer to their questions. This resulted in apprehension among parents before the program even could be explained to them.

As the concepts underlying the program were made clearer, some of the concern subsided. I remember speaking personally to parents as a group and one-on-one about the basic ideas behind the primary program shortly after KERA became law. Most parents could understand the potential benefit of having children of different age groups learn together if this meant their children would be with others of similar ability irrespective of their age. These parents also generally supported the idea of children progressing at their own rate (i.e., continuous progress), but they typically said they preferred that it occur within the traditional grade level structure.

As I listened to their concerns, it was obvious they were using grade levels as assurance that their children were progressing with their peers. How would they know this if there is no promotion from one grade level to the next or children of different ages are grouped together? The idea that children would be assessed based on their "continuous progress" toward some standard of performance did not satisfy their desire for the signs which had told them in the past how well their children were progressing.

Opinion surveys of parental support for the primary program have shown that it widely varies across districts and even within schools. It is difficult to know the exact reasons for support or opposition. The responses indicate that many parents still are not familiar with the rationale for the program. In some cases their opinions seem to be based on how much they perceive their children are benefiting from the non-graded classroom and the new methods of teaching. In some cases opposition is based on a simple desire to have children receive the same kind of schooling that their parents experienced. These parents have a difficult time relating to some aspects of the primary program because it lacks the traditional elements with which they are familiar. Still others are fearful that their children are part of some experiment or they are not learning the "basics" of reading, writing, and math.

Some of the parental concern over the primary program no doubt is justified based on how the program has been implemented in some schools. When teachers openly express doubt or concern about it, parents obviously will feel insecure. The mindless grouping of children of all ages in ways that do not enhance a child's learning will seem purposeless to parents. The inability of some teachers to appropriately or adequately explain the progress of children leaves parents frustrated and suspicious that their children might end up three or four years later unprepared for the fourth grade with little information to alert them of that possibility.

Multi-age grouping was one of the most serious problems to arise in the early stages of implementation. The reasons for this situation have already been discussed, but the problems that this lack of understanding created for the primary program as a whole cannot be exaggerated. Parents already were skeptical of the non-graded aspect of the program and their concerns were certainly not allayed by the confusion they saw among teachers over how and why to group children if it is not done by age or traditional grade level.

The curriculum framework was not available until a year after the elementary schools had to submit their primary school plans. This was a problem for teachers who not only had to learn how to teach in a multiage, multiability classroom, but also had to align their instruction to a new curriculum which at the time consisted only of a set of broadly stated "valued outcomes." Primary school teachers could make other changes envisioned for the primary program without the curriculum framework. However knowing that the state accountability test for their school would be based on the academic expectations, the primary program teachers felt pressured to make certain they were properly preparing their students for the fourth grade accountability test at a time when they were making many other changes in instruction.

It is my view that most of the problems that arose with the primary school program could have been avoided if more time had been allowed for implementation and better conceptualization of the program by the Task Force on Education Reform to guide those who had to implement it. It certainly would have been helpful to everyone if the task force had developed a working paper containing the "architectural drawing" of a model primary program from which the people who had to implement the program could draw a clearer picture of what the finished product was to look like.

In the absence of a clear picture of what the task force had in mind, I believe the department of education probably created a program that was much more complex then originally envisioned. An example of this is the inclusion of multi-ability grouping as an essential attribute of the primary program. There was no mention of this in the language of KERA although it probably is appropriate in the narrower context of providing educational opportunity for exceptional children. I am not suggesting that what the department staff did was not desirable. The point is that much more was wrapped up in the primary program package than would have been necessary to satisfy the non-graded classroom requirement in the law.

Certainly the expectation of "full implementation" within two years was unreasonable. Implementing the primary school program as it finally took form involves more then just learning new skills. It requires teachers to re-conceptualize their professional practice. It demands a whole new approach to the instructional process. The most common complaint of teachers and administrators right from the start was the lack of sufficient time and opportunity to work through the practical issues and to acquire the necessary skills and knowledge to properly implement a high quality primary program. Resentment over the short timetable for implementing the primary school program was evident even among teachers who basically supported the program.

A change in professional practice as dramatic as is required by the primary program should be carefully orchestrated over a period of three to five years. It is my opinion that implementation would have gone more smoothly if various elements of the program had been sequenced to provide a systematic, orderly transition from the traditional to the non-graded classroom. Some of the features of the program as it came to be defined could have been delayed until other more critical elements were firmly in place. Such a "scaffolding" approach would have given time for intensive training to occur before each stage in the implementation rather than expecting teachers to be able to "eat the whole enchilada" in one big bite.

NOTES:

[1] See HB 940 Section 3 (1) (a). [KRS 158.6451 (1) (a)]

[2] Kentucky Supreme Court, in *Rose, et al. v. Council for Better Education*, June 8, 1989.

[3] See HB 940 Section 25(2) [KRS 158.030(2)]

[4] National Association for the Education of Young Children position statement on developmentally appropriate practice in the primary grades, serving 5-8 year olds. *Young Children*, 1988, Vol. 43, 64-81.

[5] Wallace G. Wilkinson, *Q. A. Improving Kentucky Schools*, undated but released in Fall 1988.

[6] David Hornbeck, memorandum to the Curriculum Committee titled "*Initial Working Paper on Recommendations Related to Curriculum*," dated December 19, 1989.

[7] *The Wonder Years*, Frankfort, KY: Kentucky Department of Education, 1991, 8.

[8] See KAR 3.440. Primary school program guidelines. The General Assembly amended KERA in 1992 to incorporate these seven attributes into the statute. See KRS 158.160(1)(a)

[9] 704 KAR 3:440.

[10] See HB 940 Section 31(1)(a) [KRS 156.160(1)(a)]

[11] See HB 940 Section 25(1) [KRS 158.030(1)]

[12] Betty Steffy, *The Kentucky Education Reform: Lessons for America.* Lancaster, PA: Technomic Publishing Co. Inc., 1992, 119-120.

[13] KRS 156.160(1)(a) as amended in 1992.

[14] See University of Kentucky/University of Louisville Joint Center for the Study of Educational Policy, *A Review of Research on the Kentucky Education Reform Act 1995.* Frankfort, KY: Kentucky Institute for Education Research, 1996, 127-130. Most of the observations cited here are based on this report or appear in one or more of the documents cited in this report.

---

[15] See data tables in *Primary Program Progress Report*, Frankfort, KY: Kentucky Institute for Education Research, 1995, 25-26.

[16] See University of Kentucky/University of Louisville Joint Center for the Study of Educational Policy, *A Review of Research on the Kentucky Education Reform Act 1995.* Frankfort, KY: Kentucky Institute for Education Research, 1996, 114.

[17] Ibid., 117-119.

[18] See HB 187 [KRS 156.160 (1)]

[19] See *State Regulations and Recommended Best Practices for Kentucky's Primary Program*, Revised Edition, "Position Statement," 1994, 24.

[20] See Patricia Kannapel, Lola Aagard, Pamelia Coe, and Beverly D. Moore, *A Qualitative look at Kentucky's Primary Program: Interim Findings from a Five-Year Study,* A research paper presented at meeting of American Educational Research Association, New Orleans, LA., 1994.

[21] See *A Review of Research on the Kentucky Education Reform Act*, Frankfort, KY: Kentucky Institute for Education Research, *1995*, 118.

[22] Ibid., 122-123.

[23] See HB 940 Section 25(2) [KRS 158.030 (2)]

[24] See 703 KAR 4:040.

[25] See 703 KAR 4:040 Section 3.

8. Support for Students

The task of educating children extends beyond the schoolhouse. The Task Force on Education Reform fully understood that when it wrote the following as a preamble to KERA:

> *The General Assembly recognizes that public education involves shared responsibilities. State government, local communities, parents, students and school employees must work together to create an efficient public school system. Parents and students must assist schools with efforts to assure student attendance, preparation for school and involvement in learning. The cooperation of all involved is necessary to assure that desired outcomes are achieved.*[1]

KERA created three new programs specifically designed to deal with environmental conditions generally thought to contribute to poor academic performance. These are (1) preschool and early childhood programs for children from economically disadvantaged families; (2) extended school services for children who need more time to learn; and (3) human resource centers located at or near schools to connect them with community agencies serving children with emotional or health problems.[2] In addition to these programs, KERA required the Kentucky Board of Education to set requirements for student health standards to be met by all students in the accountability grades of four, eight, and twelve.[3]

Preschool and Early Childhood

Preschool programs for economically disadvantaged children are intended to help them acquire interpersonal and social skills similar to those possessed by children from more privileged families when they first enter school. Preschool programs are thought necessary to provide equality of educational opportunity to these children.

Preschool programs were not new to Kentucky at the time KERA was enacted. Education reform legislation enacted in 1985 created an early childhood education commission to study the issue and make recommendations. Kentucky for many years benefited from the federally-funded Head Start program that provides educational and child-care services to children of economically disadvantaged families, but prior to KERA there was no state-funded preschool program to meet the need for preschool educational opportunities in communities not served by Head Start.

Beginning with the 1990-91 school year KERA required all local school districts to assure that a developmentally appropriate half-day preschool education program is provided for each child who is four years old by October 1 of each year and "at risk of educational failure."[4] A school district that could show a lack of facilities to comply with this section of the law by the 1990-91 school year was given one additional year to make necessary arrangements.

The policy for this element of KERA is based on the widely held belief among educators and child development researchers that children from economically poor families are disproportionately "at risk of educational failure" in an educational system based on middle class values and life experiences. A "developmentally appropriate preschool program" is defined in KERA as:

> *a program that focuses on the physical, intellectual, social, and emotional development of young children. The preschool program shall help children with their interpersonal and socialization skills.*[5]

The criteria for family poverty used in the federal school lunch program guidelines was selected as the criteria for eligibility to participate in the new preschool program.

Handicapped children continued to be selected according to federal guidelines for such programs. Also included are three and four-year-old children with an identified speech disability, developmental delay, or are severely handicapped.[6] The program could serve other four-year-old children "to the extent placements are available."

<u>Coordination of Services was Required</u>

When this element of KERA was discussed by the Task force on education reform and in public hearings, concern was expressed about the potential for duplication of services such as those offered by some daycare centers and particularly the Head Start program. In order to ensure coordination with other agencies serving preschool children, KERA created a Kentucky Early Childhood Advisory Council to advise the Commissioner of Education and the Kentucky Board of Education in development of program guidelines and to help them work through issues of implementation and administration.

The advisory council consisted of a member of the state board of education and 16 others appointed by the Governor. The statute specified that 12 members of the council consist of one representative each from nine stakeholder groups and three state agencies which provide or fund social and health services for preschool age children. The council also had a representative of the Interagency Task Force on Family Resource and Youth Services Centers created by KERA, the Head Start Association, the Head Start director, and the Infant/Toddler Coordinating Council which brings the total membership to 17. The advisory council continues indefinitely with members serving four year staggered terms.

To further ensure coordination, KERA required school districts to work with existing preschool programs to avoid duplication of programs and services and to avoid supplanting federal funds.[7] School districts are given the option to provide the program themselves or to contract with one or more community agencies to provide it as a way to enable state preschool program funds to flow through the district to other agencies. In either case the school district remains responsible for oversight of the preschool program and for enforcement of the guidelines for them.

Funds for preschool programs appropriated by the legislature are granted to local school districts according to an allotment system approved by the state board of education. School districts submit proposals for these grants, which are approved by the department of education based on criteria in the law and regulations adopted by the state board of education. Proposals may be submitted for implementing new services, enhancing existing preschool education services, or contracting for services from public or private service providers in the community. The department of education approves the proposal and the school district then implements the proposed plan. The school district receives a stipend from the state for each child served based on a formula approved by the state board of education.

Potential loss of Head Start funds was a serious concern at the outset of the program. Federal law does not allow states to use federal funds in place of funds they would otherwise appropriate for programs similar to Head Start. If it were found that state funds have been supplanted by federal funds, the state would have to return to the federal government the Head Start money that was considered to have supplanted the state appropriation.

The department of education took several actions to avoid the possibility of losing Head Start funding. A memorandum of agreement was signed by Head Start program administrators and the department of education which specified how the Kentucky preschool and Head Start programs would coordinate their services so as to avoid any supplanting of funds. A data collection system was put in place to track children in all preschool programs so that Head Start children could be clearly identified even when a Head Start program serves children funded by the Kentucky program. The initial memorandum of understanding was later redrafted as a formal agreement that has guided the articulation between these two programs since that time.

Preschool Program Guidelines

KERA required the Kentucky Board of Education to adopt guidelines for the program, which included eligibility criteria, program guidelines, and standards for personnel by the beginning of the 1990-91 school. The Kentucky Early Childhood Advisory Council was supposed to advise the commissioner and board of education on such matters, but the council did not hold its first meeting until February 1991, six months after the first programs were to begin.

With less than six months in which to draft guidelines, the board of education proceeded to approve the process and regulations for funding these programs without input from the advisory council in order to meet the beginning deadline. In this case KERA was very specific regarding the criteria to be used for funding preschool programs.[8] The board of education adopted guidelines and application procedures based on the 16 criteria for program approval specified in the law so school districts that were prepared to offer preschool programs the first year could be funded.

Various implementation issues surfaced early in the program such as transportation for children participating in the program, assurance of program quality, and qualifications for professional staff. The state board of education approved regulations dealing with these issues including creation of a new interdisciplinary preschool teacher certification program that was just going into effect at the time of this writing. Most children are provided free transportation. Various licensing and accreditation options are available to both public and private preschool service providers and most of them either have or are actively pursuing some form of quality certification. All in all, implementation of the preschool program has been one of the most trouble-free of all KERA initiatives.

Implementation of the Preschool Program

School districts quickly responded to this element of KERA. In the initial 1990-91 school year, the department of education approved 130 proposals for preschool programs. The department of education estimated at the time there were about 54,000 four-year-olds in Kentucky, about 21,000 or 39 percent of whom were estimated to be at risk of educational failure based on the federal school lunch criteria. During this initial year these programs provided services to 13,470 children or about 64 percent of eligible children. The department estimated there were approximately 10,800 three and four-year-old children with identifiable disabilities the first year of which 3,259 were served by all providers.[9]

Over succeeding years the number and percentage of eligible children served by the state-funded preschool program and Head Start steadily increased. In the sixth year, the preschool program served 29,348 children including Head Start children. Head Start served about 42 percent of the total at risk children enrolled in preschool programs.

Preschool programs are voluntary, so it is not expected that the number served will ever reach 100 percent of all eligible children. In the 1995-96 school year about 74 percent of all children eligible for free lunch and 90 percent of all three and four-year-olds with identifiable disabilities participated in preschool programs. A relatively small number of children (2,531) not eligible based on the free lunch criteria also were served in 1995-96 on a "space available" basis. These statistics show that a significant proportion of the target populations now participate in preschool programs.

The level of coordination with other service providers appears to be high based on the number of "blended" programs. In the 1995-96 school year, 141 school districts (80 percent) operated programs in conjunction with some other agency or source of funding. The most frequent partnership is with Head Start, but nearly one-fourth of the school districts secure additional support for their programs from local district funds, donations, tuition, and fees. Only 35 districts (20 percent) that year operated preschool programs supported entirely with state funds.

The Office of Education Accountability received complaints from some for-profit service providers in a few areas of the state who contend that the free service provided by the state has hurt their business. Applications for state grants require local districts to document that they have held meetings with all local providers and they were involved in the design of the program. Of course, this involvement doesn't necessarily lead to a contract between the district and these local providers. Head Start is a unique situation because of the necessity to avoid supplanting state funds with federal funds. Head Start administrators must affirm that their programs are being fully utilized, and recruiting and child counting methods are synchronized with the state.[10]

The growing level of participation among eligible children resulted in a budget shortfall in the 1996-98 biennium. In order to keep the program within budget, the Kentucky Board of Education reduced the per-child rates below the second year level of funding, an action which has the potential to reduce the number of children served in future years. The level of participation could fall in the future if the state reimbursement doesn't keep pace with costs or if "caps" are placed on enrollments by the state in order to stay within the budget for this program.

Impact of the Preschool Program

Preschool programs are primarily directed toward socialization of the child, but the primary interest the Task Force had in these programs was to ensure more equality in educational opportunity. There are many important contributions the preschool program makes to the general welfare of these children, but the measure of success ultimately would be how well these children fared in school compared to their peers who did not participate in these preschool programs.

During the first year of the preschool program the department of education contracted with the University of Kentucky to conduct a longitudinal study of the preschool program.[11] This study is still ongoing, but the early results of this research indicate that the policy objective of equalizing educational opportunity for at risk children appears to be met up to this point. The researchers compared cohorts of at-risk children who participated in the preschool program with a random sample of children who did not participate.

The data from this study indicate that preschool children generally have done as well or better during their first two years in the primary school program as children who did not participate in terms of attainment of Kentucky's six learning goals. Positive gains also were observed for children with confirmed disabilities while in the preschool program. Given their unique differences, the progress of these children could not be compared with other children, but improvement during their participation in the preschool program was significant for most of them.

The most recent research indicates that some of the early gains demonstrated by preschool participants seem to diminish by their third year in the primary program. It appears that the preschool preparation given these children at least puts them in a much better position to succeed. But it also suggests that primary school teachers must realize that these gains can only be sustained over time by continued attention to the same factors that put these children at risk when they were four-year-olds.

A key element of the program is involvement of parents in the early education of their children. Both school personnel and parents indicate problems in achieving this objective, mostly due to lack of awareness of the opportunities being offered for parental involvement, unavailability of transportation, and scheduling conflicts. A large number of the parents of children in the preschool program do volunteer work in the school or classroom, which promotes communication between the school and parent.

At this point, the preschool program appears in the main to be meeting the policy objectives for it. Opinion surveys of school administrators, teachers, and parents show a high opinion of the preschool program.[12] However, there needs to be a seamless integration of the same developmentally appropriate learning experiences these children have in the preschool program on into the primary school program if this investment is to have its maximum impact.

The Extended School Services Program

The question of whether or not to increase the length of the school year came up at various times during the deliberations of the curriculum committee of the task force on education reform. Proposals included going from the current 175 instructional days to as much as 200 days over a period of time. The general consensus was that Kentucky children do not spend a sufficient amount of time in school when compared to children elsewhere in the United States and in the industrialized nations of the world.

Extending the school year had significant fiscal implications, but money wasn't the only concern of the committee. Time is a fixed variable in American education, but for the learner time is not standard. Some students require more time than others to learn certain things. When the school year is fixed, the assumption is that all students will learn everything they are supposed to know in the exact same amount of time. The policy question then was whether to increase the school year for all children or make more time available for some children on the basis of their educational need. In other words, should time be variable rather than fixed by the school calendar.

David Hornbeck offered the following proposal in his initial "working paper" submitted to the curriculum committee dated December 1989:

> *Financial provision must be made for at least one third of all students to attend school for as many as 240 days per year including time on the weekends, summers and longer school days. Some students require substantially more time to learn the same amount.*

Later on Hornbeck also recommended that the basic school year be extended immediately to 190 days with an additional five days added in each of the next three years.

The decision of the Task force on education reform was to retain the current 175 instructional days and create a new program under which teachers could be paid to spend extra time as needed to tutor or provide additional instruction to students who require it. This new program would provide both teacher and student additional time to re-teach or review material at the time it is most needed — when it is currently being studied in the classroom.

The language describing the nature of this program is as follows:

> *Schools shall provide continuing education for those students who are determined to need additional time to achieve the outcomes defined in Section 3 of this Act, and schools shall not be limited to the minimum school term in providing this education. Continuing education time may include extended days, extended weeks, or extended years.*[13]

The policy intent of the "continuing education" provision of KERA was to make the school day, week, and year a flexible element in the educational experience of the child. It was envisioned that teachers would determine a need for additional assistance. The teachers would both schedule *and deliver* the additional instruction, either before or after the regular school day, on Saturday, or after the regular school year had ended. Special funds would be available so those teachers could be compensated for the time they personally spent with these students after regular school hours. Based on these concepts, KERA created what later would be called the "extended school services" program. *

The program was supported through grants to local school districts in the initial two years, but then it was expected that these services would be funded somehow through the regular funding formula for school support (SEEK) as provided for in HB 940:

> *The State Board for Elementary and Secondary Education shall promulgate administrative regulations establishing criteria for the allotment of grants to local school districts for the 1990-1991 and 1991-1992 school years for continuing education. These grants shall be allotted to school districts to provide instructional programs for pupils who are identified as needing additional time to achieve the outcomes defined in Section 3 of this Act. The chief state school officer shall recommend to the Division of School Finance of the Office of Education Accountability by June 30, 1991, a method for funding continuing education for these students through the state supported funding program.*[14]

As was the case with other KERA program initiatives, the language in the legislation did not communicate very well the policy intent of this initiative or how the funds appropriated to support it should be distributed by the state or by school districts.

Implementation of the Extended Services Program

Money was appropriated for the 1990-91 school year but the state board of education had to determine a method of allocating it before schools could actually use the funds. The amount of the appropriation was based on an estimated cost to provide ten additional days of instruction for approximately one-third of the entire school enrollment statewide. The board approved regulations and a reporting system in June 1990 and the first allocations were made in November that year. Under the guidelines issued by the department of education, eligible students can be referred to the program by parents, teachers, or students can self-refer.

---

* The department of education changed the terminology for this initiative from "continuing education," the terminology in the law, to "extended school services" because the former terminology historically referred to adult education programs. The current name of the program is used hereafter.

An interesting situation arose very early as to whether students referred to the program could be required to participate. Several local school boards had made participation mandatory early in the program, but the legality of this action was challenged. In 1992 the General Assembly gave statutory authority to local school boards to take such action.[15]

Transportation for extended school service students was a serious financial and logistics issue. Students required to participate in an after-school, weekend, or summer extended session presumably must be transported just as if they were attending a regular school session. Local school districts had to make such arrangements in a manner that assures that transportation staff and buses are available when needed. Some districts had to spend as much as one-third of their extended school services allotment on transportation while others apparently spent nothing for this purpose.[16] Obviously this situation creates an inequity from one district to another because a standard allocation leaves very different amounts of money available to provide services to students. As of this writing, this inequity still had not been addressed by either the legislature or state board of education.

The Office of Education Accountability noted significant differences in compensation paid to teachers who provide extended school services.[17] In the spirit of local control, the department of education has not established regulations regarding compensation for those who provide services funded by this program. I believe task force members assumed that teachers would be working with their own students at their personal rate of compensation. In practice, regular teachers apparently accept the assignment at rates often applied to extra duty work or to substitute teachers. While I think it would be inappropriate for the state to establish a pay schedule for this program, in the interest of parity there probably should be a state level policy to guide local districts when they set their district compensation policy.

The use of extended school services funds to underwrite the cost of regular summer school programs was an unexpected interpretation of the intent of this program. As I indicated earlier, it was presumed that most of the money would be used to compensate teachers who would devote time beyond the regular school day to help students in their classes who would otherwise fall behind or fail. If the school year ended with some students still not where they should be or in a failing condition, the teacher could extend the instructional year by as many days as considered necessary, presuming that the additional instruction had a reasonable likelihood of allowing the student to move to the next grade level or course.

Obviously summer school was not specifically referenced in the language of the statute. I don't think the task force anticipated that extended school services funds might be used to replace local expenditures for regular summer school programs. In fact, I don't recall that summer school was even mentioned when the extended school program was proposed. Summer school generally consists of regular course offerings provided for students who want to make up courses or improve their grades. Students who repeat a failed course during the summer no doubt are doing the proper thing, but this is not what I think was intended when "extend the school year" language was put in the statute.

In fiscal terms this has been a financial windfall to districts, which prior to KERA underwrote the cost of summer school from their own funds, tuition, or some combination of the two. In fact, in the first year of the program, 18 school districts only offered the extended school services program in the summer. Perhaps one could argue that this use of the money is good policy even if it wasn't originally intended. The point is that policy makers failed to foresee how the legislation would be interpreted later on and therefore did not speak to the appropriateness of using funds appropriated for this program in conjunction with or in support of regular summer school offerings.

In any case, the state now is underwriting some or all of the cost of summer school programs in some school districts with funds from a program that was created with something quite different in mind. It is unlikely that use of extended school services money for summer school programs will be denied without an outcry from the school districts which now use it to help pay for their summer school programs, so summer school programs probably will continue to be subsidized in part at least by the extended school services program.

Interestingly, in April 1994, the Franklin County Circuit Court ruled that private school children in Campbell County and Fayette County could not be denied access to extended school services provided in the summer solely on their status as private school children. School districts across the state were advised to abide by the ruling unless advised otherwise by legal counsel. If the intent of this program is to extend the school year for students enrolled during the year, then students not enrolled during the year could hardly have their school year extended. The situation on which this case was based arose because the local districts that were defendants in this case did not actually extend the school year. They offered a summer school to which all students in the county had previously been able to attend whether or not they were in private schools during the regular school year and used extended school services funds to pay for it.

Impact of the Extended School Services Program

Opinion surveys indicate great support for this element of KERA from parents, teachers, administrators, and board members. It is considered by many of the respondents to be the best program in KERA.[18] Data provided by teachers on students who participate in the program indicate that a majority of them are able to increase the grade they receive by one or more letters. There are no data on the correlation between state accountability test scores and participation in the extended school services program although a study is currently under way to do this. On the surface, at least, it appears that the program is meeting its primary objective to help students improve their academic performance, but the extent to which these students are achieving the state academic expectations is not objectively established as yet.

Anecdotal information provided to the author and observations reported by department of education staff reveal some practices that might be considered inappropriate for this program. For example, in some schools the teacher responsible for the student's regular instruction is not tutoring students. Students are "referred" to the program as if it was an add-on or remedial program rather than a continuation of classroom instruction. Some teachers reported poor communication between the teachers making these "referrals" and the teachers providing the service regarding the specific needs of the student. There also are reports that some students are working on regular schoolwork such as homework instead of receiving special help. While the extent of these practices is not documented, there appears to be sufficient evidence to indicate that the extended school services program may not be as useful in some schools as in others.

The initial vision for the extended school services program was that it would become an integral part of the instructional program of the school. The intent was to facilitate learning by giving children more time to grasp a particular concept or to master a skill if the time available during the regular school day was not sufficient. It seems obvious now that this vision of the program was not properly communicated at the outset, so some of the potential impact of this innovative attempt to make learning time variable for all children has not been realized. In some schools the program apparently is used primarily as a remedial program or a safety net for students who are failing a subject or grade.

Family and Youth Service Centers

It is widely believed that a direct relationship exists between the physical and social well being of children and their capacity for learning. Students who are suffering abuse, neglect, hunger, family breakup, alcohol or substance abuse, fear, and unattended medical problems are ill prepared to concentrate on academic achievement. When these children do not perform well in school, teachers often recognize these conditions are a contributing factor.

Although such problems are found in families at all socioeconomic levels, families living in poverty have less resources with which to remedy them. Almost two-thirds of Kentucky schools are located in communities with high levels of poverty. In the interest of achieving equality in educational opportunity, the task force felt it was very important to address the impact poverty has on learning beyond the preschool years.

Some members of the Task Force also were concerned about what had come to be known as "latch key" children because they were going home to an empty house. It was their belief that it would be much better for these children to remain at school where they could be engaged in after-school activities or work on homework.

KERA creates a network of family resource and youth services centers to provide a variety of health and social services to economically disadvantaged children and their families. Initially these centers are to be located at or near school facilities where twenty percent or more of the students are eligible for free school meals. The family resource centers located at or near elementary schools are expected to provide at least the following services:

(a) Full-time preschool child care for children two and three years of age;

(b) After school child care for children ages four through twelve, with the child care being full-time during the summer and on other days when school is not in session;

(c) Families in training, which shall consist of an integrated approach to home visits, group meetings and monitoring child development for new and expectant parents;

(d) Parent and child education (PACE), a pre-KERA program which promotes parental literacy and child care education;

(e) Support and training for child day care providers; and

(f) Health services or referral to health services, or both.

The youth services centers located at or near middle and high schools are expect to provide at least the following services:

(a) Referrals to health and social services;

(b) Employment counseling, training and placement;

(c) Summer and part-time job development;

(d) Drug and alcohol abuse counseling; and

(e) Family crisis and mental health counseling.

KERA specifically continued a popular program known as Parent and Child Education (PACE) created in 1995 to provide literacy training for parents who could not read while at the same time offering them an opportunity to acquire good parenting skills. The program was considered an educational program where parents and their preschool children could learn together. The law made this program explicitly part of the array of services that were to be made available at a family resource center. The PACE program was then linked with a concept called "families in training" which is to consist of an integrated approach to home visits, group meetings and monitoring child development for new and expectant mothers.[19] The family resource centers would provide a convenient site for these services and also help to build linkages between schools and new parents.

Implementation of the Resource Centers Program

The legislation initially envisioned a five-year schedule to implement this network of service programs under the guidance of a sixteen-member Interagency Task Force on Family Resource Centers and Youth Services Centers.[20] The interagency task force was to complete an implementation plan for the program prior to January 1, 1991. Local school districts were to develop initial plans for their centers by June 30, 1991. By June 1992 family resource centers and youth services centers were to be established in or adjacent to at least one-fourth of the eligible schools, with expansion by one-fourth of eligible schools each year thereafter until all eligible schools have a center.

The interagency task force was required to monitor implementation of the plan and review grant applications until December 31, 1995, at which time it would cease to exist. This schedule assumed full implementation of the program within five years after KERA was enacted. In the 1994 session of the General Assembly, the sunset date for the task force was extended until the end of 1997 and the number of members was increased to 21.

Although these centers were created as part of an education bill, fiscal and regulatory responsibility for them was vested with the cabinet for human resources. Historically, there had been relatively little coordination between schools and community human service agencies. Under KERA, the cabinet for human resources can fund but not operate or directly control the centers. The centers must form an advisory council comprised of school personnel, parents of children in the school, and community representatives.

Each school hires its service center staff, selects the center site, and establishes its own program focus based on advice of the local advisory council. On the other hand, school districts must satisfy criteria set by the human resources cabinet before they can receive state funds to create and support a center. This division of responsibility was intentionally created to force schools and health and human service agencies to work together in this program. Neither party can achieve its objectives without the participation and cooperation of the other.

The centers are supported with annual grants to school districts rather than to individual schools or the centers themselves. The human services cabinet secretary is required to establish criteria for awarding these grants with oversight of the interagency task force. Grant applications first are reviewed by the interagency task force, which then makes recommendations to the secretary of the cabinet for human resources who authorizes and administers the grants.

The law as initially written in 1990 provided no guidance to the cabinet regarding the criteria it should use for the grants other than the free school lunch eligibility criteria and the list of mandated services each center should provide. The interagency task force five-year plan for the program must promote identification and coordination of new and existing resources to maximize the use of local, state, and federal funds that might be available to support specific elements of the plan and to avoid duplication of effort.

School district funding for these centers is based on the number of eligible children enrolled in the school being served by the center. Initially the minimum grant was $10,000 per center regardless of the actual number of eligible children in the school. The maximum award was $90,000. Each center is encouraged to secure additional funds, gifts, and grants to support various services. In the first year of the program, local school districts augmented the state allocation of $8.6 million with an additional $3.3 million from local school districts and $1.7 million from community resources.

Over 1,000 school sites were eligible for grants in the first year, but only 133 grants were made that year. Another 89 centers were opened in Fall of 1992 bringing the total to 222 the second year. These 222 centers served 414 of the eligible schools. Of these initial centers, 127 were family resource centers serving elementary school children and 55 were youth services centers serving middle and high school children, with 40 more centers being combined family resource and youth services centers. Over 51,000 persons participated in one or more of the services provided by these initial centers. In fiscal year 1997, the number of centers reached 560 serving 912 or approximately 80 percent of all eligible schools. These 560 centers will make services available to over 418,000 students and their families.

The only statutory constraint on the centers is a ban on providing abortion counseling or making referrals to a health care facility for the purpose of seeking an abortion.[21] In 1992 the initial statute was amended to prohibit centers from offering contraceptives to minor students without the express consent of their parents. The 1992 amendment also included a clearer definition of a center, criteria for awarding grants, and a requirement that services be available to all students in the school and their families, with the most economically disadvantaged having priority status.[22]

Several implementation issues surfaced as the program evolved. At the local level a question arose about the relationship and line of authority between the center advisory councils and school-based decision making councils. It is understandable that the centers appear to be outside the sphere of the school councils given their affiliation with the cabinet for human resources. However, the issue seems primarily to be less one of whom should control the centers and more one of the school councils wanting a working relationship with the center advisory councils, something KERA did not address. Center coordinators have been advised to work more closely with their school councils to avoid the need for a legislative resolution of this issue.

Another administrative issue is accountability of the centers for use of the funds they receive and the services they provide. The cabinet for human resources has fiscal responsibility for the program, but the centers are administered by and are under the control of local school districts and their school boards. Lines of authority between the center coordinators, local school administrators, and state officials were not made clear in the law. Local policies and practices sometimes are developed and implemented by the coordinators of the centers with the advice of their advisory councils but without much consultation with anyone else.

Some Policy Confusion Emerged

Task force on education reform members held different views of whether a new agency was being created or a center was only a coordinating point where schools and human service agencies can intersect. Language like "center" and "located at or near a school" no doubt communicated the idea of a new agency that has a specific locale. This idea was further confirmed when one of the services to be provided is day care for preschool children and after- school care for others.

The language used for the preschool program is very clear that the school districts are not to duplicate services already available in the community. Contracting for services is the preferred method of providing preschool programs. A school district is to create its own program only if other resources are either unavailable or fully utilized. However, similar language was not used with the family resource and youth services centers section of the legislation. Consequently, the family resource and youth services centers provide some services on their own and broker others.

There is nothing inherently inappropriate from a policy perspective that a center be the locale where various services are provided. In fact that is perhaps a major reason for locating a center at or near a school. In 1988 then Governor Wilkinson established a pilot program called the Kentucky Integrated Delivery System (KIDS) at ten school sites to demonstrate the viability of providing certain human services at or near school sites. This program was designed to provide easier access to social and health services for children and their families. The program also sought to improve collaboration between these agencies and schools when working with families of children enrolled at the school.

A key concept underlying the KIDS demonstration project was that the person in charge of the local KIDS site was to broker services on behalf of school personnel, children, and their parents. The actual delivery of services was to be provided by the professional staff of various community agencies and to be paid for in the same manner as if these services were provided at the offices of the agency. The KIDS director was a person who monitored the interaction between the professional staff and school personnel to ensure appropriate communication occurred among and between them. A KIDS "center" was a transaction point where social and health agency staff, school personnel, students and their families were brought together.

The language of the statute did not address the issue of whether these centers should broker or provide services, but I believe the level of financing provided for the centers by the legislature since the passage of KERA has clearly sent a signal that the state intends only to fund a coordination or brokering function. With the maximum level of funding set at $90,000, the funds available could never support the full range of services listed in KERA.

The presumption of the legislature seems to be that the services itemized in the legislation will be paid for at the centers in the same manner as if the services were provided at the primary location of the agency. In fact, funds for some of the specific services named in KERA such as PACE are appropriated elsewhere in the budget. One could conclude, therefore, that the center's primary function is intended to be a transaction point where children and their families can access these services and not another service delivery agency. Centers that create their own services must use other means to finance them than the money appropriated directly to support the centers program. Perhaps the centers should do both, but the policy intent probably should be clarified to give clear direction to the future development of the centers.

Impact of the Service Centers Program

Initial data on services provided by the centers was very inadequate largely because a reporting system was not developed until after the initial grants were awarded. The accountability system consisted primarily of reports and statistical data, which were cumbersome to prepare and often late in submission. In the third year of the program the state instituted a computerized reporting system that gradually has been enhanced to perform other information functions for the local centers. At the present time a significant database of information on the centers and the nature and volume of the services they provide is being assembled.

State oversight of the centers is carried out by liaisons from both the cabinet for human resources and the department of education. In July 1995 the cabinet and the interagency task force made a decision to reduce the number of cabinet liaisons from eight to five with each liaison responsible for overseeing an average of 115 centers each. In 1996 Governor Paul Patton split the cabinet for human resources into two cabinets, one of which is now called the Cabinet for Families and Children which assumed responsibility for the program and its state liaisons. During hearings on the reorganization, the new cabinet pledged to restore the number of liaison members to eight.

The reorganization also transferred the functions of the interagency task force to a newly created Kentucky Commission on Human Services Collaboration. The new commission on human service collaboration was created by executive order in June 1996 to focus attention on ways to improve coordination of services to Kentucky families and children. The previous interagency task force created by KERA was disbanded effective December 31, 1997. It appears to be a logical body to oversee the family resource and youth services centers program but unlike the interagency task force it will have other responsibilities. Whether this results in better coordination and program oversight remains to be seen.

The 1994 office of education accountability annual report cited examples of fiscal and management practices which the staff felt were inappropriate and deserved review by the cabinet for human resources. The OEA staff expressed concern that there was "insufficient monitoring" of local center operations. Obviously the issue here is over how much direct control the state in general, and specifically the cabinet for human resources (now the cabinet for families and children), should have over centers created by and under the direct control of local school districts.

It probably was inevitable that the control issue would surface eventually given the way the program was structured at the state level. Both the department of education and the former cabinet for human resources took steps to address the issues raised by the OEA staff. However the philosophy remained that the centers were first and foremost the responsibility of local school districts which were admonished to provide closer oversight of the actions taken by the coordinators of their centers.

One issue that arose during the public hearings on HB 940 was the placement of social workers and guidance counselors at every school. Advocates of this proposal contended among other things that teachers are increasingly confronted with disruptive behavior, violence, and substance abuse, which they are not prepared professionally to handle. Besides the need for more professional help, teachers maintained that dealing with these disruptive students seriously detracted from the learning of other students.

Guidance counselors had been hired in the past to help students and parents make educational decisions rather than to counsel students with behavioral problems. Most of these counselors were at middle and high schools. The idea of hiring social workers was to provide professional help to troubled students whose behavior is interfering with the learning of other students or threatens the safety of others in the school. We believed that having such people at the school site would result in immediate intervene when students are disruptive in class or on school property.

The decision to create the family resource and youth services centers was considered a better approach than hiring human services staff for all schools. Presumably these centers would be able to access a much broader range of services than could be provided by a few staff people employed by or assigned to a school. Furthermore, it seemed unwise to duplicate in the school system a social service system that already existed in the state. A review of research on the operation of the centers and my own personal observations leave open the question of whether the centers are providing schools with the assistance they need to manage crises or help control disruptive behavior *as it occurs* at the school site.

One of the reasons for requiring that the centers be placed "at or near" a school site is to enable center staff to quickly intervene when troublesome situations arise in the classroom or at the school site. On various occasions I have been in schools where students were sent directly from a classroom to the family resource center because of their disruptive behavior. The influence of the center staff was immediate and effective in terms of helping these students return to the classroom under control. In these schools the center staff and teachers see their centers as an extension of their schools and work closely to resolve problems on the spot. If additional services from a community agency are needed, the center staff members are in a good position to make an appropriate referral.

On the other hand, I have been in schools where the centers are treated as if they are independent agencies to which teachers must make formal referrals. In some cases the center staff provide little or no feedback to teachers regarding actions they took to deal with the behavior which led to the referral. It never occurred to me that center staff might not realize that part of their mission is to work closely with school personnel to help them deal with students whose behavior clearly indicates a need for human service intervention. The center staff might not be the people best able to provide all the services needed, but at the very least someone on the staff should have the professional training and skills needed to help moderate or defuse dangerous or disruptive situations at the school.

The centers have received broad support from school personnel, the families served, and various researchers who have evaluated them.[23] The consensus of various evaluations done on the program is that the objectives are being met, the services are perceived to be of value by both school personnel and clients of the services, and children generally seem to benefit academically from participation in the services the centers provide. Definitive connections between academic achievement and the existence of centers cannot be verified, and perhaps they never can be. However, those who are close to the operation of the centers seem convinced that they do have a positive impact on the children and families served.

Health Screening

Recognizing the importance of good health to learning, KERA requires the Kentucky Board of Education to set requirements for student health standards to be met by all students in grades four, eight, and twelve.[24] Each school is expected to provide health screening at these grade levels to identify deficiencies that might adversely affect learning. This aspect of KERA has not received specific attention in terms of state regulations.

Personal discussions with the Secretary of the Kentucky Cabinet for Human Resources prior to passage of KERA indicated this was a good idea, but it probably was more an issue for the public health departments than for schools to address. The task force was not clear as to how this provision might be implemented or paid for by schools. No specific appropriation was made to finance this activity and local schools historically had no funds with which to pay for such examinations.

Obviously schools could require parents to provide evidence that their children had received such a medical examination. Schools in high poverty areas undoubtedly would turn to the department of public health to secure health services for extremely poor families. In any case, this element of KERA has not been operational, and it probably will remain so until the legislature determines how and by whom it should be implemented and financed.

NOTES:

[1] See HB 940 Section 2. [KRS 158.645]
[2] Federal and state programs for handicapped and exceptional children that existed prior to KERA were continued under this legislation.
[3] See HB 940 Section 31(1)(f). [KRS 156.160 (1) (f)]
[4] See HB 940 Section 16(1) [KRS 157.3175 (1)]
[5] See HB 940 Section 16(2) [KRS 157.3175 (2)]
[6] See HB 940 Section 17 [KRS 157.226]
[7] See HB 940 Section 16(4) [KRS 157.3175 (4)]
[8] See HB 940 Section 16(5) [KRS 157.3175 (5)]
[9] The participation data reported here are based on information appearing in various annual reports of the Office of Education Accountability.
[10] See Kentucky Department of Education program advisory No. 92-PRES-013, April 15, 1992.
[11] See the four annual reports issued by the study authors, *Third Party Evaluation: Kentucky Education Reform Act (KERA) Preschool Programs*. Frankfort, KY: Kentucky Department of Education. A summary of this research appears in *A Review of Research on the Kentucky Education Reform Act 1995* prepared by the University of Kentucky/University of Louisville Joint Center for the Study of Educational Policy for the Kentucky Institute for Education Research, Frankfort, KY.
[12] See opinion data on the preschool program in the annual opinion surveys conducted by the Kentucky Institute for Education Research.
[13] See HB 940 Section 27(7) [KRS 158.070 (7)]
[14] See HB 940 Section 27(7) [KRS 158.070 (7)]
[15] See HB 596 enacted in the 1992 session of the General Assembly. [KRS 158.070 (7)]
[16] *Annual Report 1992*, Frankfort, KY: Office of Education Accountability, 1992,
48.
[17] *Office of Education Accountability Report 1995*, Frankfort, KY, 73.
[18] See T. Wilkerson & Associates, *The 1995 Statewide Education Surveys*. Frankfort, KY: The Kentucky Institute for Education Research, 1995.
[19] See HB 940 Section 18 (3c) [KRS 156.497 (3) (a)]
[20] See HB 940 Section 18 (1-3) [KRS 156.497]
[21] See HB 940 Section 18 (6) [KRS 156.497 (6)]
[22] See Senate Bill 86 enacted in the 1992 session of the General Assembly.

[23] The findings of this research are summarized in *A Review of Research on the Kentucky Education Reform Act* prepared annually by the University of Kentucky/University of Louisville Joint Center for the Study of Educational Policy for the Kentucky Institute for Education Research, Frankfort, KY.

[24] See HB 940 Section 31 (f) [KRS 156.160 (1) (f)]

9. Technology in the Classroom

Technology is a major element of KERA. The task force envisioned using technology for both administrative and educational purposes. The primary administrative goal was to create an electronic network that schools could use to share information. The law also called for electronically linking all school districts with the state education agency to improve the state's ability to monitor and administer the system as required by the court decision.

The educational goal was to use technology to enhance teaching and learning, which is the element of the technology program of primary interest here. The task force envisioned both students and teachers using technology to enhance learning and personal productivity. We also intended to facilitate communication among teachers, parents, students, and others through various forms of telecommunications including access to a telephone in every classroom.[1]

The term technology is defined comprehensively in KERA as video and computer systems, software and hardware, multiple delivery systems for satellite, microwave, cable, instructional television fixed service, fiber optic, and computer connections products, the preparation of school buildings for technological readiness, and the development of staff.[2] Thus the use of technology was to be more than just buying computers for schools, although deployment of computer technology eventually became the primary focus of the program.

When KERA was enacted the task force on education reform envisioned spending as much as $600 million to create a state-of-the-art technology system to serve all schools in the state and the state education agency. The task force wanted to ensure that the money for this program would be available across future budgets, so all appropriations for the technology program were and continue to be placed in a special trust fund. Under this statute, the state finance cabinet can only release these trust funds if the proposed expenditure conforms to a technology plan approved by the state board of education.

The Plan for the Technology System

A plan for the technology system was to be developed by a nine-member Council for Education Technology appointed by the governor with the consent of both the Kentucky House of Representatives and Senate. The technical aspects of the plan would be developed under contract with a private sector company with experience in system integration technology and implementation based on specifications established by the technology council.

The technology council was given six duties and responsibilities in the statute:

> *a. developing a long range plan for the efficient and equitable use of technology at all levels from primary school through higher education, including vocational and adult education. The plan shall focus on the technology requirements of classroom instruction, literacy laboratories, instructional management, distance learning, and communications as they relate to the Commonwealth's outcome goals for students described in Section 3 of this Act;*
>
> *b. creating, overseeing, and monitoring a well planned and efficient statewide network of technology services designed to meet the educational and informational needs of the schools;*
>
> *c. working with private enterprise to encourage the development of technology products specifically designed to answer Kentucky's educational needs;*
>
> *d. encouraging an environment receptive to technological progress in education throughout the Commonwealth;*
>
> *e. recommending a policy governing the granting of right of ways for the laying of fiber optic cable in a manner to insure that all of Kentucky's citizens are served equitably, that the fiber optic system is available for educational technology purposes, and that the private and public sectors are partners in the venture; and*
>
> *f. receiving, holding, investing, and administering all funds received by the council for the purpose of carrying out its duties and responsibilities, as set out in this section. These funds shall be spent with the aim of achieving equality of education throughout the Commonwealth.*[3]

As with other elements of KERA, a very short timeline was provided to accomplish a very complex set of tasks. The members of the council for education technology were to be appointed by the Governor by July 1, 1990, just a little more than two months after passage of KERA. The appointments actually were made August 8th and the council held its first meeting two weeks later.

KERA required the council for education technology to develop a five-year plan "for the efficient and equitable use of technology at all levels from primary school through higher education, including vocational and technical education."[4] The policy objectives of the five-year plan for the technology system are spelled out in the legislation as follows:

(a) *Improve learning and teaching and the ability to meet individual students' needs to increase student achievement;*

(b) *Improve curriculum delivery to help meet the needs for educational equity across the state;*

(c) *Improve delivery of professional development;*

(d) *Improve the efficiency and productivity of administrators; and*

(e) *Encourage development by the private sector and acquisition by districts of technologies and applications appropriate for education.*[5]

Because of the large expenditure anticipated to finance this project, the legislature wanted to approve what the task force called the "broad parameters" of the five-year plan before any money could be spent on it.[6] Implementation of the first stages of the plan could begin immediately upon approval of the "broad parameters" of the plan.[7] This meant the council had to produce at least a detailed outline of the essential elements of a five-year plan and submit it to the Legislative Research Commission for its approval by January 1, 1991, less than five months after its appointment.

The statute was quite specific about what the legislature wanted to see as the "broad parameters" of a five-year plan. Among these expectations was a requirement that the plan include administrative regulations that could be submitted to the board of education for approval by January 1, 1991, and a plan for implementation of an administrative system to be operational by the beginning of the 1991-92 school year. It was these elements that the council found impossible to include in the initial draft of the "broad parameters" of the five-year plan.

The Technology Plan Encounters Problems

The council met the deadline for submitting a "broad parameters" plan by January 1, 1991.[8] However, the 51-page plan was deemed by the legislative research commission members to be inadequate. The commission voted to reject the plan as written, and returned it to the council with specific recommendations for changes in the proposed plan. This proved to be only the first of several setbacks for this high priority program.

The council struggled for nearly six months in an attempt to satisfy the legislative subcommittee on education technology. Finally, the newly appointed Education Commissioner Thomas Boysen and Representative Pete Worthington, chairman of the legislature's subcommittee on education technology, agreed to create a 7-member Kentucky Educational Technology Steering Committee to resolve the outstanding issues. The Legislative Research Commission subsequently delegated to this steering committee its responsibility to approve the technology plan.

The steering committee consisted of the following: the chair of the council on education technology; the governor's secretary of education who also served on the council; the chair and vice chair of the subcommittee on education technology in the legislature; one member of the state board of education; the commissioner of education; and the technology project director employed by the council.

Formation of the steering committee effectively diminished the role of the technology council created under Section 21 of KERA, but it ended a protracted struggle that had developed between the council and Representative Pete Worthington who was the primary author of this portion of KERA. The legislation creating the council on education technology was subsequently amended by the legislature in 1992 to change its composition and to formalize the role of the steering committee. Further changes in the approach to implementation of this component of KERA occurred during a special legislative session in 1993 when the administrative structure and control of the project was altered, ending the role of the steering committee.

Major Policy Issues to be Resolved

The delays in implementation described above largely were caused by the inability of members of the council for education technology and the leadership in the legislature to resolve major policy issues that had not been addressed in the legislation.

The drafter of the technology component of KERA thought the detailed description of issues to be addressed in the technology plan would provide the guidance the council would need to create the "broad parameters" plan. However, it was quickly apparent that a number of important issues were not addressed in the legislation, issues which the technology council members thought they had to resolve before they could submit an outline of a five-year plan.

In large measure the dispute between the council members and the legislature was over priorities. The legislature expected the program to evolve along two parallel tracks: (1) development of the infrastructure for a statewide information network linking every school with the state education agency; and (2) deployment of technology to every school in the state for instructional use.

Technology was viewed as a significant way to deal with the equity issue raised in the court case, but the legislature also wanted technology to help fulfill its mandate to "monitor the system." A state-of-the-art information system was considered just as important to the education system as the availability of technology to teachers and students in the classroom.

Development of a statewide information network proved to be a much more complex task than coming up with a plan for distributing money to schools for the purchase of technology. Extensive technical and engineering information had to be prepared before such a system could be designed. Furthermore, the state was in the midst of designing a new telecommunications system for use by all agencies of state government. Obviously, the department of information and telecommunication services wanted assurances that whatever was done here would be compatible with what the state was designing.

Given this set of circumstances, members of the council for education technology decided that decisions about how to build the statewide education information system would have to await the resolution of issues related to the telecommunication infrastructure the state had committed to build for other purposes. The plan the council submitted for this component of the technology system proposed that the department of education enter into a contract with a consulting firm as quickly as possible. The consultant would study the problems such a system must overcome, estimate the cost, and propose a plan and timetable for its construction. Once this work was completed, the council would then submit a plan for the design and implementation of the administrative system.

In the interim, the council thought it was unreasonable to withhold the distribution of much needed technology money intended for instructional purposes until the complicated information system plan could be designed and approved by the legislature. Council members wanted to push money for the purchase of technology out to the schools as quickly as possible and proposed a plan for doing so in an equitable manner. Although the legislature had concerns about the proposed plan for distributing technology money to schools, the absence of a plan for the administrative system in the initial draft of the "parameters" plan probably was the main reason the legislature rejected this initial draft of the technology plan.

A Plan is Finally Approved

After the initial version of the "parameters" plan was rejected, the council asked the department of education to expedite its request for technical assistance. It took almost six months to prepare and distribute the request for proposals, evaluate them, and select a contractor. A contract was finally awarded in mid-summer in 1991 after creation of the steering committee described above.

In the meanwhile, the finance cabinet refused to release any money from the trust fund, except a small amount needed to finance the activities of the council for education technology, until a technology plan was approved by the legislative research commission as required in the legislation. Because the legislature's leadership was unwilling to approve a technology plan until the administrative component could be included, money appropriated for the technology program when KERA was enacted in 1990 was withheld by the state until well into 1992.

As was the case with so many other elements of KERA, the time allocated to achieve the goal of developing a technically sound plan for developing such a complex computer and telecommunications system was clearly unrealistic. The first six months was devoted to hiring an executive director for the council, obtaining information about the current status of technology in the schools, reviewing technology plans in other states, and holding general discussions about policy issues that would have to be resolved before a plan could be finalized. Only a very rough sketch of what the technology program might look like was feasible in such a short time frame.

Finally, after sixteen months of frustration and public debate, the legislative research commission finally approved on May 6, 1992 a "broad parameters" plan called the Master Plan for Education Technology. The master plan was approved by the state board of education the next day and was effective immediately. The document was as much a statement of policy as it was a plan. But the "master plan" did bring closure on the critical issues that were the primary source of disagreement between the council for education technology and the legislature. The overall system was given the name Kentucky Education Technology System (KETS.)

Major Policies for the System

Many issues surfaced in the months following delivery of the initial "parameters" plan that were not addressed in the legislation. The task of accommodating the competing interests of all interested parties proved to be much more difficult to accomplish than most had thought when KERA was enacted. Here are the key issues that were resolved.

The Equity Issue

A plan for the equitable distribution of technology, particularly computers, was more difficult to get agreement on than was thought at first. Some school districts already had significant investments in desktop computers for student use and automated management systems. An argument was made that districts with less technology should initially get a larger share of the money in order to "catch up" with districts that already had computers. The counter argument was that such a policy only punished districts that had the foresight to invest in computers on their own prior to KERA.

Ultimately it was reasoned that, because of the rapid rate of obsolescence in computer technology, much of the existing hardware base would have to be replaced before the technology program could get very far along. Furthermore, some of the older computers currently in use would not meet the standards that the master plan had set for new equipment and should be replaced as a matter of policy.

Based on this logic, the state took the position that previous investments in technology probably do not constitute a significant advantage. Ultimately, the policy was to distribute technology money to schools in equal units based on student enrollment without regard to existing technology.

A Local Financial Match is Required

Initially, the intention of the task force was to have the technology program fully funded by the state as part of its obligation to provide equitable support to all schools. However, before the program actually reached the stage where technology money could be awarded to local school districts, the legislature decided to require a match by local school districts equal to 50 percent of the cost. Since the original legislation did not call for local participation, this change in policy meant that local school districts now had to find ways to raise the local funds for participation in the program. This unanticipated change in state policy further delayed deployment of technology for instructional use.

Local Decision Making

Given the general policy commitment to instructional autonomy at the school level, it was decided that individual schools should determine how they want to use the technology money they receive. This decision, of course, meant that every school had to evaluate its need for and intended use of technology. It took a full academic year for the guidelines for the planning process to be developed and distributed by the department of education. Then a second year was needed for schools to assess their technology needs, set priorities, prepare their technology plan, and submit it to the state education agency for approval.

Each school district was initially required to prepare a six-year education technology plan that is consistent with the state Master Plan for Education Technology. The state education agency published guidelines for the planning process and issued several documents containing standards for the system. A statewide network of technical assistance, coordinated by the state regional service centers, was also provided. While all of this was helpful and necessary, it further delayed getting technology into the hands of teachers and students for their use.

Hardware and Software Standards

Concurrent with development of the technology planning process, the department of education had to develop minimum standards for equipment and software to ensure sound investment of technology money. These standards had to conform to the design standards being set for the statewide education information system, so their development was in part linked to the standards set by the system integration contractor. The system integration contract was disputed shortly after it was executed by the state. The contract had to be renegotiated, which in turn delayed decisions about computer and telecommunications equipment standards and decisions about management and financial software.

Setting standards also made obvious the need for a plan for the replacement of technology that did not meet current standards. The rapid improvements in technology meant that standards had to continually change. Many school districts found they could not use technology money to upgrade some hardware to meet the new standards because the cost was greater than could be justified. My personal observations indicated that they just continued to use the equipment anyway. Often the older computers were moved to the elementary grades where they were used for "drill and practice" sessions which do not require high performance hardware.

Standards also had to cover the building and wiring requirements of modern computer and telecommunication systems. Most school buildings, even new ones, were not constructed or wired to accommodate the electronic and telephonic equipment the new technology system would require. Thus the department of education also had to come up with technical and engineering specifications that construction contractors and architects must follow when designing and constructing new facilities or upgrading existing ones.

Another standards issue was the incompatibility between computer operating systems. The state computer system was essentially based on the Unix operating system. Computers currently in use in schools throughout the state were a mix of Intel-based (IBM compatibles) and Apple computers that did not "talk" to each other. The KETS had to accommodate this diversity in operating systems so as not to render obsolete existing hardware, but also to accommodate different preferences for one operating system over another among teachers and administrators.

Furthermore, some school districts and consortia of districts had invested in proprietary management software that was designed to run on a specific operating system. A statewide information system must be able to convert data created by the older system software to the new system software without loss of historical information unique to the district. It also had to give local districts the ability to create their own reports and to collect information in addition to what the state would require. Decisions about management software had to await a decision about the nature of the operating system that the state would use for the department of education. The linkage between these elements of the system posed a timing problem for the rest of the program.

This diversity in the existing equipment and software base also posed serious technical problems for networking these diverse computer systems. Eventually, the state mandated that the system must have an "open architecture" which means the interchange of information has to accommodate the various operating systems currently in use.

The issue of absorbing the cost of data conversion continued to be a matter of concern to school districts. The state finally agreed to absorb part of this cost, but it had to come out of the technology money the district would receive from the program. It also unlinked the decision about management software and the distribution of technology money to schools. The latter decision removed a major obstacle in getting the program off the ground.

Finally, there was concern that schools invest in high quality instructional software at the lowest possible price. In the beginning, the state gave local schools clearance to purchase anything that would support their local curriculum. In the meanwhile, the state secured statewide license agreements from major software vendors that made acquisition of their software both easier and less costly. In later years the state created an approved list of instructional and other software based on teacher evaluations of its merit in the classroom. The state policy now is that state technology money can only be used to purchase software on the approved list.

The Deployment of Technology in Schools

The initial contract for the technical design of the system was delayed, changes were made in the administration of the program, and the master plan went through various revisions. All of this vacillation resulted in an extended delay in the deployment of computers and other technology that were called for in the original legislation. These fits and starts had serious consequences for the program.

Recognizing the urgency of moving money into school districts as quickly as possible, grants were made beginning with the 1992-93 school year. The master plan, building standards, software guide, and a planning workbook were issued at various times in 1992. While other problems would arise later, at least the program now had reached a point where the money could begin to flow to the schools and classrooms. In spite of all the initial problems and implementation delays, money for technology was available to schools within two years after KERA was enacted.

The earliest money was awarded with less than adequate control or documentation of actual use. A total of $53,700,000 in state funds was distributed between 1992 and 1995 that was matched with an equal amount from local school districts. Actual allocations were based on average daily attendance and a demonstration of "need" as detailed in the district technology plan. The initial state award was $33.35 per student and grew to $34.54 in the second year of the program. However, this amount dropped dramatically thereafter to a low of $23.72 for the 1995-96 school year.

In 1996 the legislature's office of education accountability did a review of the program's implementation. Based on a survey the staff conducted, the respondents indicated significant deployment of technology in schools, although it was primarily in the form of computers. Several tentative conclusions can be gleaned from the data the office was able to collect. With just under 30 percent of the surveyed schools responding, the following observations must be considered only a rough estimate of what has occurred in the first four years after money was made available to schools.[9]

The respondent schools reported having 31,642 workstations. Of these, a vast majority (85%) were student workstations. No data was given in this study on the ratio of workstations to students. The ratio for teachers was 2.7 teachers for each teacher workstation. This ratio probably suggests that access to computers by students is a higher priority than providing computers to teachers.

The respondents reported that almost 36% of their computers did not meet state standards, which indicates that about one of every three computers still in use in 1996 was purchased prior to 1992. Apparently schools are using their technology money primarily to expand availability rather than to upgrade their existing equipment base. Although frugality is a virtue, the older equipment must soon be replaced, something that will no doubt slow down the expansion of the number of computers available to students and teachers in the future.

Access to the information world at that time was limited. More than half the schools reported no access to the Internet or availability of high-speed transmission lines. This problem was being addressed at the time, but no information was available regarding the status of the state telecommunication system at this time. No information was gathered on the requirement that telephones be installed in every classroom.

In 1995, just three years after final approval of the technology plan, a report on the program issued by the department of education indicated that through March of that year, 54 percent of the technology money available to school districts purchased student workstations; 13 percent purchased teacher workstations; and 11 percent was used to purchase instructional software.[10] Clearly, the acquisition and deployment of computers and software had the highest priority. The goal is to reach a ratio of 1 computer for every 6 students by the year 2000. Kentucky has spent nearly $467 million on education technology since 1992, a figure that is getting close to the $600 million projected by the task force in 1990.

The Role of Technical Assistance

Only a relatively few school districts had much experience with computer technology prior to KERA. The law made no mention of training beyond requiring that the education technology council address this need in the five year master plan for technology. It was obvious that school personnel would need considerable training and technical assistance in the acquisition, deployment, maintenance, and proper use of the technology that would be available to them in this program.

Various initiatives emerged in the early years of the program that proved to be very helpful. The department of education created a Technology Assistance Team in the Fall of 1992, the members of which were stationed in each of the eight state regional offices. The technology team members provided direct, on-site assistance to districts and schools to help them with technology decisions. Their primary mission in the first six months was to help school districts prepare their first five year technology plans. District plans had to be submitted to the state by April 1993 in order to receive financial assistance for technology purchases in the 1993-94 school year.

As time passed, these team members became regional technology coordinators stationed at each of the state regional offices. The department of education required school districts and local schools to identify at least one staff member as the technology coordinator. The local coordinator served as the point person for all technology issues at the local level.

While the state coordinators were required to have technology expertise, most local coordinators were classroom teachers who had little experience with technology beyond using computers and multimedia equipment for instructional purposes. The technology program required local expertise in the technical aspects of the equipment acquired by the district or school including such things as networks and servers. Only a few local coordinators had any training or experience with this aspect of computer technology. Obviously an extensive training program was necessary to ensure that proper decisions are made at the local school and district level.

Recognizing the urgency of providing training to local technology coordinators, the department of education offered annual training programs to upgrade the knowledge and skills of school and district level technology coordinators. In 1995 this training program was expanded to include a Principal's Institute on Education Technology designed to provide technology awareness training for school level principals and administrators.

In addition to these direct technical assistance programs, the department of education created an 8,500 square foot Education Technology Assistance Center in the state capital city to provide both a test and demonstration site for education technology. The center manages the state technology program (KETS) help desk which is operated privately under contract with the state. It provides network management for the entire KETS network and technical consulting services through a regional engineer program. It also maintains an electronic bulletin board and toll-free telephone access. The center, supported by a $1.25 million budget, serves both the instructional and hardware needs of Kentucky educators.

Every component of the KETS information network such as workstations, printers, computers, and software applications is tested and on display in the center. Educators use this facility to examine and compare various technology available through state contract before making their purchase decisions. It also is a meeting place for technology coordinators and other technology personnel. The center is a real asset to educators throughout the state and is widely used.

The state education agency sponsors an annual technology conference that has become nationally recognized as one of the best in the nation. Over 4,000 educators and others attend the annual conference for seminars and training sessions. Vendors of educational technology exhibit their latest offerings, which allows teachers and others to stay abreast of what is available for their schools.

The state education agency has sponsored various innovative programs to reinforce the use of technology by teachers and students beyond the annual technology conference. One such innovation is the "Academic Village" sites on the internet. These villages offer the opportunity to read or download various state documents such as the curriculum guidelines document

Transformations, content guidelines, units of study development criteria and materials, and assessment design manuals. Resource materials are available at these sites such as units of study, portfolio prompts, bibliographies, resource guides, and professional development modules.

The web-based Academic Village received its name in an effort to promote an electronic community of learners. To promote this aspect of the village, there is a library where "villagers" can go to get information and learning resources; a community center where discussions are held on topics of interest to the villagers; and a newspaper to post announcements, classified ads, and up-coming events. There even is a town council that maintains order in the village, directs the selection of materials for the library, and selects new avenues to be explored by the village. These academic villages also are linked by the Web to other internet resources.

The department of education also created the Student Technology Leadership Program (STLP), a student driven program designed to develop student leadership and technology skills that will also benefit their peers, their school, and their community. The program involves having a STLP student coordinator at a school site whose primary role is to facilitate student involvement in developing and implementing program activities that accomplish the program's goals. Information on this unique program is available on the internet.

Kentucky Educational Television

Kentucky was a national leader in educational television for many years predating KERA. Prior to KERA, the legislature financed the installation of television antennae on every school building in the state to make these resources available to every student in the commonwealth. KET has for more than a decade produced and broadcast an award winning program series called Star Channels, which offers classroom instruction via interactive television.

Kentucky Educational Television (KET) is independent of the public schools and university system, so it is not part of the KERA technology program. Nonetheless, KET played a very important role in advancing the goals of KERA in the early years. KET and the department of education collaborated to produce a number of special informational and professional development programs based on different elements of KERA. The KET network made these programs available to every school in the state. Many of these programs were live and interactive, allowing the participants an opportunity to pose questions to the presenters during the program. KET continued to provide instructional programs for Kentucky schools, but they are funded and produced outside of the scope of the KERA technology program. Therefore, KET's role will not be discussed further in this context.

Impact of Technology on Teaching and Learning

There is little more than anecdotal information available about the use of technology in Kentucky classrooms statewide after the program finally got off the ground.[11] The impression one gains from this information is that fewer than one-third of all teachers appear to be using computers in their instruction and then it is usually for "remediation" or "drill and practice" type activities. While attitudes about the potential of technology for improving instruction and student learning are positive, over 90 percent of the teachers in one survey reported that their training for computer use was inadequate or ineffective. The primary reason they cited was that computing technology still was not readily available to them to follow up on the training.[12] The results of this research suggest that training needs to be tailored to individual needs, but it is only effective if computers are available for regular use by teachers.

The delay in purchase and deployment of computers discussed earlier resulted in a slower integration of technology in classrooms for instructional purposes than was envisioned by the task force on school reform. This situation might explain in part why the use of computers as a tool in instruction has been slow to develop. But another factor in the slow use of computers in classrooms is the low level of expertise many teachers have in the use of computers to improve their own productivity. Many teachers readily admit that their students know much more about computers and software than they do, which is a circumstance that can only be overcome through extensive training.

The vision for technology in KERA is for students to do more than just learn to be "computer literate." Computers and other technology are to be used to create charts, graphs, data records, and visual images based on work in mathematics, science, art or other subject areas. Various technologies are to be used as tools for learning, information sharing, and productivity just as they are used in the workplace. At the very least this meant that access to technology should be freely available to all students and teachers.

Schools that used computers and other technology for instructional purposes prior to KERA usually had installed them in computer laboratories or media centers rather than in regular classrooms. Consequently, it wasn't necessary for most teachers to be proficient in their use. Relatively few teachers regularly used technology for instructional purposes in their own classrooms. Whatever children learned about the use of technology was taught or managed by the person in charge of the computer laboratory or media center.

It may be too early yet to evaluate the impact of the investment in classroom computers and other technologies on student learning, but the initial evidence strongly suggests that a critical mass of teachers who feel competent in their preparation for the use of technology has not yet been reached. It is highly unlikely that a measurable impact on either students or teachers will be discerned until the technology is more widely distributed and teachers have been better trained in its use.

Experts in the field of education technology generally agree that it is very difficult to document a direct link between technology and learning. However, in the Kentucky case the use of technology is itself a learning objective. Thus the investment is considered a success if students learn to be productive with technology whether or not it helps them learn specific subjects. The primary objective is for them to learn to use technology to do science or mathematics, not just to use it to learn about science and mathematics.

NOTES:

[1] HB 940 Section 22 (5) See KRS 156.670.
[2] HB 940 Section 22 (2) See KRS 156.666.
[3] HB 940 Section 21 (7) (a-f) [KRS 156.666 (7)]
[4] HB 940 Section 20 [KRS 156.665 repealed in 1992]
[5] See HB 940 Section 22(1) [KRS 156.670]
[6] Since the legislature would not meet in regular session again until 1992, the task force decided to delegate this responsibility to the Legislative Research Commission, the administrative agency of the legislature.
[7] See HB 940 Section 22(1). [KRS 156.670 before amended in 1992]
[8] Council for Education Technology, The Kentucky Education Technology Plan: Broad Parameters Report, January, 1991.
[9] See *Office of Education Accountability Annual Report*, December, 1996, 141-155; 273-277.

---

[10] See *Kentucky Education Reform: The First Five Years*, Frankfort, KY: Kentucky Department of Education, June, 1995.
[11] See *A Review of Research on the Kentucky Education Reform Act*, Frankfort, KY: Kentucky Institute for Education Research, *1995,* 154-158.
[12] *Op. cit*, 155.

10. A School is Redefined

The changes in curriculum and teaching envisioned in KERA are supported with a dramatic change in school organization called school-based decision making, a feature of KERA that empowers people at the school site with authority to make the professional judgments necessary to meet the learning needs of every child. Understanding the origins and intent of this policy is very important to understanding Kentucky's strategy for improving schools.

We will begin with a review of how the idea of school-based decision making entered the discussion and became a central element in the new public school system in Kentucky. Then we will examine in detail how this innovation was expected to work. Finally, we will examine how this policy was implemented and what effect it has had on school performance.

The Policy Origins of School-Based Decision Making

A series of important and influential studies of American public education, including a presidential commission, were published in the 1980s. Each study pointed to the approach educators were taking to the learning process of children as a major reason so many children were not reaching the level of achievement needed to be productive citizens and workers in the United States.

Among the many findings of these studies is the observation that schooling in America is a regimented process of covering textbook material based on age-graded increments in the cumulative knowledge children are expected to absorb. Teachers are not personally accountable for the results of their work. Teaching the curriculum is the primary focus of their work, not the success of individual children.

The focus of the workforce in public education all too often is on responding to and complying with rules and mandates rather than on finding ways to achieve the best results with children. Teachers are treated as technicians who are supposed to work according to the manual rather than as clinicians. In a word, improvement in the way children should be taught is a victim of the bureaucratic way schools are organized and operated. Innovation, to the extent it occurs, comes from the administration rather than from classroom teachers.

School-based decision making is designed to give teachers at the school level the authority they need to engage in a clinical approach to managing student learning. The idea is to give teachers direct control of the key variables in the learning environment such as the characteristics of the staff, the use of teacher and student time, classroom management techniques, assignment of students, curriculum and learning materials, and the use of equipment and space. Using this authority, teachers are expected to use the instructional methods they believe are most appropriate to improve the learning of their students rather than simply "teach the textbook."

The idea of giving personnel at the school site more control over instructional matters received considerable public attention toward the end of the 1980s.[1] The most notable examples of this innovation at the time were found in school systems in Rochester, New York; Dade County, Florida; and San Diego, California. Governor Wallace Wilkinson introduced the concept of school-based management into the debate over how to improve schools in Kentucky when he included site-based management as a key element in his agenda for school reform in 1987.[2] His proposal was to provide teachers a maximum amount of freedom to teach children in the manner they think is best, and then hold them professionally accountable for improving the learning of all students, not just the "brightest and best."

Many Kentucky educators and legislators considered the idea of school-based decision making controversial at the time, but it eventually gained acceptance by the Task Force on Education Reform and became an integral part of KERA. There are some differences between Wilkinson's ideas and the specific form school-based decision making eventually took in KERA, but clearly many of the elements of his proposal are in the legislation.

Instructional Authority Granted to the School Site

Fully aware that teachers had little previous experience with making instructional decisions of the kind we envisioned, it was felt that some kind of organizational structure would be necessary to facilitate the decision process. School councils were created solely to facilitate a transition from a bureaucratic type organization to a professional practice model for local schools.

The instructional nature of the responsibilities of the school council are clearly spelled out in KERA to assure that the decisions at the local school level do not gravitate into management responsibilities of the principal, superintendent, or local school board. The section of the law quoted below gives school site personnel control over those elements of the school that have a direct impact on their ability to influence learning such as materials, space, time, and teaching strategies. As will be shown here, the scope of authority granted to the local school is tightly circumscribed and is limited to matters that most directly affect the ability of teachers to create an effective learning environment for all the children in their care.

Here are the specific decisions that KERA says must be made by personnel at the school site if there is a school council in place:

1. *Determination of curriculum, including needs assessment, curriculum development, alignment with state standards, technology utilization, and program appraisal within the local school board's policy;*
2. *Assignment of all instructional and non-instructional staff time;*
3. *Assignment of students to classes and programs within the school;*
4. *Determination of the schedule of the school day and week, subject to the beginning and ending times of the school day and school calendar year as established by the local board;*
5. *Determination of use of school space during the school day;*
6. *Planning and resolution of issues regarding instructional practices;*
7. *Selection and implementation of discipline and classroom management techniques, including responsibilities of the student, parent, teacher, counselor, and principal; and*
8. *Selection of extracurricular programs and determination of policies relating to student participation based on academic qualifications and attendance requirements, program evaluation and supervision.*[3]

The Structure of School Councils

KERA requires every local board of education to adopt a policy for implementing school-based decision making not later than January 1,

1991, which was just 6 months after the law took effect. The law requires the board policy to address and comply with the following organizational issues:

(a) *Each participating school shall form a school council which shall be composed of two (2) parents, three (3) teachers, and the principal or administrator. The membership of the council may be increased, but it may only be increased proportionately. The parent representatives on the council shall not be relatives of any employee of the school.*

(b) *The teacher representatives shall be elected for one (1) year terms by a majority of the teachers. The parent representatives shall be selected for one (1) year terms. The parent members shall be elected by the parent members of the parent teacher organization of the school, or if none exists, the largest organization of parents formed for this purpose. The principal or head teacher shall be the chair of the school council.*

(c) *The school council shall have the responsibility to set school policy which shall provide an environment to enhance the students' achievement and help the school meet the goals established by Sections 2 and 3 of this Act. The principal or head teacher shall be the primary administrator and the instructional leader of the school, and with the assistance of the total school staff shall administer the policies established by the school council and the local board.*[4]

The particular structure created here is intended to have these special features:

(1) the ratio of educators to parents is two-to-one but council membership can be larger so long as this proportionality is retained;

(2) the principal or head teacher is the chairperson of the council and is recognized as the instructional leader for the school;

(3) the selection process for membership on the school council is to be democratic rather than appointive; and

(4) the total faculty is to be involved in the decisions of the council through a broad-based committee structure.

The following sections of the law make these features explicit:

(d) *All certified staff at a school may be participants in the school-based decision making. The staff shall divide into committees according to their areas of interest, such as, but not limited to, grouped grade levels, subject areas, and special programs. Each committee shall elect by a majority of the committee a chair, who shall serve for a term of one (1) year. The committee shall submit its recommendations to the school council for consideration.*

(e) *The school council and each of its committees shall determine the frequency of and agenda for their meetings. Matters relating to formation of school councils that are not provided for by this section shall be addressed by local board policy.*

(f) *The meetings of the school council shall be open to the public and all interested persons may attend. However, the exceptions to open meeting provided in KRS 61.810 shall apply.*[5]

The model set forth above is mandated to ensure a somewhat uniform implementation of school councils across the state. The number of council members is important, but it is not as important as the balance between the professional educators and parents and the retention of the principal as the instructional leader. We knew that membership size would be an issue for large schools where a group of six people could hardly be considered representative. Thus the law makes provision for increasing the membership so long as the ratio of professional educators to parents is retained.

Recognizing the possible limitations inherent in the structure that was mandated above, we made provision for alternatives to be considered and approved by the state board of education.

> *A school that chooses to have school-based decision making but would like to be exempt from the administrative structure set forth by this section may develop a model for implementing school-based decision making including, but not limited to, a description of the membership, organization, duties and responsibilities of a school council. ... The application for approval of the model shall show evidence that it has been developed by representatives of the parents, students, certified personnel and the administrators of the school and that two-thirds (2/3) of the faculty have agreed to the model.*[6]

The caveat in this language is that the school first must choose to have school-based decision making based on the two-third vote of the faculty. Once that decision is made, the school can develop a proposal for a different structure for its school council than the one specified in KERA. However, the alternative structure for its school council must satisfy the criteria given above, which documents that all the key stakeholders have been involved in the development of the plan. The alternative plan must then be approved by the state board of education.

Issues of Local School Leadership and Autonomy

Many of the actions of the school council would be meaningless without resources to implement them, whether they are financial or human in nature. Therefore, KERA gives school councils the ability to influence faculty appointments, the selection of a principal, and the use of instructional and professional development funds made available to the school.

The law on personnel matters and instructional funds is clear.

> (g) *After receiving notification of the funds available for the school from the local board, the school council shall determine within the parameters of the total available funds the number of persons to be employed in each job classification at the school. The council may make personnel decisions on vacancies occurring after the school council is formed but shall not have the authority to recommend transfers or dismissals.*
>
> (h) *The school council shall determine which instructional materials and student support services shall be provided in the school. Subject to available resources, the local board shall allocate an appropriation to each school that is adequate to meet the school's needs related to instructional materials and school-based student support services, as determined by the school council.*
>
> (i) *From a list of applicants recommended by the local superintendent, the principal at the participating school shall select personnel to fill vacancies, after consultation with the school council. Requests for transfer shall conform to any employer-employee bargained contract which is in effect. If the vacancy to be filled is the position of principal, the school council shall select the new principal from among those persons recommended by the local superintendent. Personnel decisions made at the school level under the authority of this subsection shall be binding on the superintendent who completes the hiring process. The superintendent shall provide additional applicants upon request.*[7]

Employment decisions generally are regarded as managerial in nature and therefore should be beyond the authority of a school council. The rationale for giving school councils a role in personnel decisions *at the school site level* is based on the reality that people are the most important resource in a school. We did not think teachers should be hiring each other. On the other hand we did not think they should be subjected to the consequences of central office decisions to place people in certain schools for political or other non-instructional reasons, especially when such persons do not fit the personnel or instructional needs of the school as determined by the school council. We wanted a local school through its school council to have a meaningful role in personnel decisions within the system.

Although school councils cannot be forced to accept someone unacceptable to them, they are not given authority to recruit or employ personnel on their own. Only the school district can employ, discipline, or dismiss school employees. The school district is the employer, not the school council. A school council informs the district of its personnel needs, which includes non-certified personnel as well as teachers. The district then is expected to find people qualified to fill the positions the school council has identified. If the school council finds a nominee unacceptable, the superintendent must offer additional names until someone acceptable to the school is found.

In addition to involvement in personnel decisions, the local board must allocate instructional funds to each school site the use of which is to be determined solely by the school council. These funds are to be budgeted for purposes determined by the local school through the school council. Authority to decide what instructional materials to use would be empty unless financial resources were available to implement these decisions.

Prior to KERA there was a common practice of schools using fund raising programs, often involving students, to finance the purchase of instructional materials and equipment. We felt strongly that it was a duty of the local school board to *adequately* fund the instructional program of each school, so that teachers would not have to resort to fund raising activities in order to meet the instructional needs of their students. Giving discretionary funds to local schools was not a common practice, so KERA made it a requirement.

The reference to "student support services" was inserted to give schools the opportunity to define the need for and the role of non-certified people hired to assist teachers in the classroom. Previously these people generally were called "teacher aides" who were hired according to a state formula. The change in terms now gives schools the ability to define the role of non-certified people in the classroom in ways that best suit their unique instructional needs.

The local school board was given other responsibilities that had to be addressed by the board policy for school-based decision making that included but is not limited to the following:

(a) *School budget and administration, including: discretionary funds; activity and other school funds; funds for maintenance, supplies, and equipment; and accounting and auditing;*

(b) *Assessment of individual student progress, including testing and reporting of student progress to students, parents, the school district, the community, and the state;*

(c) *School improvement plans, including the form and function of strategic planning and its relationship to district planning;*

(d) *Professional development plans developed pursuant to Sections 12 and 13 of this Act;*

(e) *Parent, citizen, and community participation including the relationship of the council with other groups;*

(f) *Cooperation and collaboration within the district, with other districts and with other public and private agencies;*

(g) *requirements for waiver of district policies;*

(h) *requirements for record keeping by the school council; and*

(i) *A process for appealing a decision made by a school council.*[8]

Clearly the local school board is expected to provide guidance to school councils in areas of district-wide importance.

Every effort was made to clarify the respective roles and responsibilities of school councils and the district board of education. Still some local school boards raised questions about the degree to which they could dictate, influence, or approve decisions made by school councils. There were some instances where local school boards attempted to influence school council decisions in various ways, usually by trying to require board approval of certain school council actions.

In 1992 the legislature clarified at least the issue of undue interference in school council action by adding the following provision to KERA:

> *No board member, superintendent of schools, or district employee shall intentionally engage in a pattern of practice which is detrimental to the successful implementation of or circumvents the intent of school-based decision making to allow the professional staff members of a school and parents to be involved in the decision making process or working toward meeting the educational goals established in KRS 158.645 and 158.6451 or to make decisions in areas of policy assigned to a school council pursuant to paragraph (j) of subsection (2) of this section.*[9]

Violation of this provision can result in removal from office, which sent a strong message to anyone who wanted to return to an earlier time of autocratic rule over schools.

The constitutionality of giving school councils such broad powers without their decisions being made subject to approval by local school boards was challenged in court. The rulings in these cases all favored the school councils. It now appears the legal foundation of school councils is secure and future challenges in the courts are not anticipated.[10]

The Role of School Principals

Some school administrators contend that there is an internal conflict in KERA with regard to the role of the principal as the school instructional leader and the authority assigned to school councils to make decisions on instructional matters. At least a decade of research on school effectiveness prior to enactment of KERA produced strong evidence that academically high performing schools had visionary school principals who were instructional leaders first and administrators second. It was our intent to preserve the instructional leadership role of principals, but at the same time engage the entire faculty in a process of changing and improving their professional effectiveness in the classroom.

Perhaps we unwittingly inhibited the ability of some principals to be effective leaders in instructional matters because the law appeared to have assigned this role to school councils. The law clearly said that the principal was to be the instructional leader of the school and with the assistance of the total school staff is to administer the policies established by the school council.[11] KERA also required that the principal be a member of the school council. Perhaps the potential for conflict between the two ideas was not clearly seen at the time.

Not making the principal the sole policy maker at a school was designed to break the pattern of autocratic leadership that was so pervasive in Kentucky schools prior to KERA. Evidence has shown that principals must assert strong leadership in a school for it to make progress even if a school council is present. Undoubtedly there are principals who are quite capable of providing effective leadership without being dictatorial. Likewise, a school council that plays its role as facilitator of a collegial decision process can be an important asset to a visionary school leader. A serious problem arises when a school council perceives itself as a governing body and regards the principal as a pawn in its hand.

A related issue is the role given to local school councils in the selection of a principal. We discussed earlier the rationale for granting school councils a role in the selection of teachers and other personnel at the school site. This same rationale was extended by the task force to the selection of a principal and essentially for the same reasons. It obviously gave school personnel a kind of "black ball" that could be used to make it very difficult for an unpopular principal to be assigned to a school. It was this very kind of situation that led task force members to give schools that kind of protection. If the school is the unit of accountability, then the faculty of the school should have some say in the selection of their instructional leader.

Personal conversations I have had with some superintendents revealed a concern they had that this provision weakened the control a superintendent has over a principal if the appointment has to meet the approval of the local school. I also hear the contention that this provision might cause some principals to be beholden to the council members who approved their assignment. My personal observations indicate just the contrary. The fact that the local faculty influenced the selection of the instructional leader actually led to a feeling of commitment to the success of that person that might otherwise be lacking. As the value of school councils is debated in the future, consideration should be given to finding a way to more clearly delineate the respective contribution of a school council and the instructional leader (the principal) in the development of sound instructional policies and practices in a school. It serves no public purpose to have conflict between the two.

Deployment of School Councils

Every school district had to have a school council established at one or more schools by June 1, 1991. A council could be created at any school in which two-thirds or more of the faculty voted to implement school-based decision making. If no school took such action, the local school board had to designate at least one school in which it would expect school-based decision making to be implemented. All schools had to have school councils by the 1996-97 school year unless exempted by the state education agency because they met their performance goal on the state accountability test.[12]

The reason for the five year implementation period was to give every school district some experience with the school-based decision making process before requiring it for every school in the state. There was much to be learned about how school-based decision making and school councils would work in practice, so a slow approach was built into KERA. Schools could take up to five years to create a school council, but all schools had to have them in place not later than July 1, 1996, unless the school received an exemption from the department of education as provided for in the legislation.

The immediate task for local school boards was to create a policy for school-based decision making by January 1, 1991.[13] The law gave specific instructions as to the issues that this policy must address. The department of education also was required to provide sample guidelines to help local school boards develop their policies. In addition to the sample guidelines, the department had to provide professional development activities to help local schools implement school-based decision making.[14]

The law established a school council discretionary fund to be administered by the department of education. Each year that school councils were in existence the department was to distribute the funds appropriated for this purpose to schools participating in school-based decision making. The amount a school could receive was based on school enrollment.[15] The purpose of these grants was to give local schools a financial incentive to participate in school-based decision making in the early years of KERA and to help offset any additional expenses a school might incur by adopting school-based decision making.

The department of education was slow in drafting regulations for the distribution of the discretionary funds. Apparently at the time the regulations to govern their distribution were being prepared, a draft was sent out for comment. Because so many schools already had created school councils without these grants, many people felt it was inappropriate to offer them to other schools at that late date. Consequently, the grants were never made.

In addition to these specific duties, the department of education provided awareness sessions throughout the state and through the Kentucky Educational Television network. These sessions provided participants with information about the law, defined the concept of school-based decision making, and described the roles of various participants in the process. Special training sessions were held to give new school council members organizational skills in areas such as consensus building, developing an agenda, planning, and running a meeting.

Capacity building efforts of the state education agency were augmented by special information and training sessions offered by education professional organizations and voluntary groups like the Kentucky Congress of Parents and Teachers and the Prichard Committee made up of citizen advocates for school reform. All of these groups recognized the potential of school-based decision making, but they also saw the tremendous need for good information about it. Each group worked with their respective constituencies to help them understand the law as well as to acquire the skills needed to make it successful. It seems that many people wanted this part of KERA to succeed, and they put forth a great effort to that end.

NOTES:

[1] See Paul Hill and Josephine Bonan, *Decentralization and Accountability in Public Education*. Santa Monica, CA: RAND, 1991

[2] See Wallace G. Wilkinson, (undated document released Fall of 1988) *Q. A.: Improving Kentucky Schools*. His views were further refined in *A Plan to Restructure Schools in Kentucky,* (undated document released Spring of 1989).

[3] HB 940 Section 14 (j) [KRS 160.345]

[4] HB 940 Section 14 (a) through (c). The law was amended in 1994 to assure minority membership on a school council if a minority parent was not elected in the regular election in schools with 8% or more minority students. The ratio of parents to teachers is increased in such cases. See [KRS 160.345]

[5] HB 490 Section 14 (d) through (f) [KRS 160.345]

[6] See HB 940 Section 14 (7) [KRS 160.345 (7)]

[7] HB 940 Section 14 (g) through (i) [KRS 160.345]

---

[8] HB 940 Section 14 (3) [KRS 160.345]

[9] KRS 160.345

[10] A major test case was *Board of Education of Boone County v. Bushee*. 889 S.W.2d 809 (Kentucky 1994).

[11] See HB 940 Section 14 (2) (c) [KRS 160.345 (2) (c) (1)]

[12] See HB 940 Section 14 (5) [KRS 160.345 (5)]

[13] See HB 940 Section 14 (2) [KRS 160.345 (2)]

[14] See HB 940 Section 14 (6) [KRS 160.345 (6)]

[15] See HB 940 Section 14 (9) [KRS 160.345 (8)]

11. The Role of School Councils

The primary rationale for creating school councils is to ensure that the instructional decision process is meaningful and to promote a collective sense of responsibility for results. Presumably a process of collegial decision making can exist without a formal structure like a school council. However, all too often what passes for collective decision making really is just consultation, and in some cases an overt effort at co-optation by school administrators. It was thought that a formal council structure would ensure true participation of the school faculty in the most important instructional decisions in the school, and replace the arbitrary, authoritarian atmosphere found in many schools with a participatory approach to the way instructional decisions are made.

The authority to make instructional decisions at the school level was granted to school councils instead of the faculty as a whole to provide a clear point of accountability. But the purpose of the council structure is singularly to enable teachers to be directly involved in implementing the transition to the new approach to teaching and learning envisioned for Kentucky schools.

Perhaps the most common misunderstanding about the purpose of school councils since passage of KERA is the perception that this meant schools could govern themselves. Legal responsibility for the local school remains with the local school board just as it was before KERA was enacted. There is nothing in the political discussion that preceded KERA or in the legislative language that supports a contention that the intent was to make schools independent of school board control. No one intended to unduly constrain the ability of school administrators to carry out their administrative responsibilities under the law. The sole intent of the school council *structure* and the school-based decision making *process* created by KERA is to *enable and empower teachers* to make decisions about their professional practice in a collegial and orderly manner at the school site.

Unfortunately, the concept of school councils that emerged after KERA was enacted is one of a body that functions like a governing board rather than a coordinating body. This interpretation no doubt stems from the authority KERA granted to school councils to make final decisions. It was never the intent to make these councils a mini-school board. On the other hand, there had to be some group at the school in a position to resolve differences and bring closure to issues under discussion. If was felt there should be a single point of accountability. This was intended to be the sole role and function of a school council.

School councils were not expected to get into administrative matters such as fixing water fountains or ordering alterations to their buildings without school board approval. KERA explicitly made a distinction between what constitutes the administration of schools as educational institutions and the professional responsibilities of the educators who are hired to work in them. The matters described in the previous chapter are considered the legitimate province of the faculty rather than the administration. In spite of the specificity of the language in the law and the extended discussion of the concept of school councils that was the center of public debate prior to KERA, some school councils over time nonetheless took on many issues that were not in their province under the law.

Perspectives on School Councils

Now that school councils have been in existence in Kentucky for eight years, how are they viewed by educators and parents? The answer to this question is examined first from the perspective of educators and then from the perspective of parents.

Educator Perspectives

A common concern among educators in schools with school councils is the amount of time it takes to be a member. Most teacher responses to surveys on school-based decision making indicate they would not want to go back to the old autocratic environment, but many teachers believe that the benefits from having a school council are not worth the effort it requires. After a school has had a school council in place for several years, it appears from personal observation that some of the more creative members of the faculty shun the opportunity to serve as members. They prefer to participate in activities more directly related to classroom needs or professional growth.

Another common concern among educators has been the focus of the training they were given in preparation for creating a school council and for council membership. The emphasis in the training, they contend, was primarily on understanding the law and on procedural issues. While they concede this may be necessary initially, many educators who serve on school councils believe they also should have received more training in the specific policy areas where they are expected to make decisions.

Research findings suggest that many teachers do not think they have the proper background or experience on which to base school policies on issues like aligning curriculum with the state mandated learning expectations and setting disciplinary policy. Council members say that the training experiences available to them have not been of much help in this regard. Policy-making is not something for which they have been prepared either by education or experience.

Assumption of the responsibilities KERA assigned to local schools was fearful for many faculties. Most teachers had been solo practitioners most of their career. The very idea that what goes on in their classroom now was to be a matter of mutual agreement among their colleagues was foreign or perhaps even distasteful. Collegial decision making in itself is a major change in school culture and operating procedure. Making decisions about the kind of matters that KERA delegated to school faculties was an even greater challenge.

It appears that we did not make sufficient provision for building the capacity in local schools to make the kind of decisions we assigned to them. Changing long-standing instructional practices and habits of mind is a daunting task. Simply creating a school-based decision process or a school council cannot bear the full burden for changing school culture.

Much of the professional development available to teachers in the early years of KERA failed to make a connection between what they were doing through professional development and the policy making process at the local school level. It was if the two had no strategic connection to each other. The problem was further compounded by the fact that the training school council members received focused primarily on procedural and legal matters rather than on what they should consider when making decisions on instructional policy. In retrospect, we should have created a knowledge base where council members can find information they need to formulate sound instructional policies and practices.

Many school councils apparently spent much of their time in the initial months on issues that were peripheral to instruction. It is natural for a new group to concern itself with its own operational issues, but it seemed to take more time than was expected and in some cases even prevented the council from moving quickly to issues for which it was responsible. Even then, some school councils seemed to gravitate to issues dealing with school procedures (often on administrative matters) rather than to issues relative to how the school would make the transition from the traditional teaching model to a clinical practice model.

As for the idea of having parents on school councils, some teachers complained that occasionally parents get on a school council to further a personal agenda rather than to serve as a representative of the community of parents who have children in the school. The perception is that most parent members don't consult with the larger parent community about matters under consideration, so the faculty members don't get much more than the opinions of the two people who get elected.

Parent Perspectives

KERA gives faculty unilateral control over the decision to create a school council and it gives them a majority in membership on the council. Our reason for having parents involved in this process is to give them a formal position at the table when issues of importance to them are discussed. All too often parents had seen things done that they only learned about after the fact. The intent was to ensure that a parent perspective would be considered before a school made important decisions affecting their children.

Although it was thought important for parents to have a meaningful way to participate in the decisions of school professionals, it was never the intent to give them control of such decisions. The ratio of two educators for each parent member on the council was intentionally designed to subordinate the role of parents in the decision process. This kind of structure for school councils was particularly important to faculty because they, not the parents of the children, are the people the state holds accountable for the effectiveness of the instructional process. Even the school council is not held responsible.

Eager to seize an opportunity to participate in important decisions at their children's schools, many parents apparently thought their membership on these school councils would give them a major role in how the local school was operated. These expectations could not be realized the way the law is written. Participation is not always control, and in this case it was not intended to be.

Research on school councils strongly indicates that parent members show the least enthusiasm for these councils once they have participated in them. Perhaps this is predictable if they sought membership thinking their presence would given them control of school decisions. The reality is that many important decisions in fact are being made through processes outside the purview of the school council and sometimes even without the members' awareness. Thus the parent members feel "out of the loop" and incidental to what is really happening in the school. Soon they begin to see the picture and lose interest or stop attending the meetings. After the first year or so these schools begin to experience great difficulty in getting parents to even run for membership on the school council let alone actively participate once they are elected.

Data from surveys of parent members of school councils indicate they often feel the educators tend to dismiss their opinions, "talk down to them" and make them feel inferior, or indicate that a decision has already been made and the parent members should be prepared to accept it. The condescending attitude of faculty in these situations is offensive and results in conflict, poor rapport, or diminished interest in being a member.

The method of selecting parent members, term lengths, and the absence of minority representation on school councils became an issue in certain schools. The legislature made certain adjustments in the law in 1994 to address these concerns. The larger question, however, concerns the efficacy of having parent representation at all. It appears that parents still want membership on school councils even if their role is marginal, because they believe it is at least one point of access to school decision making that they did not have before KERA.

Slow Adoption of School Councils

All school districts met the initial mandate to have a school council in at least one school by the beginning of the 1991-92 school year, although 40 of the 176 school districts in the state had to select a school because none had volunteered. In the first year 286 schools in 136 school districts voted to create school councils. Four years after the initial mandate, 922 of Kentucky's 1,365 schools had voted to create a school council. However, it is notable that a significant number of schools still had not yet participated in school-based decision making after four years of experience with school councils. Entering the fifth year of their implementation, 450 of the schools in the state (one-third) still had to either create a school council or be granted an exemption by the state board of education before the July 1, 1996, deadline.

From a policy perspective, one has to ask what accounts for the slow adoption of school councils. Is it a rejection of school-based decision making, or is it a rejection of school councils as the vehicle for it? The research results so far are difficult to interpret because much of it has focused on school councils rather than on the concept of having personnel at the school site be involved in collegial efforts to change the way they conduct their profession. Structure seems to have taken preeminence over function in many instances.

The most common reason given for not creating a school council is that it takes up too much time that faculty believe is better spent on other activities. Some faculties may be resisting the idea of having parents involved in their professional decision making. A more foreboding reason may be reluctance among some teachers to assume the responsibilities that school-based decision making entails. There also is some evidence that a lack of enthusiasm for the idea among school principals may account for some schools not creating a school council. In some instances, faculties are practicing school-based decision making without creating a school council. Why incur the hassle of a time consuming school council if you can exercise all the prerogatives without one?

Although the research data are not definitive on this point, evidence seems to suggest that a large number of schools have bought into school-based decision making in practice, but their reluctance to create school councils makes it appear they are rejecting it. What they may be resisting is school councils, the organizational vehicle that state policy makers thought was necessary for school-based decision making to work. Whatever the reasons, the reluctance of such a large number of schools to create school councils must be a matter of concern.

Are School Councils Necessary?

Considerable research has been done on school councils and the school-based decision making process.[1] Most of the research has focused on how school councils get organized and do their work. Relatively little has been done to assess the impact of school-based decision making on instructional effectiveness, perhaps because it is very difficult to isolate the affect of this one variable. School councils are a means to an end, but the councils seem to be an end in themselves in the mind of many people who research them.

In light of the reluctance of so many educators to support and participate in school councils, it is legitimate to ask about their importance to the goal of school-based decision making. Are they a necessary condition for delegating important instructional decisions to personnel at the school site? Have they helped or hindered the school-based decision making process?

The primary policy objective of school-based decision making is to assign responsibility for instructional decisions to the people who are in the best position to influence learning. Therefore, the policy issue here is whether such decisions are being made by faculty in a collegial manner. The answer should rest on the extent to which instructional changes are the product of a collegial process, with and without the presence of a school council.

The curriculum alignment process that was widely used in most schools clearly emulated school-based decision making. However, it should be noted that in many cases this process occurred outside the school council structure even in schools where the final product was approved by the school council. In fact in many schools this process occurred even before a decision was ever made to create a school council.

Likewise, anecdotal information indicates that significant changes in instructional practice have occurred whether they were formally sanctioned by a school council or were solely a product of a collegial decision process. It is difficult to determine with certainty the role school councils may have played in the facilitation of these changes in a school, but it seems reasonable to conclude that a school council is not a necessary precondition for collegial decision making to occur. In fact, while school councils were focused on organizing themselves and attending to procedural matters, the faculties in many of these schools made critical changes to curriculum, teaching strategies, classroom practices, and the like on an informal basis.

Collegial decision making on instructional matters is regularly occurring during planning periods and in faculty meetings totally outside the school council structure, and often without consultation with the school council until a consensus had been reached or the changes are already in place. The discontinuity between what school councils are working on and what faculty do on a day-to-day basis to implement various elements of KERA probably is inconsequential, since the faculty in these schools have found ways to achieve consensus on important instructional matters without direction from their school council.

It appears that the policy objective of ensuring collaboration on such matters was met in many schools whether or not a school council was present. Even when school councils are present, they often are not used to facilitate collaboration but rather to confirm its results. In both schools with and without school councils, teachers now are spending a great deal of time in consultation and joint planning, something most educators believe is beneficial though time consuming. Teachers seem to feel they can experience the benefits of school-based decision making without having to devote the time required to have council meetings that are seen as just an added burden.

Research has revealed that the creation of a school council has not always ensured collaboration, especially in cases where the school principal wanted to control the decision process. Power struggles emerged in these schools between faculty members on the school council and the principal who generally chaired it. In these schools the principals apparently controlled the council agenda and built coalitions within it as a way to ensure the outcome would be the one they wanted. Domination of a council by the school administrator in these cases generally was resented and usually resulted in faculty members feeling very dissatisfied with the school council concept.

If faculties can address and resolve the complex issues affecting their professional practice without a school council to make them final, then how useful is a school council to school improvement? The obvious policy intent of school-based decision making was to delegate to personnel at the school site authority to make certain decisions. School councils were the vehicles the legislature created to give structure to a decision process that was new to almost every school. However, the reason for creating school councils initially may not be a good reason for continuing them indefinitely. The experience with school councils may very well bring about changes in attitude and working relationship in ways that will continue even if the requirement that they have a council is eliminated.

Perhaps the law should be changed so that the authority to make the decisions now delegated to school councils is vested in the faculty at the school site so long as a sound, visible, and democratic process is present and operative to support the decisions that are being made. Such alternatives to school councils should still require approval of the state board of education until there is firm evidence that these alternatives are working in practice. It is important, however, that the justification for approval be based on documentation that a viable *process* exists rather than simply the presence of a school council. It probably would be wise to continue the requirement that schools formally create a structure to support school-based decision making, but it would also make sense to begin to unlink the decision *proc-*

ess from the kind of formal *structure* that KERA initially imposed as a model.

The Dissolution and Re-Creation of School Councils

An important oversight in KERA has surfaced in recent years. A few schools have sought to dissolve their school councils, an action that was not addressed in HB 940. In these cases, the faculties contend that the authority for the action is based on the exemption provision in the statute. In each case the school councils were dissolved unilaterally by a majority vote of the faculty that brought protests from parents who felt they should have had some say in the decision. Only a few schools have tried to reverse the decision to adopt school-based decision making, but these incidents point out the need to address this issue from a policy perspective.

The law was very specific about the creation of school councils but made no explicit provision for their dissolution. As noted earlier, the law allowed any school performing above its threshold level, by a majority vote of the faculty, to petition the state board of education for an exemption from the requirement to create a school council before the July 1, 1996, deadline. The state board of education must grant the exemption.[2] However, HB 940 did not deal specifically with the issue of the dissolution of school councils *once they were created.*

The issue that led to the insertion of the exemption provision in Section 14 (5) in HB 940 was the possibility that there might be some schools that repeatedly meet or exceed their improvement goal but have not created a school council within the five year time frame for their establishment. The policy question was whether such schools still should be required to create school councils notwithstanding their demonstrated success without them. Task Force members agreed that the law should not arbitrarily impose either a structure or process on a school that apparently did not need it in order to meet its performance threshold, so the exemption procedure was inserted into the bill. However, it should be noted that the exemption provision appears in the section of the law dealing only with *initial creation* of school councils and not in a separate section dealing specifically with the dissolution of a school council once it has been created.

The Task force never considered the issue of dissolving an existing school council, because school councils were presumed eventually to be the rule for all schools. As the Act was passed in 1990, the creation of school councils was an irrevocable decision unless the exemption language in Section

14 (5) of the Act could be construed to apply to any school that met or exceeded its performance threshold *whether or not it already had a school council in place*. In light of the history of the exemption provision, this did not appear to be its legislative intent.

Apart from the question of whether KERA authorizes dissolution of school councils, there are some unresolved legal issues for schools that do not have school councils. The statutory authority to make the decisions the authors of KERA wanted made in a collegial manner by people at the school site is granted by statute only to a school council. From a legal standpoint, it is a school council, not the faculty as a collective, which has the authority to take action on these instructional matters at the present time. This was done initially to give schools an incentive to create school councils, since school personnel could not exercise these prerogatives except through a school council. Therefore, unless a local school board on its own is willing to delegate to a local school the authority to make these decisions, the authority reverts to the school administrator and local board of education by default. Under present law, a school has no legal foundation on which to continue to make these decisions once their school council has been dissolved. When a school dissolves its school council presumably it also forfeits the decision-making authority the school had while the council was in place.

The dissolution of existing councils and their re-creation in the future is an important policy issue. A rational policy would not have school councils created, dissolved, and then re-created based solely on whether schools achieve a particular standing on the state accountability test. The only criteria for exemption now is whether a school is meeting the state improvement goal, something that could change every two years. While success in meeting the state improvement goal may be important in determining whether a school council should be required, the issue is whether it should be the only requirement. The answer to this question should rest on whether the school has met the policy objective for school councils, not on a score on the state accountability test.

Another issue that must be addressed in the dissolution of school councils is parental involvement in the decision and how parents will be involved in decisions if a school council doesn't exist. In light of the way the law is written, it is logical to assume that if a school council can be created unilaterally by a two-thirds majority vote of the faculty, it can be dissolved in the same manner. The political problem here is that parents have seen school councils as a point of access to school decisions that previously did not exist. They are rightfully concerned about what happens to that access if a school council is disbanded. Evidence so far indicates that parents feel their rights will have been abridged if a faculty can unilaterally "disenfranchise" them.

Clearly parental involvement in the decision to dissolve a school council and the role of parents in whatever structure or process takes its place should be addressed in any legislation dealing with the dissolution of school councils. If a school faculty elects not to create a school council, it should be required to provide an alternative procedure or structure through which parental involvement in major instructional matters can be supported and made meaningful. At the very least there should be a requirement that parents have an opportunity to review and comment on important changes in school instructional policy or practices before they are put in place.

The Future of School-Based Decision Making

It is my personal opinion that faculties will be reluctant to give up their new authority over instructional decisions. Therefore, from a management perspective, school-based decision making has met one major objective. I has helped break up the bureaucratic structure at the school level. However, it is still too early to make a judgment about the impact school-based decision making can have on school performance.

Judging the merits of school-based decision making on the basis of such things as improved test scores may miss the mark of what is most important about this innovation. Its primary benefit may be found in giving schools the ability to correct their instructional practices and policies in a more timely way when test results indicate unsatisfactory progress in student learning than if they were still operated as bureaucracies.

What we have learned is that the transition from a traditional bureaucratic structure to a consensual model based on participatory management concepts is more difficult to achieve in public schools than in the private sector. On the other hand, the Kentucky experience does seems to indicate that school-based decision making is an achievable goal if there are appropriate incentives to undertake it and there is a sound plan to provide appropriate training and support for those willing to do it. However, one must be cautious about dictating a specific structure to support the process. School councils, whatever their other values, do not seem to be necessary to foster the kind of professional behavior they were intended to support. In fact it appears that is some schools they are just another form of bureaucracy at the school level.

---

[1] Over 60 articles, books, and research papers on the subject were cited in *A Review of Research on the Kentucky Education Reform Act 1995* prepared by the University of Kentucky/University of Louisville Joint Center for the Study of Educational Policy for the Kentucky Institute for Education Research, Frankfort, KY.

[2] See HB 940 Section 14 (5) [KRS 160.345 (5)]

12. Responsibility for Results

KERA establishes clear goals for the new system of public schools. The goals are set forth in the very first sections of the law. However, the authors of the legislation wanted more than lofty goals. They wanted to see results. Perhaps the most controversial element of the Kentucky Education Reform Act is the accountability system it created to measure and reward these results.

In order to understand the approach to accountability that ultimately was used in KERA, it is helpful to understand the political and policy context in which this element of the law was drafted. The antecedents to the accountability system finally approved by the legislature are discussed in detail to provide a background for understanding what eventually became the law in KERA and how it came to be interpreted later.

School Accountability Prior to KERA

Kentucky had used accountability as a way to improve school performance for more than a decade before KERA. In the late 1970s Kentucky enacted education reform legislation that among other things required schools to document improvement in student academic achievement. In the initial years this improvement was measured by national standardized tests that compared Kentucky with other states. At first the scores were compiled by school districts and reported only by the department of education. Later on the legislature added a requirement that test results be published in a local newspaper to inform the community about the level of achievement students were making compared with other school districts and nationally.

Legislators and critics of public education often used these test scores to point out that Kentucky students were not doing well even in basic skills like reading, writing, and mathematics. Responding to this evidence, the legislature in 1982 ordered the creation of an "essential skills" test to be taken each year by every Kentucky public school student. A contract was awarded to develop what came to be known as the Kentucky Essential Skills Test (KEST). The KEST was based on elements of the Comprehensive Test of Basic Skills (CTBS) the state previously used to measure student achievement. The KEST test items were aligned with specific academic skills Kentucky teachers thought should be taught at every school, but they were not suitable for national comparisons.

The KEST was first administered in 1983 and was used for five years. Shortly after its creation the legislature asked the department of education to expand the KEST to include items that would allow comparisons with other states. Critics of the KEST said the attempt to expand the purpose of the test was asking too much of a single test. They argued it would be better to go back to the CTBS for national comparisons than to expand the KEST for this purpose.

There were other complaints about the KEST that ranged from the time it took away from instruction to the narrow focus of the test items. Because the KEST results were made public for every school district in the state, it was very important that students do well in this "horse race" to see which school district could perform the best of the state test. Teachers readily admitted they were "teaching to the test" because the results would reflect directly on their professionalism. Many teachers contended the test had narrowed the focus of their teaching to this long list of basic skills at the expense of acquiring important knowledge in other subject areas.

Responding to these latest criticisms of KEST, the legislature discontinued funding for it in the 1988 session. In the interim, school districts could continue to use the CTBS at state expense if they chose to do so, but the requirements to report their scores to the state and to publish them locally were dropped.

Consequences for Poor Performance

Gradually the General Assembly came to embrace the idea of state intervention in school districts where student test scores or management practices indicated problems detrimental to the education of children. In a special session in 1985 the legislature gave the department of education authority to intervene in the management of a school district considered to be "deficient." The inclusion of student test scores as one of the criteria for declaring a school district to be "deficient" gave a clear signal that the legislature now embraced the idea that consequences should be attached to low academic performance. This change was important from a policy perspective, because it meant that intervention now could be based on student performance as well as mismanagement.

Sanctions for poor academic performance were directed at district level school officials rather than classroom teachers in the belief that the central office was the most effective pressure point for change. The state board of education could remove local school officials from office if such action was considered necessary to improve schools in the district.

A program of management assistance was created to help districts that the department of education declared to be deficient. A deficient district was given ample opportunity to improve with help from the state before the state would take direct responsibility for the operation of the schools in the district. The multiple stages a deficient district would go through while under state supervision meant that an actual take over would not likely occur until at least five years after the district was initially declared deficient.

A Different Approach to Accountability is Proposed

Governor Wallace Wilkinson offered the legislature a different approach to accountability in 1988.[1] The most important policy change was his proposal to shift accountability for improving schools from the district to the school level. Under the existing system, poor performing schools in a school district with acceptable average test scores could continue to exist without a mandate to improve. If every school is required to improve, then these poorer performing schools would get the attention they deserve and need.

Wilkinson proposed that improvement in school performance be measured on various criteria including among other things student performance on a battery of state tests that ultimately would be based on learning outcomes the state would define through a Council on School Performance Standards. School performance would be calculated as the percentage of students who meet or exceed specific performance standards. The use of ratios rather than average test scores more clearly identifies the actual proportion of students reaching or falling below a standard.

Wilkinson's proposal defined improvement as a steady reduction in the proportion of students who fall below each performance standard. School improvement on all criteria would be calculated using an Educational Performance Index (EPI) based on the proportion of students whose educational attainment meets or exceeds the performance standards.[2] Separate indices would be developed for elementary, middle or junior high schools, and secondary schools.

The most controversial element of the Wilkinson plan was his proposal that personnel at schools that are able to improve the performance of their students be financially rewarded in the form of a cash bonus, the amount of which would be based on the magnitude of the improvement shown. Wilkinson proposed that rewards be based on the improvement a school showed over its previous performance level rather than on its relative standing when compared with the performance of all other schools. It was his view that every school in Kentucky had room to improve and should be motivated to do so. All teachers, whether good, bad, or in between, would either earn or lose the cash bonus as a group, which Wilkinson thought would encourage a collective effort to improve the school.

Rewarding teachers for their collective rather than individual success was a significant break from the common practice of identifying and rewarding only the best teachers. Believing that improving schools required a total team effort, Wilkinson proposed that certified staff in an improved school be eligible for a cash bonus equal to 80 percent of the total reward and the remaining 20 percent of the reward be given to non-teaching staff. Central office staff also would benefit from the program, receiving an award equal to 6.25 percent of the award given to the certified personnel in qualifying schools.[3]

In return for accountability for results, Wilkinson thought teachers should be given direct control over all aspects of the instructional process at the school site. Wilkinson called this concept school-based management, which later came to be known as site-based decision making under KERA. Under this concept, state regulations that educators believe are an impediment to their success could be waived by the state board of education. The only consequence for failure to improve would be ineligibility for a reward.

Wilkinson's proposals for school improvement and teacher accountability was a significant departure from previous approaches to school accountability in Kentucky and elsewhere. For various political reasons, Wilkinson's proposals were not enacted during the 1988 session of the legislature. However, they remained an important part of the education policy debate in the state until the Kentucky Supreme Court abolished the education system in June 1989. The debate about school accountability then moved to the task force on education reform.

The Task Force Considers Accountability

David Hornbeck, the consultant to the curriculum committee of the task force on education reform, proposed an accountability program based on the key policy principles set forth in the Wilkinson proposal with several important differences.[4] Hornbeck proposed that schools be given improvement goals to be met over a two-year period. Schools that exceeded the goal would receive cash rewards as proposed by Wilkinson. Improvement would be measured by an accountability index similar to Wilkinson's EPI. Hornbeck stressed that the index calculations take into account gains with both at-risk students and all students. He was concerned that schools might try to meet their improvement goal by boosting the performance of their better students and leave others behind.

The method Hornbeck proposed for calculating the size of the bonus also was based on Wilkinson's proposal, but the cash value of the reward in Hornbeck's proposal was to be based on the annual salary of the individual teacher rather than the average salary of all teachers at the school.[5] Under the Wilkinson proposal, all teachers in a school would receive an equal amount based on the total bonus amount awarded to the school, whereas Hornbeck thought the bonus award should be based on each teacher's salary.

Hornbeck also proposed that the instructional staff at each school should decide how the award money could be spent.[6] He suggested such things as sabbaticals, graduate work, and membership dues in professional organizations, all of which in some way might contribute to the professional development of the teacher rather than simply be a cash bonus. He also suggested that perhaps school councils should be involved in the decision about how award funds should be spent.

Probably the most significant difference between the two proposals was Hornbeck's idea to have a system of consequences that included sanctions for schools that do not improve. Hornbeck proposed a three tiered classification for schools that do not exceed the improvement threshold set for them. The first level is schools that improve but don't exceed their goal. The second level is for schools that actually decline from their previous level of performance. The third level is for schools that experience a decline of greater than five percent on the accountability scale and is called a "school in crisis."

He considered a "school in crisis" to be an emergency condition. Parents with children enrolled in a school in crisis would be notified of the status of their school. Parents could request that their children be transferred to another school at district expense if they so desired. All professional personnel at a school in crisis would be placed on probation. A school in crisis also would be assigned a "distinguished educator" to evaluate the school and to help the school administration and faculty develop a plan for improvement.

The Task Force Responds

The ideas Governor Wilkinson proposed for a school accountability system were extensively debated throughout the state in the year prior to the Supreme Court decision, and Hornbeck's proposals were vigorously debated at various task force meetings. While the idea of rewards for improvement was controversial and strongly opposed by educators during the months prior to the Supreme Court decision, Hornbeck's proposal to include sanctions was even more controversial. Nonetheless, the central idea that educators should be personally accountable for the results of their work had gained broad support in the task force by this time. Only the details had to be agreed upon.

After much discussion and vigorous debate, the curriculum committee adopted the essential principles of the accountability program as outlined by Hornbeck including the concept of sanctions for schools that fail to improve. The accountability elements of HB 940 went essentially unchanged through the legislative hearings and become a central feature of KERA. It was in this context that the KERA accountability program took final form.

As we examine responsibility for results under KERA, it will be helpful to make a distinction between the *accountability* system and the *assessment* system. The *accountability* system consists of the goals for schools, the concept of accountability at the school level, the establishment of school improvement goals, the various consequences for results, and the distinguished educator concept. These things taken together are the elements of the *accountability* system.

The *assessment* system, on the other hand, consists of the methods by which improvement is measured and consequences are determined. It might be thought of as the technical foundation for the accountability system. The *assessment* system includes the measurement of learning outcomes, the measurement of the so-called "non-cognitive" goals such as attendance and drop out rates, the method of calibrating rewards and sanctions, and the method of determining the improvement thresholds for schools.

In the current chapter we will review the accountability system, its implementation, and the lessons learned from it. In subsequent chapters the development and implementation of the assessment system will be discussed. Although the accountability and assessment systems are inextricably bound together, each one has its own set of issues and implementation problems. It will be easier to understand the consequences of a public policy of holding educators responsible for results if the problems associated with the technology for measuring results are examined independently. At least theoretically, the accountability system could be inappropriate or unworkable even if the measurement technology was flawless or the opposite could be true.

A Dual System of Accountability is Adopted

Task force members generally felt an accountability system had to be put in place at the earliest feasible time. It must be remembered that the previous testing program was terminated in 1988 when the KEST test was not continued. The new accountability system would be heavily dependent on development of a new assessment system that could take many years to completely develop. On the other hand, waiting until a new assessment system was fully in place would mean delaying implementation of the accountability system at least another six to eight years. This much of a delay was considered politically unacceptable, so an alternative plan was put in place which in effect created two accountability programs that would operate in parallel for the first six years of KERA.

The new accountability system needed a long time frame for implementation because it required development of a new primarily performance-based assessment system. The new assessment program was envisioned to evolve in two distinct phases. The intent was to have the earliest versions of the performance-based assessment instruments developed and implemented as early as the 1993-94 school year but not later than the 1995-96 school year. No deadline date was set for completion of the entire assessment program, although it has been interpreted to be the 1995-96 school year.

Initial baseline test data for the new program was to be collected no later than the end of the 1991-92 school year using interim tests. The school improvement goals for the first two-year accountability cycle, beginning with the 1992-93 school year, were to be set by the board of education using the first year data. The first consequences under the new accountability program would occur at the end of the 1993-94 school year. This was much too long to wait before interventions could take place in schools that clearly were poor performing even under the old system.

Three school districts were under state supervision in 1989 when the issue of school accountability was being debated by the task force. Since the Supreme Court had abolished the statutes granting the state authority to intervene, there would no longer be a legal basis on which to continue this intervention. One option was to simply abandon the current interventions and await the consequences that would come under the new system. Alternatively, the current system could be reenacted and application of consequences based on the new accountability system be delayed until the new assessment system is operational.

The compromise adopted by the task force was to have a dual accountability system for at least the first six years of the reform. The previous "deficient school district" program was amended and re-enacted. This program continued the department of education's previous authority to intervene in school districts it deemed deficient under essentially the previous terms. The primary difference was that attainment of the goals of KERA was made part of the criteria for determining whether a district can be considered to be deficient. This accountability program was effective immediately.[7]

The new accountability program was set to go into effect by the 1992-93 school year. In the meanwhile the previous accountability system would continue until June 30, 1996, at which time this section of the law is statutorily repealed and the deficient school district program is ended. Having the old system operate concurrently with the new one provided a legal basis for continuing to intervene in the most troubled school districts while the school-based accountability system is being implemented. It also enabled the department of education to proceed expeditiously with the transition to the new accountability system.

The Accountability Grades

The kind of assessments envisioned in a performance-based system were known to be time consuming when compared with the typical paper and pencil test format used in most standardized tests. The state assessment program had to make parsimonious use of both teacher and students time as well as keep the cost of the program affordable. The KEST had been given to all students, but this approach would not be feasible for performance-based tests.

In its initial report to the task force in 1989, the council on school performance standards proposed that a statewide assessment be given each year to all 3rd, 5th, 8th and 12th grade students.[8] In effect these were the exit grades for primary, elementary, middle, and secondary schools, the most common grade groupings prevalent in the state at the time. Therefore, these four grades were natural points at which to measure student progress. Without explanation, Hornbeck disregarded the council's proposal and instead proposed grades 4, 8, and 12 as the accountability grades, probably to decrease the cost of the program by perhaps as much as one-fourth. The task force accepted his proposal without discussion.

Later, after reaching agreement on the accountability grades, the task force added an exit requirement to the primary program, which meant that a state mandated assessment also had to occur in the year just prior to the first accountability assessment. The 4th grade accountability assessment actually measures the success of the primary program even though the 4th grade is not part of it. The only rationale given for inserting the primary school exit exam was to assure that children are not promoted out of the program before mastering the skills necessary to succeed in successive grades. In retrospect it might have been better if we had adopted the council's recommendation to use the 3rd and 5th grades instead of the 4th grade as accountability points and eliminate the primary school exit assessment.

Technical questions were raised about the validity of using tests scores for a single year to determine school improvement. It was argued that annual increments in improvement could fluctuate wildly in small schools. There also was the contention that classes could differ from one year to the next and distort or erase the gains or losses of the previous year. In order to accommodate somewhat the contention that there are "good" classes and "bad" classes of students, two years of classes were combined and their performances treated as though they were a single grade. The practical effect is to average out good and bad classes unless they happen to be sequential, thus mitigating the effect of any statistical aberrations that might occur from one year to the next

A more important consideration from a policy standpoint is whether one should accept the validity of the argument that a school is somehow afflicted with an uncontrollable phenomenon called "good" or "bad" classes. While practical experience might confirm that on average one group of students tends to perform on the whole better than another group, schools actually will have most students for three years before they participate in the accountability testing program. In effect, a school has as much as three years to bring the so-called "bad" class up to standard. The school staff should recognize this situation early and do something about it long before this class reaches the accountability grade. This is not a 4th, 8th, and 12th grade problem.

Accountability for the Non-Cognitive Goals of KERA

The accountability system is based on goals that individual schools must attain. Obviously, the first of these goals is to develop the ability of students to meet the six academic achievement goals as embodied in the academic expectations. These goals have been thoroughly discussed at earlier points in this book, so they will not be further explained here. However, there are other goals schools also must meet such as increased attendance, a reduction in grade retention and dropout rate, a reduction in physical and mental health barriers to learning, and student success in life after graduation. The rationale for these so-called "non-cognitive" goals is not explained in the law, so the rationale for each of them is explained here.

Reduce Truancy

The task force wanted to address learning problems created by persistent truancy in the context of school accountability. Frequent truancy is often the precursor to becoming a dropout. The task force wanted to encourage schools to work with truants before they turn into dropouts. The intent here is for the school performance index to include an attendance goal for schools defined in terms of the percent of students who reach or exceed an attendance standard set by the state board of education. Hopefully, making good attendance part of the accountability formula would encourage schools to be more aggressive in dealing with the causes of truancy before they result in students leaving school permanently.

Reduce the Number of Dropouts

Another goal for schools is to reduce the proportion of students who drop out of school. Since students are required by law to remain in school until age 16, this goal is primarily for secondary schools although it could apply to middle schools if students are held back more than one or two times. Dropouts are disastrous to the student and the community. Reducing the number of students who fail to graduate from high school was a priority in Kentucky for many years and remained so under KERA.

Although KERA does not define how the accountability index should account for dropouts, the assumption was that a dropout is any student previously enrolled in the school who did not graduate or reenroll in that school or in another public or private school. It was also assumed, I believe, that students who drop out of school should be defined as "unsuccessful" when calculating the proportion of successful students in a school for the year in which the dropouts did not reenroll.

The high stakes nature of the program for teachers is another reason for making dropouts part of the accountability index. One might assume that most students who elect to drop out of school probably are students who have not done well academically. The task force was concerned that poor performing students might be encouraged to drop out in order to improve school test scores. However, if students who drop out reduce the school's overall index score, then encouraging students to quit school would be self-defeating. Counting dropouts as unsuccessful students means they are included in the total school enrollment on which the proportion of successful students is calculated. Keeping the number of dropouts below a certain percentage should be a goal for each school.

Reduce the Number of Students Failed

The effects of grade retention are cumulative, and over time often result in students dropping out of school. As with the drop out issue, there was a concern that some schools might be tempted to hold back poor performing 3rd, 7th, and 11th grade students in order to improve test scores for the accountability grades. Therefore the proportion of students retained each year across all grades was made part of the accountability index in KERA. Hopefully, inclusion of a reduction in the proportion of students as a component of the accountability index would motivate teachers to help these students catch up rather than fail them.

Success After Graduation

Hornbeck proposed including some measure of success after graduation in the accountability index, an idea that provoked considerable discussion by the task force curriculum committee. The argument for inclusion essentially was that such a measure would provide some assurance to the public that students who graduate are actually competent to take their place in the adult world as homemakers, workers, and citizens.

Arguments against the idea were primarily based on the contention that defining "success" in this context would be difficult to do. Questions were also raised about the reliability and validity of the data on which success would be determined. Some of us thought secondary schools might find tracking their graduates an enormous burden, but it was pointed out that most schools already keep records on their alumni for a variety of reasons. Obviously, data for successful transition from school could not be obtained until some time after students left the school, which could potentially have a negative affect on the performance index for teachers several years later who may not have been involved with these students in any way.

Including this goal in the accountability index posed other problems than data collection. Presumably a successful transition from school to adult life is the cumulative result of the entire school experience, not just the effect of the secondary school. Therefore, the issue of whom to hold responsible for meeting this goal is very debatable. Certainly a secondary school in itself cannot assure this transition, especially for students with a pattern of academic failure that was formed in the lower grades.

Notwithstanding the potential difficulties such a requirement might pose, the task force agreed to make increasing "the proportion of students who make a successful transition to work, post-secondary education and the military" a goal for schools and thus by inference part of the accountability index. Whatever measurement or other problems this requirement presented would have to be worked out by the assessment consultants and contractors. Schools would be given a goal for the proportion of their students who should be expected to make a "successful" transition as defined by the board of education.

Reduce Physical and Mental Barriers

A final measure of a successful school is a reduction in what KERA referred to as "physical and mental barriers to learning." The context for this measure can be found in Hornbeck's memorandum to the curriculum committee. It was his position that many schools were slow to accommodate students with physical or mental handicaps. In some cases the reluctance is financial or staffing requirements, but in other cases there are practices that have the effect of making the teaching of these children difficult such as the absence of someone who can "sign" for deaf children.

The requirement regarding removing obstacles to learning also was expected to present significant measurement difficulties to the assessment consultants. On the other hand, not to hold schools accountable for providing an appropriate education for such children would be irresponsible. The measurement problems this goal might present were considered by the task force members to be capable of solution, so they made this a goal for schools for which they will be held accountable.

The Cash Rewards Program

Cash rewards are given to full-time, part-time, and itinerant instructional staff of a school that achieves at least a one-percent gain over its threshold. The part-time and itinerant staffs share in the reward in proportion to the amount of time they worked at the school. The state board of education is required to calculate the size of the award in the manner specified in the law.

An immediate task facing the task force was to determine the size of the award and the appropriation necessary to support it. Neither of these issues were included in HB 940, so they were developed as part of the appropriations bill needed to support the rewards program. The decision to tie the award size to salaries meant that the appropriation had to be based on the salaries of all certified staff in Kentucky schools. Since the salaries of the award winners (and their number) could not be determined in advance, the finance committee of the task force on education reform decided that the best way to finance the bonuses is to first estimate the likely success rate of schools. Then use a mathematical formula to estimate the amount of money needed to give awards of a certain size based on a hypothetical distribution of the gains that might be made.

Obviously, without any experience on which to base this model, the initial appropriation was speculative at best. To protect against a cost overrun for the program, the total amount appropriated was fixed thereby limiting the state's financial exposure. If the money that is appropriated proves to be insufficient to pay the intended award, then the actual amount paid would be prorated based on each educator's proportionate share of the actual appropriation. Even though awards would not be made in the first biennium after passage of KERA, the 1990 General Assembly created a trust fund for the program and appropriated money to it as a gesture of good faith.

The legislature determines by statute the maximum and minimum award amount and the state board of education then distributes the awards based on a schedule that ties the size of the award to the amount of gain the school made above the threshold. The maximum award was initially set at 10 percent of the average salary of the certified staff of the five highest-paying school districts in Kentucky. If the total amount to be awarded exceeds the appropriation, the amount to be distributed was capped in the budget at 1.75 percent of the total state payroll for certified educators that year. In other words, the General Assembly was willing to spend in rewards an amount up to 1.75 percent of total salaries for certified staff in the state. Using these criteria, the maximum award was initially set at $2,600 per teacher and the minimum at $1,300 or one-half the maximum.

As noted above, KERA tied the size of the reward to the current salaries of staff in a reward school. This means among other things that schools with the same level of staffing and the same level of achievement on the accountability index could receive different amounts of money if their salary levels are different. It also means teachers within an award school would get bonuses of different size unless the school council chose to divide the money up differently.

The Consequences of Failure to Improve

KERA comes down hard on schools that not only do not improve but actually regress. Schools that do not reach or exceed their improvement goal are placed in three categories.

The first category is a school that does not reach its goal, but does not fall below its baseline, which is the previous proportion of successful students. The department of education refers to these schools as improving but not successful schools. Such schools are required to develop a school improvement plan and are eligible to receive financial assistance from the state school improvement fund. If such schools do not at least meet their threshold in the next accountability cycle, they move to the second category.

The second category is a school that experiences a decline in the previous proportion of successful students, but the decline is less than five percent of its baseline score. The department of education classifies such schools as "in decline." As with the first category, such schools are required to develop a school improvement plan and are eligible to receive limited financial assistance from the state school improvement fund. In addition, one or more distinguished educators* are assigned to work with these schools. If such schools do not meet their threshold in the next accountability cycle, they move to the third category.

The third and lowest category is a school that experiences a decline greater than five percent of its baseline score. The state board of education must declare such a school to be a "school in crisis." Several consequences follow this designation. As is the case with other schools that do not meet their threshold, a school in crisis must prepare an improvement plan and can request assistance from the state school improvement program. However, unlike the other schools, the certified staff of these schools are put on probation and can be transferred or even lose their jobs.

A school in crisis is effectively taken over by the state. One or more distinguished educators are assigned to the school and among other things must evaluate and make a recommendation to the local superintendent regarding the retention, dismissal, or transfer of each full-time and part-time certified staff. Recommendations for transfer must conform to any bargained agreement between teachers and the school district. Recommendations for dismissal are binding on the superintendent. This evaluation process is to continue every six months until the school is no longer classified as a school in crisis.

The principal of a school in crisis must immediately notify parents of students in the school that they have the right to transfer their children to a successful school along with an explanation of the procedures for initiating such a request. The district superintendent must select the school to which the student may transfer if such a school is available in the district. Otherwise the student must be transferred to a successful school in another school district at the sending district's expense. If a decline in enrollment causes over-staffing at a school in crisis, the district superintendent must reduce personnel at the school according to the procedures for a reduction in force in state law.

The sanctions incorporated in the accountability system are increasingly harsh. The sentiment of those of us who supported this element of KERA

---

* Distinguished educators are described later in this chapter. Much of what is described here was abolished when changes were made in the accountability program in 1998.

was that the lives of children were being threatened by poor performing schools just as much as if the drinking water was contaminated. If the public health department were to examine the school cafeteria and find it was unsanitary, the public would demand that the cafeteria be closed until the problem is remedied. It was our view that this same logic should apply if the government determines that a school seems incapable of successfully educating all children. School attendance is compulsory in Kentucky. Even the particular school a child attends is determined by the government acting through the local school board. It was our view that it is unconscionable to force parents to send their children to schools that the state has determined to be unsuccessful.

Rewards and Sanctions for Central Office Staff

KERA requires the state board of education to develop a system of rewards and sanctions for certified staff who are not assigned to a school in the local school district.[9] The system is to be analogous to the one described above except the performance index is based on the aggregate test data for all schools in the district. Rewards are given to non-school based staff when the district's proportion of successful students increases above a threshold adopted by the state board of education and in a manner comparable to the way the threshold is set for schools.

Sanction are to be imposed by the state when the proportion of successful students in the district declines in the same manner used to determine school level sanctions. A school district that does not meet its improvement goal must develop a district improvement plan. If the proportion of successful students in the district declines by five percent or more, one or more distinguished educators will be assigned to the district to assist the district, evaluate personnel, and make personnel recommendations to the superintendent who must act upon them.

Recommendations regarding the superintendent are made to the local board of education that must take action on them. If the recommendation of the distinguished educator is to terminate the superintendent, the board must terminate the superintendent's contract following procedures set forth in applicable law. If a district has a declining proportion of successful students for two consecutive biennial assessment periods, the superintendent and local board of education are removed and the state takes over operation of the school district until such time as it is no longer in decline.

The reason for including district certified staff in the accountability program is to motivate them to help schools succeed even though they no longer have direct control over many of their instructional decisions. There are many inequitable situations within school districts that can only be remedied by district level action. Failure of schools in the district can bring sanctions upon district leadership and staff if they do not take immediate action to help these schools. On the other hand, the district should benefit from successes in the schools of the district on the assumption that the district has provided important support to these schools to enable them to be successful. As of July 1997 district staff had earned rewards but no district had been declared in crisis and taken over by the state.

The Distinguished Educators

As noted above, KERA calls for the assignment of "distinguished educators" to schools whose performance falls below their baseline. The legislature made significant changes in this element of KERA in 1998 as part of major revisions of the accountability program. The specific changes made to this program in 1998 are discussed in chapter 15 of this book. What is described here is the initial intention of the task force on education reform and the way the program operated until it was terminated in 1998.

KERA required the state board of education to establish criteria for the Kentucky distinguished educator program that is to be implemented by July 1, 1991. In the language of KERA:

> *the designation of "Kentucky distinguished educator" is to be given to the state's most outstanding and highly skilled certified educators who deserve recognition and are willing to fulfill the following purposes of the program:*
>
> (a) *Serving as teaching ambassadors to spread the message that teaching is an important and fulfilling profession;*
>
> (b) *Assisting the Department of Education with research projects and staff development efforts;*
>
> (c) *Accepting assignments in schools whose percentage of successful students declined as described in Section 5 of this Act. The assignments shall require the educator to:*
>
> (1) *Work in a school full-time for a designated period of time to assist the school staff with implementing its school im-*

provement plan. The educator shall have the authority to make decisions previously made by the school staff;

(2) *Help to increase the effectiveness of the staff, parents, the civic and business community, and government and private agencies in improving the school's performance; and*

(3) *Evaluate and made recommendations on the retention, dismissal, or transfer of certified staff in a "school in crisis."*

(4) *Complete an intensive training program, provided by the Department of Education and approved by the Kentucky Board of Education, prior to being assigned to assist a school's staff with implementing its school improvement plan. The training program shall include, but shall not be limited to instruction in the methods of personnel evaluation, school organization, school curriculum and assessment.*[10]

Distinguished educators are to be self-selected, provide a broad spectrum of instructional positions, and be representative of the state as a whole.

Clearly distinguished educators were expected to be more than a "swat team" that is sent out by the state to straighten out poor performing schools. It was hoped that these people could be used to provide support for KERA reforms throughout the state by encouraging people to enter the education profession, engage in practitioner-based research, and promote professional development activities throughout the state that would support the reforms imbedded in KERA. The first sanctions would not be imposed until after the 1993-94 school year, so distinguished educators selected in the early years of the program had no other mission than to work voluntarily with instructional personnel across the state and to be ambassadors for KERA.

To facilitate achievement of these objectives for the distinguished educators, KERA specifies that, beginning with the 1992-93 school year, special recognition be given annually to five distinguished educators in the form of a one-year sabbatical leave. These people were paid by the state so they could serve as ambassadors to the state at large.[11] The idea behind this concept was that a cadre of distinguished educators be assembled from which five would be selected for sabbaticals. It was thought this would be beneficial to the change process and it also could diminish the image that distinguished educators are nothing more than interlopers from the state sent in to take over alleged poor performing schools. The sabbaticals would be offered annually for the life of the program.

KERA did not specify how many distinguished educators should be selected and trained but did limit the number of sabbaticals to be awarded each year to five. The only constraint was the amount of money budgeted for the program which included a one-time $250 award to each educator selected for the program. Seven people were selected for sabbaticals the first year of the program, but two of them were subsequently assigned to employee positions in the department of education when office of education accountability staff contended only five such positions were authorized in the legislation. Sabbaticals have been awarded every year since then but the number has ranged from four to six at a time according to the money available for this purpose.

The number of distinguished educators grew significantly in the first five years of the program. As mentioned earlier, seven were selected the first year of the program. Fifty educators were selected in 1993 and 17 more in 1994. The total number of educators selected and trained as distinguished educators grew to 120 by 1996 although some dropped out or resigned from the program for various reasons. For the most part, however, most of these individuals were selected and trained in anticipation of assignment to unsuccessful schools.

The department of education paid all expenses relating to the work of the distinguished educators. The department reimbursed the school district for their current salary if they left their position for brief periods to provide any of the services specified above unless they were appointed to an unsuccessful school. In this case the district had to replace the educator and the state paid the salary and benefits of the distinguished educator. The distinguished educator retained all employee benefits while on assignment.

Distinguished educators assigned to unsuccessful schools initially received additional compensation equal to 50 percent of their base salary. However, the supplement was reduced by the legislature in 1996 to 35 percent of the base salary. They also were reimbursed for vehicle mileage if the distance traveled was within guidelines set by the state board of education. They were granted professional leave by their local school for a period not to exceed two years.

The total salary of an assigned educator was paid by the state including that person's share of employee benefits, but the local school district had to pay the salary and benefits of the educator's replacement. The distinguished educator also received a proportionate share of any reward the assigned school received while working at the school. The amount to be awarded to a distinguished educator is calculated on the base salary before the supplement and is paid as compensation.

The Evolution of the Distinguished Educator Program

The distinguished educator program has undergone many changes since KERA was enacted in 1990 and ultimately was abolished in 1998. One change already mentioned was a reduction in the salary supplement from 50 to 35 percent of the base salary for distinguished educators assigned to schools in crisis. Two changes made in 1994 by the General Assembly allowed part-time assignments to schools in crisis and deferred the time frame for designating a school to be in crisis until 1996 because of questions raised about the reliability of the assessment system.[12] The budget bill that year also included language that authorized the department of education to assign distinguished educators to work as consultants in any school not meeting its threshold.

The department of education created in the Spring of 1994 an assistance program called School Transformation, Assistance, and Renewal (STAR). Designed as a high quality planning and assistance process for schools in decline, the STAR program combines fiscal resources from the state with the technical assistance of a distinguished educator in schools where there is clear evidence that these resources would be used effectively. Critical to the program design are internal and external reviews of progress based on monthly reports to the school-based councils, the district, and the Kentucky Department of Education.[13]

KERA required the department of education to specifically train distinguished educators in methods of personnel evaluation, school organization, school curriculum and assessment. The department expanded the training to include principal assessment from the National Association of Secondary School Principals, school finance, school-based decision making councils, STAR, and general informational materials. In 1995 the training was delivered in four separate sessions lasting from 1½ days to two weeks each.

Both the selection and training process underwent changes as the department of education gained experience with both. Feedback from participants played a significant role in determining the nature of these changes. The result has been improved evaluations of the program by the participants each year. As with other elements of KERA, there was no precedent for selecting and training people for the kind of mission envisioned for them. Leadership of the program at the department of education sees the program continuing to evolve as field experience suggests further modifications are needed.

The distinguished educator program suffered a setback in 1996 when the legislature did not increase funding enough to support all the educators that would be needed to work with schools in decline or crisis. The gubernatorial election campaign in 1995 focused attention on technical problems with the state tests. During the 1996 legislative session, newly elected Governor Paul Patton and legislative leaders reached an agreement that a special task force should be created to examine the entire accountability system as well as other issues that had been raised about KERA. Apparently the legislature was reluctant to appropriate more money to this program until the viability of the accountability program was determined in 1998.

Notwithstanding the fiscal position taken by the legislature in 1996, the department of education faced a new round of schools requiring assistance because their first round assessment scores would place them in decline for the first time. In order to meet an expected demand for additional assistance, Commissioner Cody approved a plan in 1996 to use staff from the regional service centers to augment the existing cadre of distinguished educators. The regional staff members were used as consultants to schools that are in decline but not in crisis. They were called "advocates" rather than distinguished educators. Cody considered the measure only a way to fulfill the intent of the law until the legislature decided the future of the distinguished educator and accountability programs in 1998.

Dealing with Cheaters

A high stakes accountability program like the one Kentucky created with such potentially severe sanctions as job loss places great stress on the people held accountable. Critics of the use of sanctions based on tests of student achievement cautioned the task force on education reform that some educators will be tempted to cheat in order to save their jobs. They urged that procedures be put in place to minimize the opportunity for cheating and to maximize the probability that cheating will be quickly discovered and severely punished.

The issue of cheating is not addressed directly in KERA. However, the department of education issued ethical standards for testing that educators must follow. Failure to do so can result in test scores being lowered or discarded and a school could be declared in crisis as a result. Authority for this action is granted in KERA under the broad powers given to the state board of education to adjust accountability scores if fraud is proven.[14] Both the department of education and representatives of the assessment contractor appear at schools on a random basis during the administration of state assessment tests to assure adherence to the ethical standards and to make certain that proper test procedures are being followed.

Responsibility for dealing with educators guilty of unprofessional conduct is vested in a education professional standards board which has the legal authority to suspend or revoke teaching certificates. Cheating and fraudulent reporting or manipulation of test data certainly qualifies as something the standards board should take a firm stand on. I believe the task force on education reform assumed this new oversight body would deal swiftly and harshly with educators found guilty of such conduct. On the other hand, the task force did not give the standards board either the responsibility or resources to discover instances of cheating or fraud.

For many years all reports and anonymous tips about suspected cheating received by the department of education were referred to an informal group of department employees for review. This small *ad hoc* group advised state testing officials how they thought each situation should be handled. In most of these cases the information was passed on to the district superintendent for investigation and disciplinary action if warranted. Very serious breaches of ethics in several cases led the department of education to adjust school scores and censure the school personnel who were responsible for the cheating.

In mid-1997 the *Lexington Herald-Leader* newspaper published several stories critical of what it considered the department of education's reluctance to take vigorous action in following up on complaints of cheating.[15] The articles cited various examples of known cases of cheating and what appeared to the newspaper editors and writers as a soft response from the state. The newspaper quoted others who believed there was insufficient deterrent to cheating because the department personnel who are called upon to investigate allegations of cheating are too involved in administration of the accountability program to devote appropriate time to them.

Officials in the department of education initially defended their process and the actions previously taken. However, soon after these news accounts were published, Education Commissioner Cody announced a significant change in the way complaints of cheating and other testing irregularities would be handled by the department of education in the future. Essentially he promised a better follow up on anonymous tips and vigorous investigations when warranted by the evidence. He also said the department would not rely on local officials to take appropriate action in cases where misconduct has been alleged. Cody said he would take personal responsibility for decisions about what should happen to schools and school personnel in situations where cheating has been verified and documented.

While the department of education has censured a small number of educators involved in verified cases of cheating, the education professional standards board has been slow to follow up with a review of the professional standing of these people. The department of education can cite educators for violations of the code of ethics, but it cannot take further action against the parties under current law. Of course, the school as a whole can suffer severe sanctions under the accountability program if the state board of education adjusts the school index scores because of cheating and subsequently declares the school in crisis.

Local school officials can dismiss staff that violates the code of ethics. However, dismissal is not a revocation of the professional license of the dismissed educators. Only the professional standards board can revoke the license of an educator. It is critical to the integrity of the accountability program that the standards board take quick and strong action against all educators who are cited for ethics violations. Failure to do so will weaken public confidence in the accountability program and diminish the fairness of the rewards and sanctions that are based on it.

The legislature's office of education accountability proposed in 1996 that a separate agency be created to review and investigate complaints of cheating and fraud. The task force on education reform considered this option in 1990. Initially there was some support for the idea as a way to keep the accountability program insulated from outside influences and potential manipulation by the department of education. Early versions of the proposal called for an oversight agency that would administer the accountability program including the testing program and the certification of rewards and sanctions.

The main argument against the idea of a separate assessment agency was a perceived need to closely integrate the assessment program with curriculum and professional development. The latter programs were part of the mission of the new department of education and not an independent agency. Based on this logic, the assessment program also should be a responsibility of the new department of education.

As other elements of the draft legislation started to take form, a proposal was made that the accountability functions be assigned to the legislative office of education accountability rather than create an independent executive agency. Governor Wilkinson strongly objected to this proposal. David Hornbeck, consultant to the curriculum committee of the task force, also objected to separating the assessment program from other key elements of KERA.

Consequently no independent agency was created for the specific purpose of administering the accountability program separate from the department of education. However, the section of KERA that details the investigative authority of the office of education accountability could be construed to include investigation of charges of cheating, which in effect is fraud and a criminal act if bonus money is received based on fraudulent acts. However, until the present time all complaints of this nature received by the office are referred to the department of education for disposition.

The Impact of the Accountability Program

The consequences of the program became a reality in 1994 at the end of the first accountability cycle. Although concerns about the reliability of the assessment test led the legislature to defer the most severe sanctions until the end of the second accountability cycle, rewards were paid to 480 schools (38 percent of the 1,238 public schools in Kentucky) in 1994 and to 502 schools (42.5 percent) in 1996. In 1994 the state paid out $26 million in the first reward cycle and awarded a similar amount in 1996. In the latter year the maximum average award earned per teacher was $2,311.

After the first award cycle, the department of education created a category called a "successful" school which is defined as a school which reaches or surpasses its improvement goal the second year of the accountability cycle. Since the average accountability index score for the biennium does not meet its improvement goal, the school is not eligible for rewards. In 1996 there were 157 schools (12.68 percent) in the successful category.[16] In all there were 659 schools (53.23 percent) which met their improvement goals. In the 1996 reward cycle 394 schools (31.83 percent) improved but were not eligible for rewards.

As noted earlier, the legislature in 1994 suspended the imposition of sanctions until the next biennium. Nonetheless, the department of education did report the number of schools determined to be in decline or in crisis after each assessment period even though the consequences of this classification were not imposed. Less than five percent of schools were classified as in decline after the first cycle. The number in decline after the second cycle increased slightly to about seven percent. Only nine schools were found to be in crisis at the end of the second accountability cycle.

Although some critics of the accountability aspect of KERA thought it was draconian in nature when the legislation was enacted, the most severe of all sanctions will be applied to less than one percent of all schools after being in place four years. Clearly most schools can at least show sufficient improvement to avoid being declared in crisis. Those schools that are found in decline receive extensive help in determining how to move toward a successful school status. In reality the threat of losing one's job because of poor performance will affect a very small number of schools.

Experience with the first accountability cycles also shows that a significant proportion of schools can achieve the improvement goals. Furthermore the goals appear to be set high enough that considerable effort is required to earn a reward for exceeding them. On the other hand, a comparison of schools that earned rewards the first cycle with schools that earned rewards in the second cycle indicates that consistent gains from one accountability cycle to another may be difficult to sustain.

In its 1996 annual report, the office of education accountability noted that 68 percent of the schools that did not earn rewards in the second cycle were classified as either reward or successful schools in the first cycle. Eight of these schools fell all the way to schools in crisis, meaning they fell more than five percent below their threshold in the second accountability cycle. Questions were raised about how schools can move from rewards and success to crisis in such a short time when in most cases the school staffs have essentially remained the same with no change in leadership.

There are several possible reasons why sustaining a steady growth trajectory will prove to be difficult for many schools. The high gains some of these schools made in the first cycle may have caused their threshold to be set higher for the second cycle than what they could repeat. In other words, extraordinary success in the first cycle may have set these schools up for "failure" in the second cycle. Also research should be done to see if any of these fluctuations correlate with school size. Theoretically a few students who score exceptionally well or poorly on the state assessment test could explain wide variations in accountability scores in schools with small enrollments.

Obviously this is an issue which must be examined and addressed. Depending on the source of these rather dramatic shifts from one category to another in the first two accountability cycles, the state board of education may need to consider modifying the procedure used to set the threshold for schools that earn rewards. Perhaps the previous threshold rather than the actual level of performance attained should be the baseline for the next cycle. Such a policy would maintain the desired improvement rate over time, but it would not penalize schools that attain something greater than what was expected. A few more schools might be rewarded under this approach, but it might moderate such wild swings in classification that are very difficult for people to understand and accept.

A positive aspect of the accountability program is the help that is provided to schools that do not meet their threshold during an accountability cycle. In August 1994, 22 distinguished educators were placed in schools presumed to be in decline that volunteered for early assistance prior to official release of their accountability scores. These schools were voluntary participants in the STAR program that later would become the state's intervention strategy for schools in decline or crisis. These distinguished educators included 13 classroom teachers, four building-level administrators, and four central office personnel including one superintendent. Initially, they provided assistance to approximately 150 volunteer schools. Fifteen new schools volunteered for participation in the STAR program after their assessment results were known.

Even though some of the original participants in the STAR program turned out not to be schools in decline (none could be declared schools in crisis at that time), 120 of these schools elected to stay in the program until January 30, 1995, which was the deadline for making a transition out of the program for schools not in decline. The STAR program probably is an excellent example of what was envisioned for the distinguished educator program beyond assignment to the schools that the state determines to be in crisis.

While providing meaningful assistance to schools that voluntarily participated in the STAR program, the distinguished educators also gained experience in helping schools improve, experience that would be invaluable when the time came for them to enter schools in crisis under the sanction provisions of KERA. It was a trial run for the critical mission to which many of them would be assigned the next year.

The office of education accountability staff visited schools with distinguished educators and found the response from faculty to be very positive. According to the 1996 OEA annual report, having an additional person to work with staff in the areas of curriculum and instruction was considered a benefit by these schools. School personnel thought this help would translate into gains on their test scores in subsequent years.[17] It should be noted that none of the 52 schools assigned distinguished educators in the 1995-96 school year because their test scores placed them in decline or in crisis remained in decline the following year.

Accountability has put stress into the system. In some cases the stress has been a negative. Teachers feared getting fired more than they wanted to earn rewards. The anxiety created by this threat has been given as a reason to both keep and abolish the system. Those who see the anxiety as motivation to change see this as a desired outcome. Those who believe anxiety distracts and divides people see the system as destructive. It is not possible to know if Kentucky would have experienced as much change as it did if the accountability program had not been part of the reform. However, my own discussions with educators indicate they are definitely concerned about looking bad in a professional sense and have worked harder than ever before to avoid the sanctions.

Clearly school personnel have gotten the message that they are being held accountable for the learning of their children. Some teachers contend the accountability program takes too much time away from instruction and will eventually lead to a poorer rather than better-educated child. Nonetheless, most teachers now appear to accept the reality of the consequences of the accountability program and for the most part have tried to change what and how they teach accordingly. In this regard, the accountability system at least in part is serving as an engine for change.[18]

A question that often is asked about the Kentucky accountability program is whether it has improved student learning. I don't think many of us on the task force on education reform expected the accountability program to have a direct "cause and effect" relationship to learning. On the other hand, I think we expected the accountability program to at least encourage educators to find ways to improve the effectiveness of their instructional practices, knowing that the results of their efforts will be made public and carry consequences.

As can be seen in this chapter, an effective program of school accountability with consequences for educators can be developed and implemented successfully provided all the important issues are properly addressed at the outset. Perhaps most important is the care given to the procedures and technology used to gather data on school performance. The Kentucky experience demonstrates how quickly the program can fall apart if the assessment element is not defensible. The opponents of accountability will quickly seize upon any weakness, perceived or real, and use it to discredit or dismantle the program.

NOTES:

[1] The final version of the Wilkinson proposal was presented in *A Plan to Restructure Schools in Kentucky*, Frankfort, KY: Office of the Governor, Spring, 1989.
[2] For an illustration of how the EPI might be calculated, see Appendix A of Wilkinson, *A Plan to Restructure Schools in Kentucky*, *Op. cit.*, A-1
[3] See "Allocation of the Incentive Bonus" in Wilkinson, *A Plan to Restructure Schools in Kentucky*, *Op. cit.*, Appendix B.
[4] The consultant recommendations discussed here and elsewhere in this chapter are the ones adopted as presented in a memorandum from David Hornbeck to the curriculum committee dated February 23, 1990. Earlier versions are disregarded here in the interest of brevity.
[5] An example of the calculation appears in Table 2 of the memorandum submitted by Hornbeck to the task force curriculum committee dated February 23, 1990.
[6] Wilkinson thought there should be no restrictions on how the money could be used by those receiving the awards.
[7] See Sections 8-11 of HB 940, which amended the language in KRS 158.650 to 158.710.
[8] See the council's initial report *Preparing Kentucky Youth for the Next Century: What Students Should Know and Be Able to Do and How Learning Should be Assessed*, Frankfort, KY: Department of Education, 1989, Vol. II, Appendix E.
[9] See HB 940 Sections 6 and 7 [KRS 158.6455 (e)]

[10] See HB 940 Section 6 (1) [KRS 158.782 (1) (c)]
[11] See HB 940 Section (2) (b) [KRS 158.782]
[12] See HB 256 enacted by the 1994 session of the General Assembly.
[13] See *Kentucky Education Reform. The First Five Years*, Frankfort, KY: Kentucky Department of Education, 1996, 52.
[14] See HB 940 Section 5 (8) [KRS 158.6455 (8)]
[15] See *Lexington Herald-Leader*, July 10, 1997.
[16] Schools that exceed their improvement goal on the biennial index are called "reward" schools.
[17] See *Annual Report December 1996*, Frankfort, KY: Office of Education Accountability, 32.
[18] For example, see Daniel M. Koretz, Sheila Barron, Karen J. Mitchell, and Brian M. Stecher, *Perceived effects of the Kentucky Instructional Results Information System (KIRIS)*. Santa Monica, CA: Institute on Education and Training, RAND Corporation, 1996. Also relevant information can be found in several reports of a longitudinal study of four rural Kentucky school districts published by the Appalachia Educational Laboratory, Charleston, West Virginia.

13. School Improvement is Defined

The school accountability program specifies that consequences are to be based on a specified increase or decrease in the proportion of "successful students" in the school. While the term "successful students" never was defined in KERA, the goals of KERA clearly indicate they are students who master the academic expectations, regularly attend classes, do not drop out of school, make satisfactory progress from year to year, and enter adulthood as productive members of their family, community, and work group.

Although it was necessary to define a successful student, it also was necessary to define a successful school. Presumably a successful school is one that steadily increases the number of successful students it produces. This chapter is devoted to a review of how success was defined and applied to the awarding of bonuses and sanctions.

A "Successful School" is Defined

Development of a methodology to determine school improvement is the responsibility of the Kentucky Board of Education within the guidelines set by KERA. The state board of education must establish a threshold level for school performance on the basis of which to determine that a school qualifies to receive a reward.[1] The term "threshold" refers to an accountability score a school must exceed over a period of two years to be eligible for a reward.[2]

The only condition set in the law is that consideration be given to the fact that a school closest to having one hundred percent successful students will have a lower percentage increase required. The assumption is that it becomes increasingly more difficult to make further gains as the proportion of successful students is increased. Therefore the absolute amount of gain expected grows less as the school improves its performance.

The threshold value is computed against a baseline performance. The term "baseline" refers to the point from which the gain in the index score is measured. The difference between the baseline and the threshold values on the accountability index represents the amount of improvement each school is expected to make. The Kentucky Board of Education has the responsibility to set a threshold for each school based on its baseline score, but KERA did not specify how frequently this must be done. Presumably it is to be done prior to each accountability cycle, the two years over which improvement will be measured.

The formula for calculating the threshold was not specified in the law except for the provision that consideration be given to the fact that a school closest to having one hundred percent successful students must have a lower percentage increase required.[3] The theoretical roots of these concepts can be found in the documents prepared by Wilkinson and Hornbeck, since the main elements of the KERA accountability program are based on the ideas they put forth in the discussion prior to KERA.

In order to frame the results of the calculation in positive terms, the threshold is expressed in terms of the percentage of successful students a school must have in order to qualify for rewards. However, the underlying computational concept is that schools must decrease the proportion of students who are unsuccessful in order to improve their performance. The threshold determines how much that proportion of unsuccessful students must decrease in order to meet the threshold. Using this methodology, the percentage of improvement required decreases as the proportion of successful students increases, as required by the law.

For example, if the baseline percentage of successful students is 60, then the threshold is calculated on a desired decrease in the remaining 40 percent of unsuccessful students over the next two years. If the rate of decrease desired is set at five percent, then the threshold is calculated by taking five percent of 40 (the proportion of unsuccessful students) which is equivalent to a 2 percent increase in successful students. In other words the threshold goal is to have at least 62 percent of the school's students considered successful (the baseline proportion plus the expected increase).

If the baseline percentage of successful students for another school is 70 percent, when the five-percent rate of improvement is applied to the 30 percent of students that were unsuccessful you have an expected gain of 1.5 percent or a threshold of 71.5 percent of the students considered successful. Using this methodology the school closer to having 100 percent successful students will always have a lower percentage of gain. It was assumed that the rate of decrease in unsuccessful students would be constant for all schools, but the absolute amount of decrease would obviously differ based on the proportion of successful students at each school.

As the examples above illustrate, a school with a higher success rate has a smaller actual gain to make than a school with a lower success rate. However, implicit in the law is the expectation that each school will attain or exceed the same rate of improvement. Only the magnitude of the differential between the baseline and the threshold would vary.

The Accountability Index Concept

The accountability index is a summary of the performance of the school on all the goals. It was intended to be straightforward and easy to compute and understand. A standard of performance is set and students are tested against the standard. The percentage of students who meet or exceed the standard is calculated and the results are averaged to get the "index" percentage.

For example, the index for the academic goals might look like this for a school that had an improvement ratio of 10 percent with these percentages of students reaching or exceeding the standard in the baseline years:

	Baseline	Increase	Threshold
Science	30.0	7.0	37.0
Mathematics	15.0	8.5	23.5
Social Studies	32.0	6.8	38.8
Writing	40.0	6.0	46.0
Reading	50.0	5.0	55.0

The index could be computed as an average of these respective percentages. In this illustration the index baseline would be 33.4, the increase would be 6.66, and the threshold would be 40.06. The average percentage of students meeting or exceeding the standard would have to be at least 40.06 percent to qualify for rewards.

The law did not specify how the accountability index should be constructed, so the illustration shown here is not necessarily the way it had to be done. It does illustrate how the intent of the law could be implemented in a simple and understandable manner.

The key to the index, of course, is the standard against which the students are measured. Standards also must be set for the non-academic goals. Now we will examine the index the department of education created and the state board of education approved to see how this aspect of the accountability program was implemented.

The Initial Accountability Index

The law left the design of the accountability index to the state board of education and the assessment consultants the board had to hire to help with the selection of an assessment contractor. Any form the index takes that accomplishes the intent of the law obviously is acceptable. However, all references in the law are to percentages, so it should be expected that the index the board ultimately approved would use percentages as its base. The following review will show that the accountability index the department of education eventually developed and the state board of education approved differs from the examples given above in important respects.

It must be noted here that in 1998 the legislature significantly altered the entire accountability program including revisions to the statutes referred to in this chapter. Since the primary purpose of this book is to examine the original intent of the KERA legislation enacted in 1990, the discussion here is focused strictly on the way the program was initially designed and implemented. A discussion of changes made in 1998 and the rationale for them can be found in chapter 15 of this book.

The official accountability index initially approved by the board of education is the sum of two scores: an academic score and a "non-cognitive" score. Student scores are calculated for each state test subject. These scores are then averaged. The academic and the "non-cognitive" scores are then summed to create a single index score that determines each school's level of performance.

The Academic Component of the Accountability Index

The academic score is derived in the following manner. The state test covers specific knowledge domains, each of which is measured through various testing approaches such as open-ended questions, performance events, multiple choice questions, portfolios, and on-demand writing prompts. Each testing approach carries a different weight in determining the overall performance score depending on the subject area being tested.[4] The purpose of the weighting is to diminish the impact of testing approaches that are less reliable such as performance events.

Student performance on the test in each subject area is calculated separately and receives a numerical score, which in turn is transformed into a performance classification described from lowest to highest as novice, apprentice, proficient, or distinguished, terms that will be described in the next chapter. Each performance classification carries specific accountability "scale points."

> a novice performance is worth 0 scale points;
>
> an apprentice performance is worth 40 points;
>
> a proficient performance is worth 100 points; and
>
> a distinguished performance is worth 140 points.[5]

Each student who takes the test is given a classification for each subject area and the school then is credited with the scale points earned based on the number of students in each classification. All the scale points for each subject area are then averaged to obtain the score for the school. The computation of the academic element of the accountability index can be illustrated in this manner: A test of mathematics yields the following student scores:

10	Novice Performances x 0 points	0
15	Apprentice Performances x 40 points	600
5	Proficient Performances x 100 points	500
1	Distinguished Performance x 140 points	140
31	Student Performances	1240

The scale points are then averaged to obtain the academic accountability score for that subject. In this example the academic accountability score is 40 (1240 total scale points divided by 31 students). This computation is made for each subject area tested and the resulting scores for all subject areas are then averaged to obtain an overall academic accountability score for the school.

As noted earlier, KERA required the index to be based on the proportion of successful students in a school. Improvement is to be based on the ability of the school to increase the proportion of successful students (or reduce the proportion of students who do not meet the standard). While the department of education does report the proportion of students who were placed in each classification (novice, etc.) for each subject area tested, the index scale is not based on the proportion of successful students. Rather it is based on weighted "scale points" assigned to each performance level. Furthermore it doesn't explicitly define a "successful" student in terms of these values.

The position of the department of education is that the nominal value to be reached by every school is a score of 100 on the academic scale. That is to say, the implied goal is to have every student perform at least at the proficient level in every subject area covered by the state test. Thus a proficient performance is the *de facto* definition of a successful student even though it has not been officially identified as such. However, the total scale score on which the index is based is an average of scale scores rather than a percentage of students who met or exceeded the standard of a proficient performance. In this respect it does not fulfill the literal intent of the law.

As the example above illustrates, the values given to each level of performance do not represent a true scale. Each value is arbitrarily set. Furthermore, the scale is skewed toward the proficient level that is worth two and one-half times the value of an apprentice performance. Moving students from novice to apprentice and from proficient to distinguished are not rewarded nearly as much as moving students from apprentice to proficient. The rationale for this is not intuitive to either educators or the public.

The Non-cognitive Component of the Accountability Index

The non-cognitive score consists of measures of a school's attendance, retention in grade, dropout, and student transition to adult life upon graduation. The dropout measure applies only to middle and high schools, and the transition to adult life applies only to high schools. The values on these measures are combined and reported on a scale of 100 which is the highest score a school can attain.

The components of the non-cognitive score are weighted differently for each grade level as follows:

Component	4th grade	8th grade	High School
Attendance	80%	40%	20%
Retention	20%	40%	5%
Dropout	NA	20%	37.5%

Transition to Life	NA	NA	37.5%
TOTAL	100%	100%	100%

These weights reflect the applicability of the various components to the various grades.[6] Beginning with the 1994-95 school year, the data for the non-cognitive component of the accountability index was based on previous year data due to difficulties in securing timely data on some of the elements that make up this part of the index.

The attendance index score is calculated by dividing the average daily attendance for the year by the total enrollment in the school. The retention-in-grade rate is based on the total number of students in the school who did not progress to the next grade at the end of the current school year. The number of students retained is divided by the total enrollment of the school to get the retention index score. The dropout rate is calculated only for middle schools and high schools. A dropout is defined as any student who doesn't reenroll in school anywhere and has not graduated. The number of students enrolled the previous year who did not reenroll is divided by the total number of students enrolled that year to obtain the dropout index score. All schools are required to report to the state the data on which these indices are calculated.

The transition-to-life index is based on survey data gathered one year after a student graduates. Students are defined as having a successful transition if one year after graduation they are enrolled in a post-secondary academic, technical, or vocational program; are in one of the military services; are employed full-time; or are a homemaker by choice. The total number of students considered successful is divided by the total number of students in their graduation class to obtain the index score for this element. The department of education provides help to schools in locating their graduates if they are not able to do so on their own. Students who cannot be located are counted as unsuccessful which encourages schools to work hard to locate every graduate.

Up to the present the goal of reducing physical and mental barriers has not been included in the accountability system primarily because no acceptable method of measuring the goal has been devised. The index scores for all four components are averaged to secure the non-cognitive index score for the accountability index.

The Final Accountability Index Value

A school's actual accountability score initially was computed by adding the average scale points for each academic area tested to the non-cognitive score which is then divided by the number of academic areas tested plus one for the non-cognitive portion of the index. The initial test covered five subject areas,[7] so the raw accountability score was divided by six (the five subject area index scores plus the non-cognitive score) to derive a single accountability score for the school. Using this methodology, equal weight was given to each subject and the collective score for the non-cognitive performances. Each component of the test was worth 1/6th of the total score or roughly 16 percent.

Beginning with the 1995-96 accountability cycle, indices for the arts and humanities and for practical living and vocational studies were added to the state assessment. New weights then were given to all the indices that make up the accountability score. Each of the original five subjects make up 14 percent of the score; each of the two new subject groups make up 7 percent of the score; and the non-cognitive score makes up the final 16 percent of the score.[8] The percentages represent "weights" given to the various elements that reflect their relative value in the scheme of things.

Implementation of the Accountability Index

Computations are done separately for each accountability grade in a school since the assessment test is different at each grade level. Each accountability grade is given an accountability score regardless of the number of accountability grades in a particular school building. An elementary school that includes grades K-8 will have two scores, one for 4th grade students and one for 8th grade students.

The accountability system posed problems in situations where a school building does not have an accountability grade or has two accountability grades with scores that could place the school as a whole in two different categories. The department of education resolved these problems by combining schools in various ways. For example, a school consisting only of the primary program is combined with the school its students would attend for the fourth grade to form a single accountability unit. Similar arrangements were made for schools with other configurations.[9] Presumably sanctions and awards follow a similar pattern.

The accountability test is given annually in each accountability grade, which assures that all students are tested as they pass through the accountability grades. The results are reported to every school after each year's tests have been scored. However, determination of whether a school has earned rewards or deserves sanctions is based on an average of two consecutive academic years as required by KERA. Combining the two years is intended to smooth out idiosyncratic differences from one year to the next and to give schools a reasonable time for instructional changes to have an impact on students. It also increases the numerical base for small schools, which improves the reliability of the results.

Predictably, people start to draw conclusions about the status of schools based on how near they are to reaching their threshold in the first year of the two-year cycle. Unwarranted pessimism or optimism is fostered and undesired attention is given to annual changes in scores. In some cases this information gives a school a "heads up" signal that they need to press even harder in order to increase scores enough in the second year to meet or exceed their threshold, a situation that might be considered salutary.

On the other hand "good news" the first year can lead to disappointment if the second year scores fall below those of the previous year enough that they do not reach their threshold when the two years are combined. There is no administrative solution to this dilemma. Only constant reminders that the accountability system is based on two years of improvement hopefully will help educators and the general public put annual scores in proper perspective.

The accountability test is given to all students in the accountability grades regardless of perceived disability or learning impairment. This was important from several perspectives. The practice conformed to the general policy of "mainstreaming" exceptional students to the extent practical. It also minimizes the temptation to mislabel poor performing students as learning disabled in order to have them exempted from the accountability testing program. The state has made some accommodation with regard to the appropriateness of certain testing methods for some disabled children, but these students are not excluded from the program even though some educators maintain that such students tend to "pull down" their accountability score if they are included.

The work load on teachers in the accountability grades eventually led to modifications in the accountability grades, so accountability testing was spread out over several grades with different elements of the test being taken at different grade levels. This decision complicated the practice of combining schools for testing purposes. Now they must have contiguous accountability grades since all subjects are no longer tested in the original three grades.

The accountability index turned out to be more complicated than it probably had to be in order to satisfy the requirements of KERA. A single measure of the proportion of students who scored in the proficient range or above in each subject area would have sufficed for the academic component. Obviously it is helpful for schools to know the percentage of students in all the other categories. The scale as it existed then gave credit for movement from one category to another across all categories and not just movement into the proficient category or higher. A downside is the cost of scoring the tests when so many criteria must be used in order to determine just where each child is on the continuum in every academic subject.

It is my opinion that the work of standard setting also was made more difficult than necessary because of the decision to use the four categories (novice, etc.) rather than a single "benchmark" standard at least for purposes of school accountability. I also think it made the accountability index more difficult to calculate and interpret. A continuum of progress is appropriate for continuous assessment instruments, assuming the terminology is made consistent, but I do not think it was necessary or appropriate as a measure of school improvement in achieving the academic goals of KERA.

Finally, assigning a weight of only 16 percent to all the non-cognitive goals means that performance improvements in this area will have relatively little impact on a school's overall performance rating. This is not enough of an incentive for schools to improve performance on these goals. Nor will it deter the undesirable behavior that the "high stakes" nature of the accountability program might encourage such as holding poor students back or encouraging them to drop out of school in order to improve the performance score of the school.

Estimating Real Improvement

KERA specified that rewards are to be given to schools that achieve at least a one-percent gain over their threshold.[10] This element of the law caused considerable confusion for the assessment consultants and contractor. The idea behind this provision in the law deserves some explanation.

The amount of improvement expected presumably should be large enough that the observed gain or loss in performance is greater than what might occur due to random behavior and measurement errors. The statistical assumption is that if the data on student performance is gathered numerous times there would be a natural variation in the observed scores that would tend to fall within a specified range at least 66, 80, or 95 percent of the time, depending on the level of statistical confidence one desires.

Given the desirability of ruling out as much chance effect as is reasonable in a "high stakes" accountability program, the rate of improvement desired should be beyond the boundaries of chance. Therefore, as an example, if chance variance is estimated to be plus or minus 3 percentage points and a school baseline score is 60, then scores could be expected to fluctuate between 57 to 63 points due to chance factors. Any value within this range would be considered equally predictable, although as the score reaches the higher and lower limits of the range the greater the probability that the score is not due to chance alone.

The amount of change deserving of a reward or sanction should be greater than what might occur by chance. In order to be certain that a school is rewarded for true improvement or sanctioned for true decline, both an upper and lower threshold should be established. In the example above improvement should not be considered to be beyond chance unless the score attained is greater than 63 even though the baseline is 60. Likewise, decline would not be indicated unless a score of less than 57 was achieved. This "band" of six points around the baseline score is the range within which any observed change can be attributed to chance factors and not real improvement or decline.

Obviously, before a threshold can be set, statisticians have to estimate the amount of variance that normally could be expected in the test instruments and the statistical data (e.g. attendance data) used for calculating the percentage of successful students. Then a judgment must be made about how much gain can reasonably be expected over a two-year period that is beyond what one might expect by chance. Once these two variables are given statistical values, the board of education can proceed to set the threshold for each school using the two values that represent the upper and lower limits of what might be observed due to measurement factors.

The "one percent gain" provision was meant to say that a school has to demonstrate a gain that is greater than what might be achieved due to testing error. Unfortunately, the "one percent" has no clear referent in the law and thus was left for others to interpret. While the law said that there had to be at least a one percent gain over the observed score, this was not intended to be the actual value. The estimated measurement error could be set at a higher value if the research data warranted it. We just didn't want an arbitrary goal to be set that could be reached by chance alone.

The department of education adopted the interpretation that the intent was that schools had to exceed the threshold by one scale point on the accountability index. This interpretation of the law totally missed the legislative intent. Furthermore, it missed the expectation that there be a research base for setting the actual amount of improvement required before a school is eligible for a reward or sanction. The one-percent was only to indicate a *minimum* that should be expected. A higher requirement would clearly have been justified under the intent of the law.

The Amount of Improvement Required

Using the interpretation of the department of education, the board of education adopted the following formula for determining the thresholds for defining improvement. Individual school awards are calculated on a sliding scale starting with the minimum award being paid for accountability index scores that are "one percent" above their threshold. The size of the award increases by one percent of the maximum award for each increase of two percent of the difference between the school baseline and its threshold. Here is an example of how the formula works out for a school with a baseline index score of 30 and a threshold index score of 37. The difference between the two scores is 7 points.

An index score of 38 is one scale point above the threshold and earns exactly 50 percent of the maximum award. In 1994 that would have been $1,300. A score between 37 and 38 does not earn a reward. The amount of the award increases one percent of the maximum ($26 in this example) for each additional two percent of the difference in scale points. In the example this is an increase in the index score of .14 points (2 percent of the 7-point difference). Thus an index score of 38.14 (the threshold score of 37 + one scale point + 2 percent of the 7 point difference = 38.14) would earn a bonus of $1,326. To earn the maximum award a school has to double the expected gain. The school in this example would have to have an index score of 45 (the threshold score of 37 + one scale point + 100 percent of the 7 point difference) in order to earn the maximum award. A score higher than this only earns the maximum award.

KERA placed a caveat to this formula when it said a "school shall be rewarded for an increased proportion of successful students *including those students who are at risk of failure* (emphasis added)."[11] The policy roots of this provision can be found in the memorandum Hornbeck prepared for the curriculum committee of the task force on education reform in which he stressed that the percentage gain "should reflect gains with both at risk students and all students."[12] His concern was that schools might be tempted to try to increase their test scores by concentrating on improving the better prepared students, leaving the less well prepared behind.

The state board of education implemented this element of KERA by requiring that at least 10 percent of a school's novices, on average across the cognitive areas, move to apprentice or higher for it to qualify for rewards even if it exceeds its threshold by one point.[13] Schools with less than 10 percent of its students at novice level on average during the previous two years of an accountability cycle will satisfy this requirement if they maintain or reduce this percent in the current accountability cycle.

Setting Improvement Goals

Under the law, the initial baseline is to be calculated using data from the 1991-92 school year assessment. However, the law as written is unclear about when or how a new baseline is to be established thereafter, especially for schools that exceed their threshold. This was an oversight in the law that is of considerable importance from an operational and policy standpoint.

A literal interpretation of the law indicates that both the existing baseline and threshold (improvement goal) are to be carried forward into the next biennium for schools that do not meet their original threshold or decline in performance.[14] In other words, the goal must be pursued until it is met. Failure to do so in successive accountability cycles only leads to more severe sanctions. The goal is not changed for these schools. However, the law is silent about schools that meet or exceed their threshold of improvement. I believe it was presumed that they would be given a new threshold each biennium based on their performance the previous biennium. The previous accountability score is the baseline for the next cycle.

The state board of education approved regulations that kept the baseline and threshold the same from one accountability period to the next one if schools do not meet or exceed their goal. New thresholds based on previous accountability index scores are to be calculated biennially for schools that earn rewards. The practical effect of this interpretation is that every school is working either to exceed its previous threshold or one based on its best accomplishments. It also fulfills the apparent original intent.

The percentage of improvement required has been set by the state board of education at ten percent of the difference between the baseline and 100 each biennium.[15] Every school is expected to reduce the deficiency in successful students by the same percentage each biennium. Obviously, using a 10 percent reduction of the residual can mathematically go on into infinity. In recognition of this, the legislature amended KERA in 1998 to require a straight-line increase in successful students. Under this approach all schools are striving to reach the goal of having all students successful at the same point in time regardless of their starting position when compared to other schools.

Although the situation may not occur soon, eventually the board of education should realize that it is unreasonable to expect a school to reduce the proportion of unsuccessful students below a certain level because circumstances beyond the control of schools will not permit it. In such cases a school that can *maintain* that level of success should be considered successful and be rewarded for maintaining a high level of performance.[16]

Several technical problems arose during implementation of this aspect of the accountability system. The planned evolution of the measurement system obviously meant that the technical basis for computing the baseline, threshold, and accountability index would likely change from one biennial period to another. Also, school performance from one accountability period to the next would be measured by tests that contained elements not included when the threshold was established against which improvement is measured. How to equate values based on different tests was a serious issue for the assessment contractor to resolve. How this was done will be discussed further in the next chapter, but suffice it to say here that technical reviews of the accountability tests have identified this as a major problem inherent in the accountability system.

One way to address this problem would be to only introduce new elements at the beginning of a two-year accountability period and not include the results when calculating the current biennial performance index. Teachers and students would have a two year period in which to experience the new elements before they would be included as part of the accountability index. The performance data gathered from the new elements could be used to set a new baseline just as was the case at the outset of the program if the two years of experience proved the new elements were reliable and valid. The department of education did follow this policy when the arts and humanities and practical living/vocational studies elements were introduced in 1994.

Other changes were made in the accountability index in the early years that also affected the stability of the index. The department of education altered the weight given to various types of academic performances at different points in time. For example, initially the writing portfolio constituted 100 percent of the writing score. Later this was changed so that portfolios represented 75 percent and writing "prompts" 25 percent of the score. The mathematics test was altered three times as the nature of the test items changed. The overall weight by subject area changed after the arts and humanities test and practical living/vocational studies test was introduced.

After a negative review of the accountability tests in 1995, the department unilaterally decided to drop the performance events from the system. It also made a controversial decision not to include the score of performance events in the preceding testing period because of their alleged incomparability with events given in previous years. While this decision did not change the index itself, it changed the weight given to other methods of measurement used in the test battery. Indirectly this change had an impact on how the threshold should be calculated since it was calculated using test versions that included the performance events.

Although all of these changes were necessary to accommodate changes in the nature of the test as it evolved, educators and others affected by these changes felt the accountability index had become so unstable it was not a fair measure of the school's effort. The practical problems inherent in implementing an evolving measurement system weighed heavily on its credibility as a basis on which to determine rewards and sanctions. The controversy over the reliability of the accountability system seriously distracted from its potential benefit.

NOTES:

[1] See HB 940 Section (5) (1) (d) [KRS 158.6455]

[2] See HB 940 Section 5 (1) (b) [KRS 158.6455 (1) (b)]

[3] The example which appears as Table I in Hornbeck's memorandum to the curriculum committee of the task force was based on the example I prepared for Governor Wilkinson to illustrate his proposed Educational Per-

formance Index. This formula will be the basis for discussing the intent of the law in this regard.

[4] See regulation 703 KAR 4:010 Section 6 for a description of the approaches and their respective weights.

[5] According to regulation 703 KAR 4:010 Section 4 these values are set at 0, 2, 5 and 7 for each classification. But Section 5 of this regulation requires that these values be transformed to a scale such that a school with all of its students at the proficient level shall receive a score of 100. This is done by multiplying each of the raw values by a factor of 20.

[6] See regulation 703 KAR 4:010 Section 10.

[7] Reading, mathematics, science, social studies, and writing.

[8] See regulation 703 KAR 4:010 Section 12.

[9] See regulation 703 KAR 3:060 Section 2 through 4.

[10] See HB 940 Section 5 (1) (e) [KRS 158.6455 (1) (e)]

[11] See HB 940 Section 5 (1) (c) [KRS 158.6455 (1) (c)]

[12] Op. Cit., 22 and 24.

[13] See regulation 703 KAR 3:060 Section 7.

[14] The language in HB 940 Section 5 (4) regarding a school that does not meet its threshold says "if a school does not meet its original threshold after the next biennial review ..." which indicates the threshold for such schools is to remain constant until it is met or exceeded.

[15] See regulation 703 KAR 4:010 Section 14.

[16] A comparable example is the unemployment rate. It is unlikely that it can be reduced to zero because people will always be out of the workforce for some period of time for reasons other than poor economic conditions. The employment rate can be considered healthy even when there is a degree of unemployment.

14. Measurement of Improvement

KERA called for the creation of an essentially performance-based assessment system to measure the progress schools are making toward attainment of the six goals for schools. As might be expected, the most important goal in the mind of most people is the goal regarding what students learn and can do with what they learn. Thus at the heart of the accountability system is the state's ability to accurately measure student success. An assessment system had to be created to provide the data on which bonuses or sanctions are determined. The assessment of student learning would necessarily be the most important element in the accountability system.

Task force members were very aware of the challenge facing those who would design and build an assessment system strong enough to justify the rewards and sanctions that they had in mind. Because there were no models on which to build it, the task force was necessarily committed to trusting experts to actually design the system. However, there were certain specification the system had to meet. Among these directives was the desired evolution of the assessment system, certain aspects of the methodology to be used to determine rewards and sanctions, and the selection, authority, compensation, and deployment of the distinguished educators to be assigned to schools in decline or crisis. Some of the specifications applied to the design of the accountability system were discussed in the preceding chapters. Now we will examine the specifications the task force wrote into the law that applied to the design of the assessment system.

An Interim Assessment Program is to be Created

The major obstacle to quick implementation of the accountability system was creation of a reliable, cost effective way to assess student learning that would be appropriate to the new goals and academic expectations (or valued outcomes). It was fully understood that development of a new set of tests could very likely encounter serious problems if quick implementation was demanded. We thought use of an interim battery of tests already available could minimize the pressure to quickly create a new set of tests.

It was believed that it would take at least five years to fully develop and validate a battery of tests to measure student performance that is sufficiently reliable to be the basis for rewards and sanctions. The earliest portions of the new test were to be ready by the 1993-94 school year but not later than the 1995-96 school year. We understood that a longer time than this probably would be necessary to complete the entire system, but some deadline was thought necessary to push the development along as quickly as feasible.

An *interim* assessment was to be created to provide the data needed to allow the accountability system to function until the new assessment system is fully operational. The interim testing approach was intended to give the state a method by which to measure school improvement in the short term, yet move steadily toward a form of assessment better designed to measure the kind of instructional results envisioned in the learning goals for students. The interim testing program was to assess student skills in reading, mathematics, writing, science, and social studies. It was to be developed for implementation during the 1991-92 school year.

It was Hornbeck's opinion that the assessment contractor could select or develop the components for the interim test within this timeframe. The assumption was that the interim testing program could be constructed from assessment instruments already on the market. The primary task for the assessment contractor presumably would be to find tests that came reasonably close to measuring the various learning goals already developed by the council on school performance standards.

Even though the company hired to develop the interim testing program likely would not be selected until early in 1991, it was assumed that the contractor still would have sufficient time to select a battery of tests for use in the Spring of 1992. Data produced by the interim tests administered during the 1991-92 school year could be used to establish a baseline for determining school success in the 1992-93 school year.[1] The first rewards and sanctions could then occur by the end of the 1993-94 school year.

The scope of the interim tests was specifically and intentionally limited to reading, mathematics, writing, science, and social studies, because it was believed that suitable tests already existed for these common subject areas. The only possible technical limitation was a preference that these tests be criterion referenced rather than norm referenced so they would more closely resemble the kind of tests students would take later on. Some performance-based instruments already were in use in several other states, particularly in reading and writing. It was expected that the contractor would try to use existing tests before attempting to build something unique to Kentucky.

There were some potential problems with this approach. The interim test had to be ready for use in the 1991-92 school year. The council on school performance standards would not finish its work until December 1991, requiring the test developers to construct the interim test before the council's final product would be available. However, it was thought that sufficient information would be available from the initial report and current working papers of the council to provide a test developer sufficient guidance to permit construction of an interim test in the specified subject areas.

Obviously, there was no expectation that schools could have their students prepared for such a test in this time frame. On the other hand, committee members thought this early testing could serve to show how far students were from knowing or being able to do what would be expected in the future. Information gathered from these interim tests could help teachers make better decisions about changes they should make in the curriculum for the coming years. The results would be used only to establish a baseline in the accountability system this first year. If students did poorly on the tests, the only consequence would be a low baseline score.

Even though these measurement instruments were considered as an interim step, we assumed that these tests would continue to be used until a full transition to performance-based measurements could be made. All or a portion of the interim tests could be retained indefinitely if they proved to be useful and consistent with the goal of a primarily performance-based assessment system. The interim tests would provide continuity and stability to the new assessment system during a transition period, which conceivable could last six years or even longer. Given the proven reliability and validity of commercial tests, it was believed that this approach also could minimize early challenges to the accountability system based on questions about the validity and reliability of the instruments used to measure student success.

Once the validity and reliability of the new performance-based instruments was documented, the scores for these new tests items then would be incorporated into the formula for determining rewards and sanctions and the weight given to the scores on the interim tests could gradually be lessened. Although this was not discussed by the task force, clearly it was assumed that the assessment contractor would administer any new instruments at least two years before they would be considered valid for use in the accountability system. This approach would provide data needed to determine the validity and reliability of specific elements of the new instrument and also give students and teachers an opportunity to learn how to prepare for such tests.

A Desire for National Comparisons

It was obvious that the kind of performance-based tests envisioned by KERA would be unique to Kentucky. It was very likely that the Kentucky tests would measure some concepts and processes not currently measured by national tests available at the time. Kentucky could potentially become an academic island even though the tests it developed would be better measures of what Kentucky wants taught than the widely used national tests. Still, many task force members wanted to continue to compare Kentucky students with others. This concern posed a dilemma for the task force.

David Hornbeck, the consultant to the curriculum committee, proposed a compromise by suggesting that the interim tests be "equated" to the National Assessment of Educational Progress (NAPE). He envisioned that the Kentucky test designers could build a bridge to the NAEP data that would provide Kentucky with national reference points with which to compare Kentucky students to others in the United States. Hornbeck recommended that:

> *... Kentucky cause to be developed a series of test instruments in reading, math, writing, science, and social studies, which can be administered at the 4th, 8th, and 12th grades, which can be equated to the instruments used as part of the National Assessment of Educational Progress (NAPE). In some instances (writing) these instruments are performance based. All have a criterion-referenced quality in contrast to being norm-referenced. At the same time, if a bridge is built to the NAEP data, Kentucky will have national reference points so that you can know how Kentucky students compare to others in the United States.*[2]

The U.S. Congress pays for the NAEP. Historically, federal law had prohibited anyone else from using the NAEP tests. Furthermore, at the time this proposal was under discussion the NAEP did not provide state-by-state data, and the items used in the test were kept confidential by federal law.

The feasibility of building a bridge to the NAEP was questioned at the time, but the NAEP officials we consulted said that the historical constraint on releasing items used in previous NAEP tests would soon be lifted. It was their opinion that it was reasonable for Kentucky to assume that the NAEP items would soon be available and could be used at least as prototypes for purposes of equating performance on similar items by Kentucky students.[3]

The language used in KERA was intended to communicate the idea that the interim testing program should have *a component* in it to permit national comparisons. The folly of attempting to do this in a test designed for other purposes was vividly illustrated by the KEST experience. There certainly was no desire to repeat that experience again. Perhaps simplistically we envisioned there could be a special component in the Kentucky assessment program that could be used at least for national comparison purposes if not for accountability.

The statement that it "shall be the same as, or similar to those used by the National Assessment of Educational Progress" was not intended to mean literally using the NAPE itself or even NAPE test items. The primary intent of the reference to NAPE was only to express a desire that the testing protocols developed for comparison purposes be "NAPE-like" meaning that their design, rigor, and scoring rubrics be similar to those used in the NAPE tests. More importantly, the NAEP was the best example of a national test that looked similar to what Kentucky was striving to create. Using items like those in the NAEP would assure that the national comparison test and the Kentucky tests would appear similar to both teachers and students. Unfortunately, the language confused the message and caused considerable problems for the assessment consultants, assessment contractor, and others who had to implement this part of the law.

The Use of Assessment Consultants

Most members of the task force on education reform believed the department of education did not have the expertise needed to design and develop the assessment system. Using consultants for these tasks was seen as the way to ensure that Kentucky would get the very best minds in the nation to design the accountability and assessment systems. These systems were to be built according to the consultants' specifications by private contractors that have experience in test construction and administration.

KERA required the state board of education to contract with three or more authorities in the field of performance assessment to direct development of the interim and full-scale statewide assessment effort.[4] It was hoped that this group of individuals would develop a thoughtful strategy for reaching the goals of the new accountability system as well as provide the technical expertise required to prepare a request for proposals from potential contractors to build the assessment system based on their design.

KERA specifically gave to these consultants the responsibility to "design the specifications for the interim and full-scale assessment development effort."[5] The consultants also were required to review the bids and to make a recommendation to the board of education regarding the company they thought should be hired for this purpose.

John Brock, Superintendent of Public Instruction at the time, formed a committee to help select the assessment consultants. A letter of invitation was sent to 39 potential candidates. Ten of these individuals responded saying they had an interest in serving in this capacity. After evaluating the qualifications of the ten respondents, Brock hired Pat Forgione of the Connecticut Department of Education, Edward "Skip" Kifer of the University of Kentucky, Jason "Jay" Millman of Cornell University, Doris Redfield of UCLA, and Grant Wiggins of CLASS in Rochester, NY, to serve as assessment consultants.

Redfield had chaired the initial assessment task force of the council on school performance standards, so she was well informed about what was under discussion in Kentucky. The others had either appeared before the council as consultants or were contributors to the work of the council task force and understood at least in general terms the intent of the assessment concepts on which KERA was based. Redfield agreed to chair the assessment consultant group.

The System Design is Completed

The five assessment consultants met several times in the late Fall of 1990 to clarify their mission, exchange views about the meaning of the relevant sections of the law, set priorities, and adopt a work plan. Many important issues were raised and resolved during these meetings. The consultants set April 1991 as the date for completion of the draft for a request for proposals.

A request for proposals went out April 19, 1991 on schedule. Six proposals were received from prospective contractors by the May 31st deadline. The five consultants reviewed the proposals as required by KERA. However, the finance cabinet maintained that the proposals also had to be reviewed by a ten-person technical review panel according to regulations governing the award of state contracts. Commissioner Boysen appointed a review panel that consisted of representatives of school districts, universities, the department of education, and myself as the Governor's Secretary of Education. The technical review panel submitted its evaluation of the six proposals to the consultants who forwarded the results to the state board of education along with their recommendation.

Four of the six prospective contractors were invited to make oral presentations and to answer questions in a two-day session at the end of June, 1991. The bids ranged from just under $13 million to a little over $35 million. Advanced Systems in Measurement and Evaluation was ultimately awarded the contract. The exact terms of the contract were subsequently negotiated along with the contract price.[6] The contract covered a five year period of development and administration of the new assessment and accountability programs.

Although Advanced Systems had limited experience with large-scale statewide testing programs, the assessment consultants' endorsement was based primarily on their confidence in the ability of this company's staff to conceptualize and design the kind of assessment system envisioned by the authors of KERA. Advanced Systems presented the most creative and responsive proposal among those submitted. The department of education would have to address the issue of the company's limited experience with the administration of large-scale testing programs when that part of the contract was negotiated.

Commission Boysen's Views of Assessment

Commissioner Thomas Boysen recognized the critical importance of the assessment system, and offered his opinions about how it should be designed in a memorandum he sent to the assessment consultants shortly after they began their work. This memorandum included his preliminary understanding of the law and an outline of how he saw the evolution of the accountability and assessment programs.[7] He listed 10 features he thought these systems should have. Conceptually he saw the assessment program as having the ability to produce valid data on "individual students, the school, the district, and the state" in order to meet all the needs previously filled by KEST; basic competency tests; and commercial norm-referenced tests. He also thought that tests should be available in all grades in the subjects that were referenced in the law as the focus of the "interim test."

The system Boysen envisioned at that time seemed to go beyond what KERA required. He believed testing for instructional purposes should be integrated into the state accountability testing program in some kind of "consolidated" assessment program. His experience in California led to a concern that schools would continue to use basic competency tests, national norm-referenced tests, and other measurements because of their perceived need for the information these tests provide or in some cases because such tests are required by certain federal programs. In his view, Kentucky needed to expand the assessment program concept beyond what the KERA accountability system required to bring uniformity to the testing practices of schools and to meet all the testing needs of public schools through a single testing program.

Tests are created to measure certain things, so there always is a problem of explaining why students get a certain score on writing in one test and a different score on another test. Unless Kentucky addressed this issue early in the development of the assessment program, Boysen felt there would be considerable confusion later on when Kentucky's measurements yielded results quite different from what schools would get from norm-referenced tests which they might use for other purposes. His concerns were well founded when researchers later attempted to evaluate the assessment program by comparing student scores on the new KIRIS test with scores attained on norm-referenced tests—exactly what he feared would happen.

Boysen questioned the feasibility of developing the assessment system envisioned in KERA in the specified time frame and with the financial resources appropriated by the legislature. He also questioned how the system could be "equated" with NAEP and still meet the unique needs of Kentucky. He noted that NAEP does not test at the same time all the subjects that KERA identified, so recent NAEP norms would not be available on a timely basis for annual or even biennial comparisons. These points all became significant issues for the assessment system as it evolved.

Clearly, Boysen had cause to be concerned about how this very important element of KERA would be designed, since he would be responsible for implementing it. However, some of his ideas went well beyond the already daunting task facing the consultants. They gave consideration to his ideas and concerns, but they also thought they were obligated to stay within the guidelines set by the law irrespective of the new commissioner's concerns and desires.

Critical Elements of the Assessment Design

The assessment system was formally named the Kentucky Instructional Results Information System (KIRIS). The KIRIS consisted technically of both the accountability and assessment system. Since the accountability element of KIRIS was discussed in the preceding chapter, we will discuss only the assessment aspect of KIRIS here.

The assessments consisted initially of a battery of mostly paper-and-pencil type items, much like items found in commercial tests previously used in the state. This was the "transitional" component of the KIRIS assessment instrument. It initially represented about 80 percent of the total KIRIS score. As noted earlier, this is the element of the assessment system that KERA required to permit early testing while the more performance-based aspects of the system are developed.

The transitional component was augmented by "performance events" and writing portfolios, which were the earliest components of the performance-based element of KIRIS. Performance events are structured activities students are required to perform to demonstrate their ability to use certain concepts or processes to solve one or more problems. Writing portfolios contain writing samples that students prepare to demonstrate their composition skills. Both of these testing approaches were used in a few states at that time, but the technology on which they were based was relatively new. The major technical issues regarding this form of testing focused on the reliability and validity of scoring the end product. More will be said about this later in the chapter.

The Use of Matrix Sampling

A sampling approach similar to what is done in opinion polls was considered sufficient to provide a reasonable estimate of whether students in a school are making progress toward mastery of the academic expectations (valued outcomes) required by KERA. This approach allows a broad range of knowledge and skills to be tested without placing an undue burden on students who have to take these tests.

A methodology called matrix-sampling was used successfully in California and Illinois, and it also is used in NAPE. There are several approaches to matrix sampling from which the assessment contractor could chose, but the one adopted involves taking literally hundreds of test questions and randomly dividing them among different versions of the test. Some questions appear in all versions for technical purposes. Each student takes only one version of the test, thus is required to answer only a "sample" of all the test items.

There were twelve version of the test initially, four for each of the three accountability grades. Presumably each version of the test is equally difficult and covers the same concepts and processes. However, all relevant versions of the test are administered in a school to ensure that all matrix items are tested. Every student doesn't answer every matrix question, but all matrix questions are answered by some students in the school.

The purpose of the accountability assessment is to determine the improvement a school has made rather than to test everything each student knows and can do. The task force thought testing every student on everything was unnecessary and burdensome. The matrix sampling approach satisfied the intent of the task force.

Classifications of Student Performance

As noted in the preceding chapter, the department of education based the accountability index on the percentage of students whose performance was at each of four levels: novice, apprentice, proficient, and distinguished. Theoretically the distinguished category was the ideal level of performance desired , but as a practical matter the goal was to get all students at least to the proficient level by the end of their 12 years of schooling. The four categories were initially defined as shown here.

Novice

- The student shows minimal understanding
- The student is unable to generate strategy; answers may display only recall effect, lack clear communication and/or be totally incorrect or irrelevant

Apprentice

- The student completes some important components of the task and communicates those clearly
- The student demonstrates that there are gaps in his/her conceptual understanding

Proficient

- The student completes most important components of the task and communicates clearly
- The student demonstrates understanding of major concepts even though she/he overlooks or misunderstands some less important ideas or details

Distinguished

- The student completes all important components of the task and communicates ideas clearly.
- The student demonstrates in-depth understanding of the relevant concepts and/or processes
- Where appropriate, the student offers insightful interpretations or extensions (generalizations, applications and analogies)

The initial wording went through some revision over time, but the key ideas remained the same. There is a gradual progression from the beginning (novice) level to what constitutes an outstanding performance (distinguished). The definitions initially were broad and designed to communicate the general idea behind each category.

Practical as well as technical questions were raised about the decision of the department of education to use the terms novice, apprentice, proficient, and distinguished to categorize performances of students on the tests. This aspect of the accountability index confused many educators and the general public. When the department of education first used these terms, teachers didn't know how they were defined or the criteria that distinguished one from the another. The department of education faced the immediate challenge of defining the terms they chose.

One source of confusion can be attributed to the choice of terms. Novice and apprentice are terms that describe the status of a person, but proficient and distinguished are terms that describe the quality of a performance. It was not immediately clear whether the terms referred to the student or the performance. Unfortunately, this has resulted in students being labeled novice, apprentice, proficient or distinguished when it is their performance that is presumed to be categorized. The language should have been changed to send a consistent message as to the intended referents for these terms.

Another issue raised by the use of these labels relates to the complexity they introduced into the task of creating performance standards. The department faced a tremendous task just to create performance standards for each academic expectation for each accountability grade level. It is hard enough to define standards for an ideal or "proficient" performance let alone try to define standards for a novice, apprentice, and the like at the 4th, 8th, and 12th grades. There was not a lot of time in which to develop an elaborate set of standards such as this scheme envisioned. An enormous effort by a large number of people was required to accomplish the task in the short time available to get it done.

As one of the people who helped conceptualize the accountability program, it is my personal opinion that a single set of high standards for each academic expectation (valued outcome) would have been sufficient for purposes of the school accountability program. The program only needed an operational definition of a "successful student" which presumably is a student who meets or exceeds the standards the department eventually established for a "proficient" performance. The proportion of students who meet or exceed that standard is all that has to be tabulated in the accountability index.

Scoring is a Major Issue

The transitional test consisted mainly of multiple choice and open response questions. Scoring these items were relatively easy and reliable. Scoring performance events and portfolios was a different matter. Only a very few Kentucky teachers had familiarity with the portfolio assessment, and performance events were entirely unique. Obviously it was important that teachers learn to assess students in the same manner as they will be assessed on the state test. The assessment contractor was required to use and train Kentucky teachers to score the portfolios and performance events. The purpose of this policy was to develop expertise in this form of assessment in Kentucky and to influence classroom assessment practices.

Scoring portfolios and performance events has two distinctly different aspects. On the one hand, the scorer uses "rubrics" or examples of proper usage that are guidelines for determining the quality of the student's work when compared against specific standards. On the other hand, the scorer must then use this information to assign the student to a specific category on the continuum from novice to distinguished.

The following chart is based on a document that was distributed to teachers to guide them in scoring the mathematics portfolios. It illustrates the kind of scoring matrix teachers had to use to score the work of each student on the math portfolios. It also illustrates how the elements of the portfolio product relate to the four categories. For brevity sake the chart only includes the criteria for the lowest and highest categories, i.e. novice and distinguished.

Mathematics Portfolio Scoring Guide

	NOVICE	DISTINGUISHED
Problem Solving Understanding Strategies	Indicates a basic understanding of problems and uses strategies	Indicates a comprehensive understanding of problems with efficient, sophisticated strategies
Execution/Extensions	Implements strategies with minor mathematical errors in the solution without extensions	Uses logical and sophisticated arguments justifying the most sophisticated, efficient, and accurate solutions with extensions
Reasoning	Uses mathematical reasoning	Uses perceptive, creative and complex mathematical reasoning
Mathematical Communication Language	Uses appropriate mathematical language most of the time	Uses elegant, precise and appropriate mathematical language throughout
Representations	Uses routine mathematical representations	Uses multiple mathematical representations accurately and appropriately and states their interconnections
Integration/ Connections of Core Concepts	Indicates a limited understanding of core concepts in mathematics	Indicates a comprehensive understanding of core concepts and interconnections throughout
Types and Contexts	Indicates the use of a few types and contexts	Indicates a use of all types and contents

Teachers who score the portfolios or performance events are first asked to judge the quality of the student's work according to specific criteria, but then they must evaluate this product in its totality to determine whether it is the work of a novice, apprentice, and so forth. The reliability of this element of the KIRIS assessment demands a high level of agreement among the teachers doing the scoring.

Obviously, there are opportunities for error or disagreement at both points. Thus the amount of potential measurement error is doubled. The experts who critiqued the assessment system found that teachers could more easily agree on the quality of the product when judged by the standards given to them for each element of the performance than they could agree on where to place a student on the continuum.

This situation is of critical importance since the accountability index ignores the actual score students receive, counting only the percent of students assigned to the specific categories on the continuum. No matter how precise the scoring of the work product might be, a serious disagreement among scorers on the category placement of students renders the reliability in scoring meaningless in terms of determining school success. Placement of students in the proper category is of greatest importance and this proved to be the most unreliable aspect of this element of KIRIS.

Test reliability is in large measure determined by the consistency with which the same score is given to the same product by all scorers. The assessment contractor and department of education conducted rater agreement studies to determine the amount of error that was generated in scoring portfolios and performance events. Initially the rate of agreement was about 80%, but this was improved to over 90% after intensive retraining was provided to the evaluators.

In addition to the rating studies, the department and contractor also conducted audits of randomly selected portfolios as a reliability control measure. Computer analysis also was made of all portfolio scores to identify any that appeared suspect. Audits were made of these portfolios and often the audits resulted in lower scores than were originally given. The scores for the accountability index were adjusted for the schools affected.

Implementation Problems Emerge

Performance assessments are at the heart of the assessment policy adopted by the task force on education reform. However, this kind of assessment is time consuming to take and expensive to create, administer, and score. The standards on which they are based also can be very difficult to create, validate, and communicate. We knew at the outset that these factors would make the transition challenging. However, we also believed that a careful, thoughtful, and staged implementation of the new assessment system would at least minimize these potential problems.

Scoring portfolios and performance events became a major issue as the assessment system unfolded. Predictably, inconsistency in scores from district to district prompted an audit of about 120 schools for possible inaccurate scoring of writing portfolios after the first round of testing. Obviously this caused concern among teachers, parents, and policy makers.

One must feel confident that writing is being evaluated the same way at every school even though for decades no one publicly questioned the validity of teacher grades for writing. Almost everyone has stories to tell about "hard teachers" and "easy teachers" even within a school. However, when grading practices of teachers become the basis for awarding bonuses or sanctioning schools, we pay much more attention to how teachers evaluate the work of their students.

The issue of students not having a stake in the outcome of the state tests was raised early, particularly by high school teachers and administrators. Evidence surfaced that some middle and high school students did not give the test their best effort because they said it had no consequence for them. Some students attempted to sabotage the test by refusing to take some parts or any of it. Still others apparently gave flippant or intentionally inaccurate answers. The response of the department of education to this issue was to ask the legislature to alter the law so that some portions of the tests could be administered in other grades. The legislature obliged and made the requested changes in 1994.

The accountability index proved to be too complex for most people to understand. Even though meetings were held to explain how to calculate the index, I found principals and teachers telling me they didn't know how to improve their performance on the index because they could not understand the computations. On several occasions I talked with principals who did the calculations only to learn that they had not done it correctly. Obviously, an incentive system must have clear rules for qualifying for the awards. Many of the teachers and administrators in the schools the state declared to be in decline or in crisis were discouraged and often very angry. Many schools that won awards in the initial round were not clear about how to do it again in future years.

The testing instruments kept changing each year as new concepts and processes were added from year to year. Even though these new items were not considered when calculating the accountability index score, it was apparent that this information did not reach all teachers. Many teachers complained that they didn't know how to prepare their students from year to year because they didn't know what would be on the next test until it was given. Teachers who didn't think the system was fair to begin with only found this to confirm their worst fears about it.

The Assessment System Gets into Serious Difficulty

After the first round of accountability test results were released, the first challenges to the assessment system were mounted. Based on rather negative reviews of the program by several independent research groups, there were calls for immediate suspension of the rewards and sanctions element of the program.

Efforts were put forth by both the department of education and the assessment contractor to deal expeditiously and prudently with the questions raised about the emerging system. Independent experts were brought in by the department of education to review the system and offer advice. The education department and the assessment contractor made adjustments to the assessments as each new one was constructed, taking into account the many recommendations they received from these consultants. In part this continuous alteration of the system contributed to the appearance of instability.

The first external technical review of KIRIS was conducted in 1993 at the request of the office of education accountability. Dr. Ronald Hambleton, an assessment specialist from the University of Massachusetts, concluded that the work done at this early point in the program was in keeping with the intent of KERA, but he thought KIRIS was flawed in various technical respects.[8] He offered some suggestions as to how the assessment system could be improved. Of course, the program had just been launched the year before, so there had been little time for the assessment system to be fully developed.

In 1994 a more detailed study of KIRIS, sponsored by the Kentucky Institute for Education Research, was conducted by the Evaluation Center at

Western Michigan University.[9] This study focused on the work completed in the first two years of the assessment program. The evaluators recognized the hard work that had been put into developing this relatively new approach to assessment. They pointed out that education, testing agencies, and the measurement profession had not yet solved all the technical and operational problems associated with a large-scale performance-based assessment program. Kentucky was breaking new ground with the mandate to create such a system within such a short time frame.

Consistent with Hambleton's initial observations, the Assessment Center researchers found the program so far was consistent with the legislative intent. They found, however, that few educators and the general public understood the method by which improvement in schools is measured. More importantly, few educators believed the KIRIS test as they had experienced it so far was a reliable, valid, useful, and fair method of documenting what their students know and can do. There also was a common belief that the test had been constructed by outsiders, even though Kentucky teachers were in fact extensively involved in setting the test standards for reading, mathematics, science, and social studies.

The Assessment Center researchers were especially critical of the accountability index, concluding that two of the three measures on which it is based were not statistically reliable enough to be used in a high-stakes assessment such as is required by KERA. Questions also were raised about the decision by the department of education to change important elements of the test between the two years it was initially used. The researchers thought these changes significantly reduced the validity of comparing the first year test scores with the second year test scores.

Notwithstanding the ongoing study by the institute, the legislature was so concerned about the public criticism of KIRIS and the work of the assessment contractor that in 1994 it also ordered the office of education accountability to conduct a full review of every aspect of the accountability and assessment programs including a review of the assessment contractor's performance. The results of this study were released six months after the results of the Assessment Center study were released.

The office of education accountability asked its previous consultant, Ronald Hambleton, to put together a panel of experts to conduct an independent study of KIRIS. The Hambleton group concentrated heavily on psychometric issues that applied not only to KIRIS but to the whole field of performance assessments.[10] This panel of experts also reviewed aspects of the accountability system. The findings of this panel of assessment experts was less positive in its conclusions about KIRIS. The Hambleton group concluded:

> *After reviewing large numbers of curriculum and technical documents and assessments, conducting a number of relevant analyses, and carefully considering our findings, the Panel is in unanimous agreement that KIRIS is seriously flawed and needs to be substantially revised. The panel is not suggesting that the educational reform movement is a failure or that educators are not working hard to implement the goals of KERA. We are not suggesting either that the educational reforms taking place in the areas of curriculum design and instruction and teacher in-service training are not worthwhile. The Panel is saying that the accountability and assessment system has major flaws which need to be corrected as Kentucky moves into the second accountability cycle.*[11]

Although the expert panel qualified its language, the main finding set off a political fire storm that ultimately caused the legislature to make significant changes in the assessment element of the law. The details of these changes are discussed below.

As one can readily see, the system was hardly off the ground before experts were asked to the judge its merits. This lack of patience on the part of policy makers pressured the department of education and the assessment contractor into making changes to the system that later proved to only further aggravate the situation. No doubt the primary reason for this haste to judgment was not so much the possibility that the assessment instruments might have technical problems. No one in a position of responsibility for the assessment system was making the case that it was or likely ever would be flawless. It was the fact that data from these instruments would determine which schools would receive bonuses or be sanctioned that provided the impetus for this rush to judgment. Nonetheless, when experts questioned the trustworthiness of the new system, confidence of policy makers, educators, parents, and the public in this new approach to accountability was seriously and irreversibly undermined.

An Attempt to Salvage the Assessment System

The legislature ended its biennial session in 1994 making only minor changes in KIRIS. But the department was warned that something had to be done immediately to address the growing criticism of the system. Shortly after the legislature adjourned in 1994, the department of education issued a position paper containing seven specific recommendations for changes in KIRIS.

In the position paper the department leadership acknowledged there were serious problems with KIRIS and hoped to move quickly to address them.[12] The recommendations dealt with most of the operational problems identified later by the assessment experts. However, the technical issues relating to the reliability and validity of the test instruments were not addressed at that time.

Portfolios and performance events were not heavily weighted in the first testing cycle, but it was expected that these elements would eventually be the most heavily weighted. The attack on the validity and reliability of these two elements of KIRIS by the assessment experts so weakened confidence in the performance-based aspects of the assessment system that the department of education finally decided to increase the use of more traditional test items, adjust the scoring methodology for the accountability index, and suspend the use of performance events, hoping to avoid a total suspension of the use of these innovative aspects of the assessment system.

The department of education made important modifications to the KIRIS design when the contract was re-bid in 1995. The new bid request incorporated most of the recommendations made in the two major studies of the system. Advanced Systems won the bid again, but shared key responsibilities with other testing companies operating as subcontractors. Changing the roles of the original contractor addressed the concerns of some critics who thought the company was not up to the task, but this did not improve the overall credibility of the testing system itself. Technical problems continued to beset the program over the next biennium.

The problems with the assessment program became a political issue in the gubernatorial campaign in 1995. One candidate promised to abolish the entire accountability and assessment system if elected. The candidate who made the assessment and accountability program an issue was not elected, but the political fallout of the controversy continued into the next session of the legislature in 1996.

In a show of political support for the assessment system following release of the two highly critical reports from the assessment experts, the legislature's OEA Oversight Committee passed a resolution during a June 27, 1995 meeting that made the following points:

The committee:

1. *Emphasizes its fundamental and strong support for an assessment and an accountability system*

2. *Recommends the Department of Education report to this committee how portfolios may appropriately be used in an accountability system.*

3. *Reconfirms its commitment to primarily performance-based testing systems and to a test that provides the state with valid national comparisons, and directs the Department to advise this committee how these objectives will be met, both in the short term and the long term.*

4. *Reconfirms its commitment to the financial reward system and demands that the Department, before further distribution of rewards, demonstrate adequate proof of the validity and reliability of the accountability system; and further recommends that the reward money be retained in the trust fund, and that the legislature proceed with the expected increase in appropriation in the 1996 session.*

5. *Recommends that the Department assure that the test emphasizes content, not just process.*

6. *Recommends that the Department take the time to make appropriate and wise adjustments to the assessment and accountability systems and solicit recommendations from teachers, superintendents, board members, interested members of the public, and test experts, keeping in mind that an accountability system is essential.*

Clearly the legislature was holding to the intent of the task force's original assessment and accountability policy, but warned the department of education that prudent action had to be taken quickly if the present policy is to remain politically viable.

While there was belief that the problems the experts had identified could be eliminated, newly elected Governor Paul Patton agreed with the legislature in 1996 to create a new task force to examine every aspect of KERA over the following two years including the assessment and accountability system. This new task force would present its recommendations to the governor and legislature in 1998 for their consideration.

Unfortunately, Advanced Systems made a computer software error in scoring the 1996-97 KIRIS tests that resulted in incorrect placement of a number of elementary and middle schools, and in turn resulted in incorrect awarding of bonuses. This was only the latest in a series of misadventures to beset the assessment contractor from the outset. After this latest snafu, the department of education canceled the contract with Advanced Systems in July 1997 after just awarding the contract to them again in spite of the concerns legislators had about the ability of the company to provide the expertise and service the program needed. These events only further eroded support for the accountability and assessment systems. In a sense this became the proverbial straw that broke the camel's back. The next year the legislature decided to make major changes in both the accountability and assessment systems that are discussed in the next chapter.

The effect on teaching and learning.

It long has been known that most teachers will teach to a test, especially if they believe their professional reputations are at stake. Thus the KIRIS tests have had a powerful influence on what gets taught and how it is taught. Of course, this is a two edged sword because this can narrow instruction if the test is too narrow. On the other hand, if the test measures what is important, then what is taught will be important as well. As indicated earlier, the task force on school reform expected the accountability test to influence instruction. The full extent of the impacts of KIRIS on instruction is not yet documented, but the early evidence indicates that the assessment component of the accountability program has definitely influenced teacher behavior.[13]

The portfolio requirement of KIRIS probably had the most dramatic effect. The early use of portfolios to measure writing in KIRIS appears to have resulted in a greater emphasis on writing in all subjects, and it had a direct impact on how writing is taught.[14] A longitudinal study comparing writing practices in 1995 with those observed in 1982 found that teachers in the elementary school classes they studied now spend twice as much time teaching writing and students are engaged in writing activities two to three times more than in 1982.[15] More importantly this study revealed that students now are spending more time on higher-level writing activities involving the composition of extended text and less time on lower-level activities such as filling in workbooks, worksheets, and copying from the board. According to the teachers studied, this increase in emphasis on writing is due primarily to the statewide accountability assessments that use portfolios and open-ended response questions. Similar results were found in studies of the impact of KIRIS on the teaching of mathematics after portfolios in mathematics were added to KIRIS.[16]

There are some unfortunate and unintended consequences to the use of portfolios. While the increased emphasis upon writing is an intended outcome of the KIRIS assessment design, all studies to date report that most teachers believe the assessment portfolios take too much time away from other important instructional activities and subject matter. However, teachers do generally acknowledge the value of portfolios in improving writing, and most teachers reported that they now use portfolios regularly in writing instruction. On the other hand, if given the option, they would prefer to use open-response questions based on writing prompts over portfolios because they take much less time to prepare and assess.[17]

The limited information available from all studies so far consistently indicate that the "high stakes" nature of the accountability system makes instructional changes imperative. Teachers generally report a greater use of broader methods of assessment which in turn require corresponding changes in how students are taught. In some studies, researchers report finding some teachers making changes primarily based on what they perceive will be covered on KIRIS rather than on sound pedagogy. Such a practice is probably to be expected, but it is not what was intended or desired.

It appears that the accountability program has stimulated important changes in instructional practices, so in that regard it probably has had at least an indirect impact on learning. Only time will tell which of these instructional changes actually improve student learning.

NOTES:

[1] See HB 940 Section 4 (1) [KRS 158.6453]

[2] See Hornbeck memorandum to the curriculum committee dated February 23, 1990, page 16.

[3] State-by-state NAPE data as well as the test items have since been made available as indicated to us at the time. However, it was necessary to resolve this issue before the question of the availability of NAPE data could be definitively answered for the task force.

[4] See HB 940 Section 4 (2) [KRS 158.6453]

[5] Ibid.

[6] The four bidders invited to make presentations were School Research and Service, Advanced Systems in Measurement and Evaluation, Educational Testing Service, and CTB Macmillan. The other bidders were Psychological Corporation and Measurement Incorporated.
[7] Memorandum from Boysen to Consultants dated January 15, 1991.
[8] See Ronald K. Hambleton, *Some Technical Comments on KIRIS Assessments*, Frankfort, KY.: Office of Education Accountability, November, 1993.
[9] See *An Independent Evaluation of the Kentucky Instructional Results Information System*. Frankfort, KY: Kentucky Institute for Education Research, January, 1995.
[10] See Ronald K. Hambleton; Richard M. Jaeger; Daniel Koretz; Robert L.Linn; Jason Millman; and Susan Phillips, *Review of the Measurement Quality of the Kentucky Instructional Results Information System 1991-1994.* Frankfort, KY: Office of Education Accountability, June 20, 1995
[11] Ibid., page 1.
[12] See *Position Paper on Recommended Changes in the KIRIS Assessment and Accountability Program*. Frankfort, KY: Kentucky Department of Education, Office of Curriculum, Assessment, and Accountability, April, 1994.
[13] Roger Pankratz prepared a summary of selected studies of the impact of KIRIS. See Roger Pankratz, *Research Related to KIRIS's Impact on Learning*. Frankfort, Kentucky: Kentucky Institute for Education Research, 1996..
[14] See Susan C. Cantrell; Cary Pappas; and Jane C. Lindle, "Preliminary Findings on Writing and Reading Instruction in Elementary Schools: Results from the First Year of a Five-Year Multiple-Case Study", *The Kentucky Reading Journal,* March, 1997.
[15] See Connie Bridge, Margaraet Compton-Hall, and Susan Chambers, "Classroom Writing Practices Revisited: The Effects of Statewide Reform on Writing Instruction", *Elementary School Journal*, 1996.
[16] See for example Daniel M. Koretz, Sheila Barron, Karen J. Mitchell, and Brian M. Stecher, *Perceived Effects of the Kentucky Instructional Results Information System*. Santa Monica, CA.: RAND Corporation, Institute on Education and Training, 1996.
[17] In addition to Koretz, O*p. cit.*, see also a longitudinal study of the primary program conducted by Patricia Kannapel, Pamelia Coe, Loala Aagaard and Beverly D. Moore, *Teacher Responses to Rewards and Sanctions: An In-Depth Look in Four Kentucky School Districts.* Charles-

ton, WV: Appalachia Educational Laboratory, 1997.

15. Accountability Revisited

As agreed upon by the governor and legislature in 1996, a new group called the Task Force on Public Education was created to conduct a review of all parts of KERA. The public education task force held numerous meetings over 18 months and made its final recommendations to the governor and legislature just before the 1998 legislative session opened.

The House and Senate prepared two quite different bills designed to deal with the recommendations offered by the public education task force. A Senate bill would have abolished the accountability system as it was originally designed. The House rejected the Senate bill and approved its own bill that retained key elements of the assessment and accountability system as originally conceived, but with major changes in their implementation. Ultimately, the House bill was enacted into law.*

Among the changes made by the legislature in 1998 was the creation of three new structures to provide guidance to the development, implementation, and evaluation of the new accountability and assessment programs:

1. A permanent subcommittee of the Legislative Research Commission (LRC) to be known as the Education Assessment and Accountability Review Subcommittee to provide continuing oversight of the implementation of the state system of assessment and accountability.
2. A School Curriculum, Assessment, and Accountability Council (SCAAC) to study, review, and make recommendations concerning Kentucky's system of setting academic standards, assessing learning, holding schools accountable for learning, and assisting schools to improve their performance. The SCAAC is to advise the Kentucky Board of Education and the Legislative Research Commission on issues related to the development and communication of the academic expectations and core content for assessment; the development and implementation of the statewide assessment and accountability program; the distribution of rewards and imposition of sanctions; and

* All of the items described below are based on language in HB 53 as enacted by the 1998 session of the Kentucky General Assembly.

assistance to help schools improve their performance. Composition of the SCAAC is specified in the law to ensure appropriate representation of all affected publics.

3. A National Technical Panel on Assessment and Accountability composed of no fewer than three professionals with a variety of expertise in education testing and measurement is appointed by the Legislative Research Commission to advise policy makers on technical issues affecting the accountability and assessment system. Among these duties is to make recommendations regarding the validity and reliability of specific tests designed by the department of education or its assessment contractors.[1]

The department of education now is constrained somewhat in its ability to develop and implement the new program. The 1998 revisions to KERA mandate that the department consult with and receive advice from all three of these groups before proceeding with promulgation of any new regulations or making any changes in the accountability and assessment system in the future.

The Assessment Program is Revamped

The name for the new assessment program is called the Commonwealth Accountability Testing System (CATS) to clearly distinguish it from the now discredited KIRIS. The CATS must have the following components:[2]

(a) A customized or commercially available norm-referenced test that measures, to the extent possible, the core content for assessment. The test must provide valid and reliable results for individual students;

(b) Open-response or multiple-choice items, or both, to assess student skills in reading, mathematics, science, social studies, the arts, the humanities, and practical living and vocational studies; and an on-demand assessment of student writing. These assessments must measure, to the extent possible, the core content for assessment;

(c) Writing portfolios consisting of samples of student work. After receiving the advice of the Writing Advisory Committee, the Kentucky Board of Education must file by September 1, 1998, notice of its intent to issue an administrative regulation that includes strategies to reduce the teacher and student time involved in preparing a writing portfolio;

(d) Performance assessment events for schools that have students enrolled in performing arts organizations sponsoring sanctioned events with an established protocol for adjudication; and

(e) A technically sound longitudinal comparison of the assessment results for the same students.

Other measures were put in place in 1998 to avoid some of the problems that confronted KIRIS. For example, the department of education must develop a biennial plan for validation studies.

> (The studies) *shall include, but not be limited to, the consistency of student results across multiple measures, the congruence of school scores with documented improvements in instructional practice and the school learning environment, and the potential for all scores to yield fair, consistent, and accurate student performance level and school accountability decisions. Validation activities shall take place in a timely manner and shall include a review of the accuracy of scores assigned to students and schools, as well as of the testing materials.*[3]

The intention is to increase confidence in the assessment process and instruments. The plan must be reviewed by the three new groups with oversight responsibility before it is implemented.

The legislation also requires the department of education to report quarterly to the Interim Joint Committee on Education as to its progress in the following nine areas:

1. Establishing a consistent structure of test components, grade-level testing distribution, and test administration procedures;
2. Beginning a new cycle of equating procedure for which their adequacy and precision can be tested rigorously and conducting appropriate equating analyses to accommodate the new accountability system;
3. Publishing more complete and informative guides for interpreting school accountability index score changes that include information about the estimated error of the accountability index, as well as information about the connections between

index score changes and estimated changes in student performance levels;

4. Reviewing school accountability classifications to assure their construct validity in all cases where they are applied;
5. Maintaining and strengthening the annual audit of portfolio scores in ways that serve to minimize the differences between teacher-produced scores and audit-generated scores;
6. Developing and implementing a validity research plan;
7. Establishing additional routine audits of key processes in the assessment and accountability program;
8. Maintaining and cataloging a library of technical documents related to the assessment and accountability program for internal and external review purposes. In addition, the department must produce an annual technical report for audiences that include educators, testing coordinators, parents, and legislators; and
9. Maintaining a vigorous ongoing program of research and documentation of the effects of the assessment and accountability system on Kentucky schools.[4]

All of these requirements are based on recommendations made in the major outside evaluations of KIRIS. Clearly the legislature is determined to maintain control over the revised assessment program in the hope of avoiding problems encountered in the past.

The 1998 revision to KERA also addressed concerns about input into the content covered by these tests, their reliability and validity, and the time demands on teachers and students they require. New language was inserted in the law giving specific direction to the department of education on each of these issues. The law is very specific about requiring public input before revisions are made to the core content for assessment.

Stability in what is tested from year to year is essential to teachers and students. No changes to the CATS can be made in the future without involvement of parents, teachers, educators at all levels, professional education advocacy groups and organizations, business and civic leaders. The process invoked here is similar to what was initially used by the council on school performance standards. These people will not be involved in creation of specific test items, but rather in the determination of what is to be tested by the CATS.

Changes in what is tested will be more cumbersome in the future, and thus less likely to be encouraged. In this sense there is the risk that the tests might grow less flexible and responsive to curriculum changes over time. On the other hand, the legislature did not want the almost annual changes in KIRIS content repeated with the CATS. The department and assessment contractors have much less latitude to quickly implement changes in the accountability tests than they had initially.

Continuous Assessment is Strengthened

The 1998 revision of KERA also addressed the role of assessment at the school district level. The task force in 1990 wanted local school districts to adopt a policy for continuous student assessment. In 1998 the legislature strengthen this provision in two ways. KERA now specifically requires the state board of education to help local school districts engage in continuous assessment to "provide diagnostic information to improve instruction to meet the needs of individual students."[5] Clearly the intent here is that the continuous assessment program cannot be limited to providing information to students and parents. It must be used to improve the ability of teachers to individualize instruction.

An annual performance report by local school districts was required in 1990, but the legislature was not satisfied with how this provision of the law was being implemented. The 1998 revision requires the state board of education, after receiving advice from the three oversight bodies, to establish the components of a "school report card" that clearly communicates with parents and the public about school performance.

The school report card must include at least the following by race, gender, and disability: (a) student academic achievement, including the results from each of the state assessments; (b) nonacademic achievement, including the school's attendance, retention, dropout rates, and student transition to adult life; and (c) school learning environment, including measures of parental involvement.[6] The school report card must be sent to the parents of students of the district, and a summary of the results for the district must be published in local news media. The intent here is to tighten up this requirement and ensure a level of uniformity in what is reported across the state.

The policy commitment to local school accountability remained strong as did the concept of a system of consequences for performance. However, major changes were made in the accountability index, the distribution of rewards, the nature of assistance given to poor performing schools, and the distinguished educator program.

The Accountability Index is Revamped

The complexity, questionable validity, and unreliability of the accountability index resulted in a mandate in 1998 that the department of education reconstruct it. The department also must consider the advice of the three new oversight bodies when the index is designed. All previous language specifying how the index should be designed was repealed, leaving open the methodology for determining school success and calculating the baseline for improvement thresholds.

After considerable debate and with advice from the oversight groups, the state board of education has approved a plan to use a "straight line" approach to setting improvement goals. Using a new baseline calculation beginning with the 1998-2000 school years, each school must improve by a fixed percentage each biennium, the value of which is set so that all schools will reach the same level of performance by the year 2014.

Originally, progress was measured against the amount of improvement made in the previous accountability cycle. This new approach eliminates the need for the department of education to recalculate a threshold for each school every two years. Now the bar is automatically raised every two years even if the school did not meet its previous goal. Only time will tell whether these automatic goals will be reasonable and attainable for schools with transient student bodies or schools in poverty stricken communities.

The 1998 legislation also changed the language for district level accountability. After consultation with the three oversight groups, the department of education must create a formula for school district accountability that includes goals for improvement over a two year period; rewards for leadership in improving teaching and learning in the district; and consequences that address the problems of the district. The department of education also must provide assistance when a district fails to achieve the goals set for it by the state board of education.[7] The legislature also abolished the "educationally deficient district" intervention program that was carried over from the pre-KERA era in 1990. This program was to have ended in 1996, but it was continued by the legislature that year.

Financial Rewards are Retained

Financial rewards for exceeding the improvement threshold are continued, but they are not considered "bonuses" or compensation. Given the centrality of this element of the accountability system as conceived in 1990, this was an expression of commitment to the basic policies of KERA as originally enacted. However, significant changes were made in how this element of KERA is implemented.

The money awarded to successful schools is now granted to the school rather than to the personnel of the school, and it is to be used for school purposes rather than as compensation. The amount of the award is now based on the number of certified personnel rather than on salaries as was the case previously. While this is not the original intent, it was a response to strong objections to cash bonuses made by educators. The legislature also specified that school councils must decide how the cash awards are spent, or the principal will make the decision if there is no school council.

The legislature continued to offer rewards during the time the new assessments were being designed, using data from the previous two years of KIRIS scores to establish the formula for measuring improvement. However, the department was required to seek the advice of the three oversight groups before setting improvement goals. The new legislation also said a school not only had to exceed its threshold, it also had to have an annual dropout rate of less than eight percent to be eligible for a reward. Dropout rates were a factor in the original accountability index, but the amount of reduction required was determined by the department of education for each school every two years. The legislature made the amount statutory in 1998.

Consequences for Failure are Modified

The 1998 legislation repealed the "school in crisis" language and the automatic probation of all school staff. It also substantially changed the nature of intervention and abolished the distinguished educator program. These changes eliminated what many educators considered the most onerous consequences in the 1990 law. Now all schools that fail to meet their threshold must be reviewed by a "scholastic audit team." The role of an audit team is very similar to the STAR program described earlier.

The department of education, after consultation with the oversight groups, is required to establish guidelines for conducting scholastic audits. These guidelines are at a minimum to include a process for the following:

1. Appointing and training team members. The team is to consist of at least a "highly skilled certified educator" as described in more detail below, a teacher, a principal or other local district administrator, a parent, and a university faculty member.
2. Reviewing a school's learning environment, efficiency, and the academic performance of students.
3. Evaluating each certified staff member assigned to the school. Only certified members of the audit team may conduct these evaluations.
4. Making a recommendation to the Kentucky Board of Education about the appropriateness of a school's classification as a poor performing school, and a recommendation concerning the assistance required by the school to improve teaching and learning.

The intent of these changes is to make certain the classification of a school as "poor performing" is accurate, to evaluate the capacity of the school staff to improve, and to take into account variables not included in the accountability assessment program that might explain why the school has allegedly performed poorly. Interestingly the legislation also requires the department of education to conduct "informational" audits of a sample of schools that achieved their goal.

The audit team will determine whether the school could benefit from "highly skilled education assistance," a replacement for the original "distinguished educator" concept. Such schools also must develop a school improvement plan and they are eligible for school improvement funds to be granted at the sole discretion of the department of education. A scholastic audit includes a formal evaluation of each staff member, an element of the original law that drew strong criticism from educators, but doesn't give anyone of the audit team the authority to order the dismissal of anyone as was the case with the distinguished educator assigned to a school in crisis.

Clearly these consequences seem less draconian than the ones adopted in 1990. The new approach is intended to focus more on helping educators rather than threatening them with their livelihood. However, there was a reason for the seemingly harsh approach taken by the task force in 1990. We wanted someone to have the authority to deal with the practice of assigning poor performing teachers to poor performing schools rather than dismissing or disciplining them. The practice was thought to be so widespread in 1990 that the task force felt it was necessary to give an outsider such as a distinguished educator the authority to rid a school of such personnel when it was clear the district authorities were not willing to do it.

Given the limited use of this authority prior to 1998, one can probably assume that the problem we intended to address under the old legislation was not being dealt with anyway. Whether this problem is real or not has never been documented, but the consequences for poor school performance now will have less direct impact on individual educators in the school than was previously the case.

Essentially the changes in assessment and accountability enacted in 1998 are designed to salvage and strengthen the initial policy intent of KERA by addressing the legitimate criticisms of the early implementation of this critical element of the reform. The legislature's commitment to accountability for results was sustained in spite of the vigorous efforts by a bloc of conservative legislators to abolish it in 1998.

NOTES:

[1] See HB 53/EN Section 2; Section 5; and Section 6.
[2] See HB 53/EN amendment to KERA Section 11.
[3] See HB 53/EN Section 11 (5)
[4] See HB 53/EN Section 17.
[5] See HB 53/EN Section 11 (6) as amended.
[6] See HB 53/EN Section 11 (7)
[7] HB 53/EN Section 12 (6)

16. Some Concluding Thoughts

Overall, I believe the concepts underlying KERA have proven to be sound for the most part. In some instances the implementation did not follow the intent as we initially envisioned the reforms. In other cases there were unintended consequences that marred the implementation. I have tried to document these observations throughout the book. However, in this last chapter I would like to share some concluding thoughts about the law and its subsequent implementation that did not fit neatly in the general format of this book.

The New Curriculum Approach

It is my opinion that the critical task of defining what children should know and be able to do as a result of a public education should not be performed by technocrats in a state agency even with the help of outsiders. The basic objectives for the curriculum in public schools should be developed and guided by a body that reasonably reflects the expectations of the public. Educators can still be granted considerable latitude in deciding how to achieve these objectives.

The idea of having a special group like the council on school performance standards conceptualize and create the design for the new curriculum I believe was a sound strategy. The process that Kentucky used involved the public as a first step that avoided having educators telling the public what they should want from the public school system. There are good reasons that such a public body should be a permanent part of the education system. No curriculum design is so self-evident there is no need for those who prepare it to resolve questions of intent. Furthermore, a curriculum design needs to be a dynamic thing that can be quickly adapted to changing needs and times.

A proposal for making the council on school performance standards a permanent body was on the table when KERA was enacted. Governor Wilkinson initially created the council on school performance standards by executive order, but his education reform plan envisioned the council as a permanent body to handle issues of interpretation and to update the curriculum and assessment design over time. The council made a similar recommendation in its final report. However, this idea was not incorporated in KERA. Instead, the council was dissolved after it submitted its report to the state board of education in 1991.

The consequences of this decision were obvious very early. Even with the extensive work the council did on the initial outcomes, within two years after their adoption by the state board of education the department of education administratively revised them to resolve issues of interpretation. When the state education agency undertook the task of creating the curriculum framework, the body that created the basis for it was no longer available to provide information and insight about the philosophy of the curriculum design and to answer questions about the specifics of its recommendations.

States evaluating the Kentucky experience should consider creating a permanent body to regularly review the curriculum design and recommend changes when appropriate. A public body like the council on school performance standards can develop expertise in various curriculum areas, assure continuity in the philosophy of the curriculum, and provide a public forum for those who want to propose changes to it. In 1998 the legislature created a School Curriculum, Assessment, and Accountability Council that in part will now perform this function in Kentucky.

Changes in Teaching

Confusion arose very soon after KERA was passed about the relationship between what students are expected to do, and how they are to be taught to do it. For example, some opponents of the new approach to curriculum raised questions about such things as the use of whole language and phonics as methods of teaching reading. This argument really is about what someone thinks is the best way to teach reading, not about what students should be able to read and understand. No doubt one can find both whole language and phonics still being used even in the same school by different teachers. Parents may have strong opinions about how they want their children to learn something. When they see a different approach being used in their school it is easy for them to assume that KERA must have mandated it.

KERA specifically avoided mandating instructional practices of any kind even in the primary program. The policy on which KERA is based leaves such decision to educators, but clearly the task force wanted educators to recognize that reliance on a single approach for all children is likely to result in some children not doing well. It is incumbent on educators to change their methods with these children rather than to simply declare that they have not learned what was taught. The goal is not to teach and grade, but to ensure that *every child* learns. When something doesn't work, the teacher has an obligation to use a different approach so that all children are able to learn, not just those who can learn in the way a teacher is most accustomed to teaching.

KERA does not endorse or require any particular methodology for teaching any subject. The state only defines the results it expects from the instructional process, i.e. students capable of doing certain things with the knowledge they acquire. Local school personnel have total control over how something is taught. If a parent wants phonics taught, this is a discussion that should go on between the parent and the child's teacher. However, neither parents nor teachers should cite KERA as the reason why a particular instructional methodology is or is not used in a school or by a particular teacher. Just because a particular instructional practice is observed in Kentucky schools, this doesn't mean it is required by or even consistent with KERA or its intent.

There was a reason for conceptually separating the end result of education from how it is delivered. The accountability system focuses on results rather than process. We wanted educators to seek out and use the very best approaches to achieving the desired results without constraint from the state. No teacher should look to the government to be told how children should be taught. Therefore, decisions about instructional practices are to be made by individual teachers at the school level, based on what works best with each child in the classroom. That's the way we wanted it.

Classroom Performance Assessments

Evaluating student progress on a continuing basis is central to education, and particularly in a system where children are expected to progress at the rate they are capable of learning. Historically, teachers generally evaluate students daily or weekly on an informal basis, and then issue official "grades" at the end of a designated period of time such as a unit or term. The perceived purpose of "giving grades" is to provide feedback to students and parents regarding progress that is being made by the student. Underlying KERA is the notion that assessment should be primarily a clinical tool for measuring the effectiveness of instruction. Just as it is desirable to know if a patient's symptoms are abating, so it is essential that teachers know if learning is occurring and at the desired rate.

Instructional practices should be based on research, but they also have to be used in the classroom with individual learning styles in mind. It was our hope that teachers would not allow students to continue very long in a pattern of non-learning before intervention with an alternative approach to instruction. Unless the progress of individual children is monitored on a regular basis, it is impossible for such a philosophy to work.

What made this emphasis on continuous assessment even more difficult for Kentucky teachers was the focus on assessing performance rather than just correct or accurate answers. All the evidence so far has shown that most teachers have limited assessment skills in general, and very little understanding of how to create and use performance assessments. It is obvious that Kentucky should have had a plan from the very beginning to train all teachers in the use of performance assessment, and such training should have been part of the training in curriculum development. These two activities should be carefully integrated in ways that did not occur under KERA. Training is critical, and it needs to be uniform throughout the state.

The need for quality standards for performance assessment done in the classroom remains a missing element in the effort to transition from the old approach to instruction to a clinical approach. Only the state accountability test gives teachers any indication of the rigorousness that should be expected in teacher-created assessments. The state needs to monitor the use of continuous assessment in schools and the quality of these assessments. This is necessary to ensure equity in the educational system. Teachers who have elected not to use performance assessments in their classrooms, or only rarely do so, should be counseled regarding the importance of this kind of assessment. Special training should be provided if necessary.

My personal experience in helping teachers develop assessments for their classrooms indicates that most teachers lack the ability to extrapolate the key elements of a good assessment from the examples that are provided in the state accountability test. An implementation policy that relies on teachers learning how to conduct high quality performance assessments by examining state test examples will not produce the kind of continuous assessment practices needed to improve student learning. Too many teachers are copying the form without understanding the fundamentals of the performance assessment methodology.

The Primary School Program

I believe much of the resistance to the primary school program in the early years can be attributed to the demand for a rapid implementation. We were much too ambition in wanting to see immediate changes in how the youngest students were taught. The three-step timetable proposed by the department of education in 1992 for *full* implementation of the program was reasonable in my opinion, and the General Assembly should have supported it. The deadline for *beginning* implementation in KERA would have been acceptable if it had not been coupled with the idea of *full* implementation. Perhaps legislators were concerned in 1992 that the proposal to delay full implementation was only a case of people "dragging their feet" instead of moving forward to do what was required to implement the primary program in a timely manner. In any case, the notion that such a complex program could be "fully" implemented in two years was not grounded in experience.

One serious consequence of the rush to full implementation was inadequate preparation of the teacher corps to put various critical elements of the program in place. Money was appropriated for professional development for all teachers during the early years of KERA, but the primary school program should have been considered a special case because of the complexity of the changes that were required. KERA should have required that a training program be developed specifically to train the elementary school teachers and administrators responsible for the program's effectiveness.

It would have been a good investment to pay primary school teachers for two or three summers to work on implementation and to receive intensive training. This might have posed some problems for teachers trying to get advanced degrees, but in this instance the goals of the state would have to take priority. If a delay in completing their academic work posed a professional hardship like missing a deadline for new certification, the Commissioner of Education could have been given statutory authority to waive the requirement for the duration of the mandatory training period.

As it turned out, many teachers did dedicate a significant portion of their summers enrolled in various voluntary professional development programs. What was lost in the laissez-faire approach was the ability to coordinate and sequence the training to properly support a staged implementation of various elements of the program. Not all teachers in a school engaged in the training, so the training did not benefit all teachers. To make things even more difficult, the training in the very early years was done while some very important issues still had not been resolved or clarified. The trainers were doing the best they could under the circumstances, but many teachers I knew often were left confused because they were told different things by different trainers regarding certain critical issues.

One other issue regarding training deserves mention. Teachers repeatedly told me they want models to emulate rather than explanations. They want to see things in practice rather than as concepts drawn in words. It would have been very helpful to have invested time and effort in the early years to create demonstration sites where teachers could see how to organize and manage multi-age classrooms, create and use learning centers, devise hands-on learning experiences, and do qualitative assessments. It appears that too much of the training teachers received consisted of talking about what to do rather than actually demonstrating it. Creating model primary school program sites might have gone a long way to facilitate implementation.

Changes in instructional practice that are as complex and diverse as those envisioned for the primary school program require strong leadership at the school site. Local school leadership, particularly the principal, plays a critical role in creating both the conditions and incentives for teachers to make significant changes in educational practice even in schools with school councils. I found elementary school principals for the most part eager to be successful in the transition from the traditional to the non-graded classroom, but they were not well equipped by education or experience to create and execute on their own a process for bringing about the transition.

My personal observations indicate that the most rapid progress in implementation of the primary school program occurred in schools with strong, visionary principals. These people were able to establish a process for consensus building that kept the faculty on the tasks they needed to accomplish in order to be successful in the transition. Schools appeared to be less successful when the faculty was left to figure things out through professional development or consultants were hired to prepare a plan for the school without faculty involvement in its development. Teachers should not be expected to take the initiative to create committees, plan changes, and execute them. This is the traditional role of the school instructional leader or principal.

There are many practical matters that have to be decided which teachers cannot resolve independent of other teachers such as moving to block scheduling, reassigning students, or altering class time. The site-based school council[1] can facilitate or make these decisions final, but the process for developing sound proposals that have the support of a majority of the professional staff usually will occur outside the school council decision process. Almost always the school principal is the person who must create and manage this process. Perhaps it would have been advisable to have given all elementary school principals intensive training in how to manage the organizational changes they would have to make to successfully implement the primary school program.

It is easy to be critical now of how the primary school program was implemented in Kentucky. Hindsight is always 20/20. This program was perhaps the most daunting challenge (other than creating the accountability system) faced by the people charged with implementing KERA. The primary lesson here is to have a plan with a reasonable timetable for accomplishing each step. Most of all provide the resources necessary for proper preparation of the workforce *before* you expect to see the program implemented in the school.

As the primary school program emerged in elementary schools, a situation arose that was unanticipated when KERA was drafted. It seems that in some schools the teachers involved in the primary school program separated themselves from upper grade teachers right from the beginning. The term "school" seemed to mean to them that they were like a school within the school. I have not been able to determine the full extent of this phenomenon, but my personal observations indicate that it was widespread. The practical effects of this behavior were many and significant.

Primary school students are expected to meet performance standards that assure success in the fourth grade. Yet I found that many fourth grade teachers were neither consulted by primary school teachers nor were they involved in any material way in the discussions that took place during the planning of the primary school program. In fact many fourth grade teachers told me they were basically unaware of what was going on in the primary program. It is hard to imagine how primary teachers can expect to prepare students for success in the fourth grade when there is such little communication with fourth grade teachers.

One consequence of this situation is an abrupt change for students leaving the primary school program. Students who are used to being in multiage classrooms suddenly find themselves being taught once again as a class rather than as individuals. Furthermore, the expectations of fourth grade teachers often are not aligned with the kind of performances students in the primary school program are being asked to demonstrate. Finally, many fourth grade teachers do not understand or appreciate the philosophy of continuous progress on which the primary school program is based.

Another consequence of this disconnection of the primary school program with the fourth grade teachers is the impact it can possibly have on student performance on the state fourth grade accountability test. For reasons unrelated to how schools are organized in the state or the existence of a primary school program, KERA designated the fourth, eighth, and twelfth grades to be the accountability grades. This meant that fourth grade teachers in schools which did not have good communication with teachers in the primary school program would have to prepare their students for the accountability test with little awareness of what they had been taught or were expected to be able to do in the primary program.

Although the exit criteria for the primary school program should provide some modicum of assurance that primary students are actually prepared for the fourth grade, it appears that in many schools the primary teachers have little idea of what fourth grade teachers actually expect. The 18 criteria for exiting the primary school program may be properly aligned with the academic expectations, but they do not necessarily represent what fourth grade teachers actually expect students to know and be able to do when they reach that grade level. The result of this situation is a complaint by some fourth grade teachers that students coming out of the primary program are not properly prepared for fourth grade.

Clearly as drafters of KERA we did not anticipate that primary school teachers and fourth grade teachers would not work closely together or we could have made this a requirement of the law. Unfortunately what is logical doesn't always happen automatically. As indicated earlier, there are no data to confirm how widespread this phenomenon is. However, if it is found that a good working relationship still doesn't exist in a significant number of elementary schools, it would be appropriate for either the legislature or the Kentucky Board of Education to bring about a closer tie between the fourth grade and the primary school program.

School-Based Decision Making

It seems very important to make a clear distinction between the concept of local responsibility and the structure that is chosen to support the decision process. In Kentucky's situation, the school council *structure* took such prominence that the reason for having the structure got lost. Furthermore, those who did not like the structure or didn't think it was necessary were statutorily denied the right to engage in the process that it was intended to support. Schools should have the right to create any structure for the decision process that best suites their needs so long as it advances the policy objectives for school-based decision making.

Although the law was quite clear that the target for school council action was instructional policy, the people who implemented school councils permitted it to be defined as part of the administration of a school. A formal structure can in some instances actually get in the way of collegial decision making if council members perceive their role as being decision-makers rather than facilitators. This distortion caused a variety of problems for Kentucky schools, not the least of which was an undesirable conflict between school councils and school principals. Policy makers should realize that even the best school council is not a substitute for a visionary instructional leader. Every effort must be made to safeguard against diminishing the leadership role of the principal or lead teacher.

If a formal school council structure is to be required for school-based decision making to occur, then consideration must be given to the time it requires. There is no professional or financial incentive for faculty members to devote their personal time to serve on a school council, only to act on matters that they participated in when they were discussed in other forums such as committee or faculty meetings. Given the amount of time council membership seems to require, faculty members who agree to serve should be given relief from other duties, or they should receive monetary compensation for their time.

Policy makers must determine if schools should be given the option not to participate in school-based decision making. It seems that the process should be employed in all schools in keeping with the overall policy of empowering people at the school site. It is my opinion that educators should be required to accept responsibility for decisions that directly affect their professional practice. Not participating in school-based decision making should not be an option. The extent of the personal involvement of individual teachers can be a matter for personnel policy, but the school as an institution should be required to accept this responsibility.

If an option to reject school-based decision making is available, then the law must be clear that the school has forfeited its authority to exercise the prerogatives of school-based decision making unless the local board of education explicitly delegates such authority. Failure to do so could conceivably result in a school not adopting school-based decision making only out of fear of reprisal from an autocratic administrator. If the faculty cannot control these decisions, then the school-site administrator should not be able to control them by default.

I noted earlier that it appears teachers are willing to participate in school-based decision making if it doesn't require creation of a school council. I personally believe unlinking the school council structure from school-based decision making would make the latter much more attractive to many teachers. If school-based decision making is mandated, then there should be considerable latitude as to the form it can take. It seems that we may have actually impeded the acceptance of local responsibility for instructional decisions by assigning this authority only to a school council rather than the school itself.

The issue of capacity building is perhaps the most critical one for policy makers who want to institute school-based decision making. The Kentucky experience clearly shows that extensive professional development is required as an adjunct to this change in responsibility. One cannot view this only as a matter of training people how to make collegial decisions and to run a council meeting according to Roberts Rules of Order. All school faculties need a sound understanding of the elements of good instructional policy and practice. They also need access to authorities and knowledge bases from which to draw expertise on matters about which they are not properly informed either by education or experience.

A final point should be considered. Kentucky had a cookie-cutter system of schools that did not meet the learning needs of all children, because every school is not alike in terms of the children or community it serves. School-based decision making results in considerable diversity among schools in terms of instructional philosophy and practice. This is an intended consequence. A "one size fits all" approach is neither expected nor desired. If diversity among schools is a problem, then school-based decision making will be a troublesome approach to school improvement no matter how well it works.

Is the Accountability System Fair?

Probably the most important issue that has to be addressed when constructing an accountability program is the degree to which policy makers believe teachers should be singularly responsible for student learning. Kentucky teachers had been giving accountability tests to their students for almost a decade, so this aspect of KERA did not trouble them very much. What was new and highly controversial in KERA was the personal consequences attached to the results of these tests. It should surprise no one that educators resented this aspect of KERA. The threat of job loss based on student test scores made the consequences even less acceptable.

Many teachers contend they should not be held accountable for someone learning something because there are too many factors that affect learning over which they have no control. For example, they point to a lack of concern for education on the part of some parents; poor home support; lack of cooperation from parents when their children are disruptive; and similar situations. They cite these factors as reasons why it is unfair and unreasonable that they alone should be held accountable for the academic failure of some students.

Some legislators on the task force were educators and expressed strong opposition to making teachers personally accountable for student learning. However, many task force members had heard complaints about or personally knew of teachers who neglected, emotionally abused, or failed to properly instruct their students. These task force members felt it was entirely appropriate to hold educators accountable for their effectiveness with all children, not just with those whom they prefer to teach.

The conditions that teachers pointed to are obviously real, but research has shown that there are ways to be successful with "problem students." The task force decided that the accountability program should make no concessions. As a matter of public policy, teachers have to improve their effectiveness with *all* children. They simply cannot continue to dump some children out of the system unprepared for life. Equitable outcomes from schooling for all children was at the heart of the supreme court decision, and this principle had to be reinforced in the legislation that flowed from it.

The rationale I have given for such a hard line position is a belief that the education system has to be pressured to do better than it has done in the past. Otherwise, the future will certainly look like the past notwithstanding the efficacy of all the other elements of the reform act. The temptation is simply too great for teachers to concentrate on students they like and leave the problem children behind. The social cost of this attitude is too great to allow it to go unchallenged. Kentucky policy makers realized at the time there are practical limits to what teachers can do, but I also think we understood that more can and must be done to elevate the learning of all children than has been done in the past.

It is my opinion that the basic policy objectives of the accountability program have been implemented essentially as intended. I have raised questions about the way some details were worked out, but the program does what it was intended to do. The most serious problems with the accountability program were created by the assessment system on which is depends. The elaborate system of consequences is based on data the assessment program provides. Weaknesses that developed in the assessment system had a dramatic and direct impact on the viability of the accountability program.

Student Responsibility

The problem of student motivation remains an issue with educators notwithstanding changes in the grade level when certain tests are administered. It cannot be disputed that some students do not put forth their best effort in the accountability tests, probably because there are no consequences for them as educators contend. Motivation is a problem for any test in which the student has no stake in the outcome, so this problem is not unique. The primary difference here is that the accountability tests have very high stakes for educators. Their professional reputation depends on students doing well on the test.

The problem seems to be most prevalent at the high school level, especially if students perceive they can hurt their teachers if they do not do well on these tests. Some schools offered rewards to students if the school did well on the tests, but they were criticized for this practice and it was discouraged by the state. A variety of proposals have been offered to deal with this issue such as tying student test scores to graduation, but none of these ideas have been adopted as yet.

In the interest of fairness, obvious cases of non-participation or random answering should be treated as measurement error and such scores should be excluded when calculating the index score for the school. Both kinds of behavior generally can be detected when the tests are scored. Scores from these tests can be set aside while the circumstances surrounding the test are investigated. If these students deliberately sabotaged the test, their scores should be excluded from the accountability index. Evidence that a teacher actively promoted such behavior, especially to purposely have the tests thrown out, should be a violation of professional ethics and be punished accordingly. Likewise a disproportionate number of such cases in a school suggests there might be a lack of diligence on the part of school personnel to motivate students to put forth their best effort. This also deserves investigation and possible sanctions.

Disregarding the scores of students who deliberately give incorrect answers or do not participate in a test might deter this conduct. They would then realize their actions will not influence the outcome for the teachers or the school. School councils also can establish procedures for disciplining students who deliberately do not put forth a sincere effort in the test. In any event, it serves no public purpose or policy objective to punish schools for student behavior it cannot control and it does not encourage.

Measuring Learning

Measurement problems occurred early in the implementation phase of the assessment program that had serious ramifications for the accountability program. Some opponents of the accountability program sought on various occasions to have it suspended, citing the problems with the KIRIS as evidence the program is a failure. However, both the legislature and the state board of education continued to support the objectives of the accountability program even through the major revisions to the program enacted in 1998.

In my opinion a major part of the difficulty with KIRIS in the initial years came from the failure to use the interim assessment test battery to provide a stable and defensible backbone to the assessment program while the new measurements envisioned in the law were developed, tested, and implemented. No doubt a large part of the blame for this can be attributed to the timelines written into the law for implementation of the performance-based tests. There also apparently was a basic misunderstanding of the nature and purpose of the interim assessment program by the assessment contractor and the department of education. These problems were compounded by their decision to build the KIRIS on test elements that had not been thoroughly validated and equated.

Most of us on the task force on education reform understood that Kentucky would have to develop new tests that would be closely aligned with the kind of curriculum we envisioned. We also knew that the measurement technology to do this in all subject areas was not yet available or even widely understood by many psychometric experts. We also knew this meant that Kentucky would have to invest considerable time and money in the research and development of new tests. What we did not want or expect was to have this occur in such a manner that the products of this effort would put the whole accountability program in jeopardy.

KERA provided for a planned transition from the best available testing protocols in 1990 to the new ones that could be brought on line after they were properly pre-tested and validated. The only thing we hoped for was that the interim assessment system would be designed around existing criterion referenced tests to the extent this was feasible. Unfortunately this is not the way the legislation was interpreted. A rush to develop and implement new performance-based tests resulted in serious technical problems, which in turn undermined confidence in the entire accountability program.

There is an important lesson here for anyone who wants to build an accountability system, and at the same time build new measurement instruments to support it. Both can be done concurrently, but there must be close articulation between what is tested and what students are taught. Teachers must have exposure to what the accountability tests will cover so they can properly prepare students for the new tests. Also the new tests must be properly validated before they are used for accountability purposes. Adjustments obviously need to be made to the accountability index as new tests are introduced, but they must occur in such a way that they do not create instability in the index. I believe our failure to do these things accounts for most of the early problems Kentucky had with its new accountability program.

Any state that embarks on a program that rewards or sanctions school personnel based on their effectiveness with students must build it on an assessment system that has credibility right from the beginning. Whether a slower development and implementation of the performance-based elements would have avoided the controversy is debatable, since there was little support from educators for the rewards and sanction element from the beginning. However, Kentucky's failure to build a solid bridge to the future using proven measurement instruments as the foundation no doubt contributed heavily to the problems it had with the accountability system.

Whose Improvement Should be Measured?

The argument is made by some critics that we should be measuring cohorts of children rather than grade levels in order to get a fair measure of a school's true impact on students. This idea was considered but rejected for several reasons. First of all, the state would have to keep individual student data for four years in order to make a comparison since each student is only tested once every four years. Such an approach simply was not feasible, because the state did not have the capability at the time to acquire or manage such data, nor would it have it in the foreseeable future. Furthermore, individual student test scores would have to travel with each student from one school to another. The baseline for each school would have to be adjusted to reflect the loss and addition of students with different scores over a period of four years. A calculation required to support this approach would be even more difficult for educators and the public to understand than the current system.

High student mobility in some schools may be a valid issue that was not addressed by KERA. Schools should have a reasonable time to have an impact on a student if it is to be held accountable for that student's performance. Schools with an annual turnover ratio in excess of a specified amount to be determined by the board of education could have their accountability scores adjusted to take into consideration the impact of students which they did not have the preceding school year.

One might hypothesize that the performance levels of students who leave are likely to be similar to the performance levels of the new students in most schools. In other words their performances actually might not be different enough to significantly change the overall score attained by the school as a whole. One way to determine this is for all students in the accountability grades to take the state tests regardless of how long they have been enrolled in the school as currently is the case. Then compare the test scores of all current students who were not enrolled the previous year with the scores of all students who no longer are enrolled in the school but whose scores were used to calculate the school's baseline score.

If the average scores for the two groups are not significantly different statistically, then the new students are performing about as well as the students who helped set the baseline. The mobility factor has been rendered unimportant in determining the school's overall performance. If the average scores of the two groups are different enough to change the classification of the school from one category to another such as from reward to decline or from one level of reward to another level, then the scores of the new students could be treated as measurement error and excluded from the final calculation.

The approach suggested here would mean that the accountability score of a few schools would have to be adjusted, but only when empirical data justified it. Student test data would only have to be retained for two years rather than four as would be required in a cohort approach. Obviously there are other ways this situation can be handled, but something like this should be considered to confirm the actual effect of mobility on the ability of a school to qualify for rewards and avoid being unfairly labeled as in decline or in crisis. Unfortunately, the law did not take this situation into account as it probably should have done.

Making concessions on how the accountability score is calculated for schools with high mobility can improve the fairness of the index, but these schools still face a serious challenge to improve the overall performance of the school when teachers have a relatively small time frame in which to impact the learning of children who move so frequently. It is incumbent upon school districts with mobile populations to help such schools deal with this problem.

Rewards and Sanctions

When writing legislation for an accountability program that awards additional compensation in the form of a cash bonus, care must be taken to make certain that the law is clear that the money is indeed personal compensation and not a contribution to the school. The failure to do so caused some problems for the Kentucky program. First of all, KERA spoke only of "rewards" and did not explicitly use the term compensation except to say that the rewards are not to be added to a staff person's base salary and shall not be defined as compensation for retirement purposes.[2]

There are two reasons why this particular language was in the law. Without it a staff person could argue that future salary increases should be based on a salary that included the reward that could in turn introduce an element of salary inequity over time if a school continued to receive rewards when other schools did not. Secondly, contributions to the state teacher retirement fund by law must be deducted from teacher salaries. The cash reward was not to be considered when calculating this contribution. Also it is not to be used to calculate the earned income of the teacher at the time of retirement.

The compensation question was further confused when KERA in the very same section of the law required certified school staff who earned the reward to decide by majority vote on the way it should be spent. The latter provision seemed to imply that the school earned the reward, but the staff had to agree on how it should be spent including keeping the money for themselves. If the reward is personal compensation, then why should the staff be required to decide how it is to be used?

Whether to grant the reward to teachers or to the school is a very important policy issue. Giving cash reward to schools could be viewed at some future time as a source of financial inequity. Giving the reward to the school also would not meet the intent to financially reward the people who work hard so their school can achieve the successful school designation. I believe everyone on the task force that drafted KERA considered the rewards to be a cash bonus even though the law as written never explicitly defined it as such or used these exact words.

Failure to clarify the compensation issue had some unfortunate and unintended consequences. After the first round of rewards, there were public accounts describing discontent in some schools over the decision of certified staff not to share their reward with support staff, teacher aides, and others who thought they had contributed to the success of the school. The law was clear that only certified staffs were to receive the rewards. Nothing in the legislation justified the complaint of other school personnel in schools where certified staff decided to take the reward as personal compensation.

The issue of giving money to others in the school besides classified staff was addressed in Wilkinson's proposal, but it was not included in KERA. I think a good case can be made that other people in a school deserve some portion of the reward. However, who should be rewarded is a policy issue that should be addressed by the legislature and not be decided at the school site level. School staff should not be put in a position of appearing to be selfish because they elect not to share the reward money with others in the school.

In retrospect it was a serious mistake to have teachers vote on how the reward is to be used because it turned out to be very divisive and contentious in some schools. KERA should have required that a reward check be prepared and sent directly to each certified staff member either by the state or the school district with no strings attached. What they choose to do with the reward money is of no more importance to the purposes of the accountability program than how teachers spend their regular paycheck. Obviously, the law should not prevent individual teachers from using their reward money to purchase things for their classrooms if they want to do so; it simply should not be a matter for others to decide.

Some teachers regarded the offer of rewards for improvement as an attempt to "bribe" them to do a better job. Some teachers complained to me that it implied they were not doing their best all the time. Some of them said it was ludicrous for task force members to think teachers would work harder just to earn the reward. It was their position that teachers are underpaid as a group and the reward money should be used to increase salaries for all teachers instead of rewarding a few.[3]

I think it is accurate to say that the reward never was thought of as a substitute for paying all educators a reasonable salary. On the contrary, funding for schools was significantly increased with KERA, which resulted in substantial salary increases for at least two-thirds of all Kentucky teachers. The only intent was to provide a form of recognition for achieving a goal that goes beyond a pat on the back or a nice certificate at an awards banquet. Much was going to be expected of educators under KERA. A monetary reward for those who achieve these goals seemed to be very appropriate under the circumstances.

As described in the previous chapter, the legislature in 1998 changed this policy. In the future the money will be awarded to the school rather than as a salary bonus. The school council will continue to decide how the award is to be spent.

Consequences for Failure to Improve

The role of sanctions must be carefully thought through because they perhaps are the most potent element in the accountability program. The gradual escalation of the sanctions was considered very important. Two years is not a lot of time in which to make dramatic changes in teaching strategies. However, intervention should not be delayed until schools are clearly not improving or are actually in a state of decline. These were the key ideas that shaped the tiered accountability structure in KERA.

What I hear most from people outside of Kentucky are questions about the concept of a school "in crisis." The approach Kentucky took regarding school accountability is grounded in a fundamental commitment to public responsibility. Schools should be certified by the state as places where learning occurs for all children. If a school's performance is below standard, the state should protect the children who attend it. As I wrote earlier, if the food in the cafeteria were found unsanitary, there would be no hesitation to close it until conditions are improved. The same concept should apply to learning. The school should either improve or be closed down.

Prior to the changes made in 1998, KERA defined a school that declined in its performance to be a school in crisis, and parents were given the opportunity to remove their children to better schools. In most school districts the attendance boundaries dictate which schools students must attend. If the assigned school doesn't meet the learning standards of the state, it was our position that no student should be required to attend it. That is the bottom line of the "school in crisis" provision of KERA as originally conceived.

The suspension of tenure of faculty in a school in crisis was controversial from the beginning. In order to avoid case-by-case litigation, KERA placed all personnel in the school in a class and treated the class equally. Decisions about the transfer or dismissal of individual teachers then could be carried out without protection of tenure since tenure for all teachers in the school was temporarily suspended. The legality of this aspect of KERA was never tested, because no teachers or administrators were ever dismissed or transferred under the authority of this statute.

As I visited schools in Kentucky and heard their explanations of this element of KERA, it came through very clearly that many teachers had been led to believe they were automatically fired if their school was declared a school in crisis. This was not true, of course, but the perception apparently was widely held throughout the state and had a very negative effect on the morale of teachers in schools that did not improve their KIRIS accountability index scores.

Actually the problem in a school may lie elsewhere than in the staff. Well-qualified teachers who are doing their best under very difficult circumstances should have had little to fear from the personnel evaluations the distinguished educators were required to perform. However, it is well known in education circles that certain schools become the dumping ground for inept teachers and political opponents. Often these schools are located in economically disadvantaged areas of a city or county populated with people who have little skill or political power to protest. This element of the accountability program is designed to address this very situation. A distinguished educator should be able to quickly recognize what is going on and take appropriate personnel actions so the remaining staff can be effective.

In speeches I made to school faculties after KERA was enacted, I often said that some schools should wish to be declared in crisis so someone could come to their aid. There is clear evidence that some schools in Kentucky have been neglected for decades. They do not have the facilities or equipment necessary to provide the kind of educational experience KERA expects for all children. This situation is found most frequently in economically poorer parts of our counties or cities, giving evidence of either prejudice or lack of commitment to equality of opportunity. In either case, the "school in crisis" concept was intended to force school districts to deal with inequitable situations that destine a large number of children to an inferior education unless something dramatic is done.

In my opinion, when a school is declared to be in crisis, we should have given the commissioner of education authority to require the school district to take immediate action to provide the facilities or equipment required for students to master the academic expectations of KERA. In my opinion these improvements should be at the district's expense with interim state assistance provided only if the commissioner declares the situation to be an emergency. If the local school authorities fail to do what is needed to help these schools, then I think they should be removed from office.

When this issue was revisited in 1998 the legislature backed away from this policy, choosing to take an approach that essentially went in the opposite direction. Individual staff are still evaluated and recommendations for their dismissal or transfer can still be made by the scholastic audit team. However, the legislature did not enhance the authority of the state to force the actions required to improve the school. It is still up to a local school district to address the problems of a poor performing school. I remain convinced that a more aggressive effort by the state to help schools suffering from historic neglect will be required if the vision of an equitable system of public schools is ever to be a reality in Kentucky.

Has KERA Worked?

In 1990 Kentucky embarked on the most historic effort in modern history to reconstitute a public education system. I am often asked if I think it is working as we expected. I have tried to answer this question throughout this book. Obviously it has not worked as I thought it might in every detail.

Still I believe what we set out to do in 1990 has for the most part been implemented as intended. Has it improved student learning as much as we expected? It is too early to know.

There is much that I see that is promising, but it is too soon to declare victory or defeat. Disparity in learning is still evident even when measured by more traditional instruments. It takes more than a few years to reverse decades of inequality. More time must elapse for the full effect of our changes to be known. When I finished this book the first children to enter the primary program were just entering high school. We need to refrain from making judgments too early on such a dramatic restructuring of a major public institution as KERA represents. Change always is slower than we desire, but I believe Kentucky is on the right track.

NOTES:

[1] This is a reference to the local School-Based Decision Making Council to which KERA granted specific responsibilities. School councils are described in earlier chapters.

[2] See HB 940 Section 5 (1) (g) [KRS 158.6455 (1) (g)]

[3] For another view of teacher attitudes toward the rewards element of KERA, see the 1995 annual report of the Office of Education Accountability, Appendix A.

Index

A

B

C

R

S

T

V

Y